Homosexuality and Ethics

edited by
Edward Batchelor, Jr.

The Pilgrim Press
New York

2d Printing, 1982

Library of Congress Cataloging in Publication Data

Homosexuality and ethics.

   Bibliography: p. 244
   1. Homosexuality—Moral and religious aspects.
2. Sexual ethics. I. Batchelor, Edward, 1931–
HQ76.25.H647 176   80-10533
ISBN 0-8298-0392-0
ISBN 0-8298-0615-6 (pbk.)

The Pilgrim Press, 132 West 31 Street, New York, New York 10001

This Book is for S.K.W.

Contributors

Edward Batchelor, Jr. is an Episcopal priest and chaplain at the City University of New York, New York.

Roger Shinn is Dodge Professor of Applied Christianity at Union Theological Seminary, New York City.

Tom F. Driver is Paul Tillich Professor of Theology and Culture at Union Theological Seminary, New York City.

Gregory Baum is Professor of Religious Studies at Saint Michael's College, University of Toronto, Ontario.

Rosemary Radford Ruether is Georgia Harkness Professor at Garrett-Evangelical Theological Seminary, Evanston, Illinois.

Saint Thomas Aquinas lived from 1225 to 1274. His treatment of homosexuality is considered by many scholars to be the definitive statement of the traditionalist position.

Karl Barth (1886-1968) taught Theology at Gottingen, Munster and Bonn in Germany, and at Basle in Switzerland.

Robert Gordis is Rappaport Professor of the Bible at the Jewish Theological Seminary, New York City, and editor of *Judaism* magazine.

John G. Milhaven is Professor of Religious Studies at Brown University, Providence, Rhode Island.

William Muehl is Professor of Practical Theology at the Yale Divinity School, New Haven, Connecticut.

Ruth Tiffany Barnhouse is a priest of the Episcopal Church, and Professor of Psychiatry and Pastoral Care at Perkins School of Theology, Southern Methodist University, Dallas, Texas.

Charles E. Curran is Professor of Moral Theology at the Catholic University of America, Washington, D.C.

Helmut Thielicke is a leading Protestant biblical theologian and ethicist, who has taught at Tubingen and Hamburg, Germany.

H. Kimball Jones is a United Methodist minister and counsellor. He is a candidate in the doctoral program in Religion and Psychiatry at Union Theological Seminary, New York City.

Hershel Matt is Acting Director of the Hillel Foundation at Princeton University, New Jersey.

The Episcopal Diocese of Michigan Report was prepared by a group of consultants and published in 1973.

The British Quaker Report was prepared by a group of Friends under the editorship of Alastair Heron.

W. Norman Pittenger is Senior Resident at King's College, Cambridge, England.

Michael F. Valente is Associate Professor of Religious Studies at Seton Hall College, South Orange, New Jersey.

Neale Secor is an attorney and priest of the Episcopal Church, who now serves as Port Missioner, Seaman's Church Institute, New Jersey.

Robert W. Wood is a minister of the United Church of Christ, and works as pastoral counsellor and minister of the Union Church, Maynard, Massachusetts.

James B. Nelson is Professor of Christian Ethics at United Theological Seminary, New Brighton, Minnesota.

Theodore W. Jennings is Assistant Professor of Theology at Chicago Theological Seminary, Chicago, Illinois.

Lisa Sowle Cahill is Assistant Professor of Ethics at Boston College, Boston, Massachusetts.

Abbreviations

AAS	*Acta Apostolicae Sedis, commentarium officiale*; Rome: 1909f.
CD	Karl Barth: *Church Dogmatics*
Ethics	Aristotle: *Nicomachaen Ethics*
ES	Helmut Thielicke: *The Ethics of Sex*
HPR	*Homiletic and Pastoral Review*
HWCT	Derrick Sherwin Bailey: *Homosexuality and the Western Christian Tradition*
PG	*Patrologia, series graeca*, ed. Migne, Paris: 1844ff.
PL	*Patrologia, series latina*, ed. Migne, Paris: 1857ff.
SCG	St. Thomas Aquinas: *Summa Contra Gentes*
Sent.	St. Thomas Aquinas: *Scriptum in IV Libros Sententiarum*
ST	St. Thomas Aquinas: *Summa Theologica*
ThE	Helmut Thielicke: *Theological Ethics*

Table of Contents

Acknowledgments

Grateful acknowledgment is made to the following authors and publishers for permission to reprint materials of which they are the copyright owners:

United Church Press, New York (Roger Shinn, "Homosexuality: Christian Conviction & Inquiry," and Neale Secor, "A Brief for a New Homosexual Ethic," reprinted with permission from *The Same Sex: An Appraisal of Homosexuality,* ed. Ralph W. Weltge). Copyright © 1969 United Church Press.

Commonweal Publishing Co., Inc. (Gregory Baum, "Catholic Homosexuals," *Commonweal,* (February 15, 1974), and Thomas F. Driver, "Homosexuality: The Contemporary and Christian Contexts," *Commonweal,* (April 6, 1973)).

Paulist Press, New York (Headings for Chapters 2 through 6 of this work taken from *Human Sexuality,* ed. by the Rev. Anthony Kosnick *et al.,* © 1977 by the Catholic Theological Society of America). Reprinted by permission of Paulist Press.

Rosemary Radford Ruether and Eugene Bianchi (Rosemary Radford Ruether, "The Personalization of Sex," from *From Machismo to Mutuality* by Rosemary Radford Ruether and Eugene Bianchi).

Sh'ma Magazine (Anon., "Must Homosexuals Be Jewish Outcasts?" from *Sh'ma* Vol. 5, No. 98 (October 3, 1978), pp. 303-305).

The Seabury Press, New York (Excerpt from HOMOSEXUALITY: A Symbolic Confusion by Ruth Tiffany Barnhouse. Copyright © 1977 by The Seabury Press, Inc. Reprinted by permission of the Publisher, and "Some Words of Caution" by William Muehl. From MALE AND FEMALE edited by Ruth Tiffany Barnhouse and Urban T. Holmes, III.). Copyright © 1976 by The Seabury Press, Inc. Reprinted by permission of the Publisher.

The Thomist Press, Washington (Charles E. Curran, "Homosexuality and Moral Theology: Methodological and Substantive Considerations," *The Thomist,* Vol. 35 No. 3 (July 1971), pp. 447-481).

Doubleday & Company, Inc., New York ("Homosexuality and Love" from *Toward*

Introduction

The past fifteen years have seen the appearance of much writing on the pastoral responsibility of religious institutions to the homosexual in general, and the ramifications of acceptance of homosexuality as a morally-justifiable life-style in particular. There are several reasons for this.

One of these is that during the last quarter of a century, societal attitudes towards homosexuality have undergone great change, especially in Anglo-Saxon countries, whose sanctions against homosexual conduct are probably the most severe and least flexible in the West.

The first attempt to change societal attitudes in the Anglo-Saxon countries took place in England and Wales. In 1950, an Anglican priest, the Reverend Derrick Sherwin Bailey, was appointed as a member of the Church of England Moral Welfare Council. In that capacity, he and others interested in the cause of homosexual law reform worked unrelentingly to persuade members of Parliament to encourage the Government of the day to set up an official Commission of Inquiry, which resulted in the appointment of a Committee under the Chairmanship of Sir John Wolfenden. The Committee's terms of reference called for it "to consider the law and practice relating to homosexual offences and the treatment of persons convicted of such offences by the courts, and to report what changes if any were in the Committee's opinion desirable."

At the same time, Sherwin Bailey was also busily engaged researching and writing a definitive historical study of the moral and legal sanctions, which was published in 1955 under the title of *Homosexuality and the Western Christian Tradition*. One of the chief features of that work is that it examines and seeks to disprove the popular misconception that the characteristic "sin of Sodom" in Genesis 19:1–26 is homosexual behavior by constitutional inverts, pure and simple. While not all of Sherwin Bailey's conclusions have been universally accepted, few scholars would question the soundness of his methodology in placing biblical and extrabiblical statements in a historical context, or would dispute David Blamire's claim that "that was not in itself a new approach to Scripture, but it was a new approach to the way in which Scripture deals with human sexuality. All subsequent serious study of homosexuality . . . either is indebted to Bailey's work or must take issue with it."

It is difficult to overestimate the significance of Bailey's work in that the ideological basis of Western legal sanctions of Justinian's time is founded upon just such an interpretation of the "sin of Sodom." For instance, Blackstone's *Commentaries*, first published in 1769, and much used as a textbook in the formation of lawyers, both in the United States and other English-speaking nations, says:

> This is the voice of nature and of reason, and the express law of God . . . Of which we have a signal instance, long before the Jewish dispensation, by the destruction of two cities by fire from heaven: so that this is a universal, not merely a provincial precept. And our ancient law in some measure imitated this punishment by commanding such miscreants to be burned to death . . .

The Wolfenden Committee issued its report in 1957. It concluded that the true function of criminal law in this field "is to preserve public order and decency, to protect the citizen from what is offensive and injurious, and to protect safeguards against the exploitation of others, particularly those who are specially vulnerable. It is not the function of the law to intervene in the private lives of citizens, or to seek to enforce any particular pattern of behavior, further than is necessary to carry out the purposes we have outlined." Moreover, the Committee went on to state that in its opinion "it is important to make a clear distinction between 'homosexual offences' and 'homosexuality' " and observed that "homosexuality is a state or condition, and as such does not, and cannot, come within the purview of the criminal law."

Ten years were to elapse before the recommendations of the Wolfenden Committee were acted upon by the British Parliament in the passage in 1967 of the Sexual Offenses Act. Since that time, Canada and 23 legislatures in the U.S.A.—Alaska, Arkansas, California, Colorado, Connecticut, Delaware, Hawaii, Idaho, Illinois, Indiana, Iowa, Maine, Nebraska, New Hampshire, New Jersey, New Mexico, North Dakota, Ohio, Oregon, South Dakota, Washington, West Virginia, and Wyoming—have decriminalized private sexual acts between consenting adults. In Idaho the legislation never took effect because the Legislature repealed the law before its operative date, while in Arkansas sexual reform was in effect for a year before the legislators re-enacted a law criminalizing homosexual conduct only.

The coming of Gay Liberation in June, 1969, also has given added impetus and urgency to the movement of liberalization of societal attitudes towards the homosexual community, and the need to critically re-examine the various sanctions against homosexual persons and their behavior. Thus, given the place and function of psychiatry and psychology in Western societies, it was perhaps inevitable that sooner or later the commonly-held view that homosexuality, as such, is a pathological condition would have to be re-evaluated.

On December 15, 1973, the Board of Trustees of the American Psychiatric Association voted to remove homosexuality, *per se*, from its official list of pathological disturbances. This action was followed by the adoption of a position statement on homosexuality and civil rights, which reads:

> whereas homosexuality *per se* implies no impairment in judgement, stability, reliability, or general social or vocational capabilities, be it resolved that the A.P.A. deplores all public and private discrimination against homosexuals in such areas as employment, housing, public accommodations, and licensing, and declares that no burden of proof of such judgement, capacity, or reliability shall be placed upon homosexuals greater than that imposed on any other persons.

A similar resolution was adopted in January, 1975, by the governing body of the American Psychological Association which, after noting with approval the action of the American Psychiatric Association in removing homosexuality from its official list of mental disorders, as well as its statement that "homosexuality *per se* implies no impairment in judgement, stability, reliability, or general social or vocational capabilities," went on to say:

> Further, the (American Psychological) Association urges all mental health professionals to take the lead in removing the stigma of mental illness that has long been associated with homosexual orientations.

We have seen that in many questions of public morality, such as the homosexual issue, there exists an interface between civil politics, the law, the mental health professions, and the religious institutions of society, which has resulted in the promulgation and enforcement of sanctions that are inter-related and mutually re-enforcing. We have also observed that the re-evaluation and removal of a given sanction has often made problematic the prudence and justice of retaining the remaining ones. We have also noted that successful homosexual law reform is usually posited on the legal premise that in a modern secular society "not all sins are properly given the status of crimes." But if consensual homosexual acts taking place in private are no longer prosecuted as crimes in an ever-increasing number of jurisdictions in the English-speaking world, and if homosexuality, as such, is not classified as a pathological condition by the leadership of the two professional organizations of American psychiatrists and psychologists, what do the Jewish and Christian religious institutions of our society have to say about the moral question? In sum, is homosexuality a sin?

Among professional moralists, there is general agreement that the ethical question is not only grave but complex. For at the present time there are at least four different schools of thought on the subject.

One school of thought re-iterates the traditional proscriptions against homosexual acts, usually based upon biblical and extrabiblical authorities and/or natural law arguments. A variant of this posture is that of the "neo-traditionalist" school which, while starting with liberal premises, nevertheless reaches equally conservative conclusions, albeit for psycho-sociological rather than strictly theological reasons. A second stance is that of scholars who, while considering homosexuality to be objectively wrong, argue that the constitutional invert may have little if any personal responsibility for his or her sexual orientation and possibly sexual acts also. Another posture is that of those who teach that all sexual acts ought to be primarily evaluated on the basis of their relational significance. Finally, there is the position of the "revisionist" school, which teaches that homosexual acts are natural and good.

This work documents all of these positions with selections taken from the writings of the leading contributors to the debate, while in the final section—part six—there appear four critiques which evaluate the relative strengths and weaknesses of the different stances. An appendix of official statements issued by Jewish and Christian religious bodies, and professional organizations has also been included.

Homosexuality and Ethics does not attempt or purport to supply simple and easy answers to the moral question. What it does is to survey the present state of the ongoing debate among ethicists, thus providing the reader with the necessary resources for reflection and determination. As we seek to find and frame the answer to this question, we might also discover more about the nature, purpose and meaning of the sexuality we all share in virtue of our common personhood.

I wish to express my gratitude and appreciation to the following persons for their assistance and co-operation in the preparation of this book: to the Rt. Rev. David Richards, Executive for Pastoral Development of the Protestant Episcopal Church in the U.S.A., who first suggested this project; to my editor at The Pilgrim Press, Esther Cohen, for her helpful comments and suggestions as to ways and means of broadening the scope and appeal of the work; to my friend and colleague, Mortimer Downing, who provided an original translation of the relevant sections of the *Summa Theologica* of Saint Thomas Aquinas; to the Faculty of the Yale Divinity School, New Haven, Conn., who awarded me a Fellowship in order to research the subject; and to Rabbi Balfour Brickner, Michael Collins, Armand De Fillipo, Bernard Gledhill, the Reverend William R. Johnson, John Klopacz, the Reverend Robert Carter, S.J., the Reverend John J. McNeill, S.J., and Rabbi Harry Rothstein.

A special word of thanks must also be given to Professor Beverley Harrison of Union Theological Seminary, New York City, and to Georgia Fuller, Ph.D., of the Quixote Center, Mount Rainer, Md., for help and encouragement in seeking to locate materials. For an explanation of the paucity of such materials written from a feminist perspective, I would refer the reader to Naomi Goldenberg's book, *Changing of the Gods*, (Boston, Mass.: Beacon Press, 1979).

Although research for this anthology began long before the publication in 1977 of *Human Sexuality: New Directions in American Catholic Thought*, prepared by the Task Force on Human Sexuality of the Catholic Theological Society of America, I would also like to acknowledge my indebtedness and thanks to Anthony Kosnick and his associates, as well as to the Report's Publisher, Paulist Press, New York, for their kind permission to reprint their descriptive titles of the four different ethical positions, which appear in the present work as the headings of parts two through five. It should be noted that the phrase, "intrinsically evil," in part two is a paraphrase of a similar phrase in the Vatican *Declaration on Sexual Ethics*, 1975, and that the phrase, "essentially imperfect," in part three is a quotation from *Sexuality and Human Community*, 1970, the Report of the Task Force on Human Sexuality of the United Presbyterian Church in the U.S.A.

EDWARD BATCHELOR, JR.

I

Toward a New Homosexual Ethic

Roger Shinn
Tom Driver
Gregory Baum
Rosemary Ruether
Anon. (from *Sh'ma*)

Homosexuality: Christian Conviction and Inquiry

Roger L. Shinn

Contemporary discussion of homosexuality, at least in Western cultures, must move through a desert of accumulated debris before getting at its subject. The debris is constituted of ignorance, fear, and guilt. The ignorance is partly a lack of accurate information and partly a collection of misinformation propagated in popular culture. The fear is of a threat, real or imagined, to acknowledged values; it is sometimes strongest among people who fear a latent homosexuality in themselves and, in retaliation, lash out against homosexuality in others. The guilt is a long legacy of persecution inflicted upon a minority of society, far out of proportion to the penalties imposed upon people who deviate from customary manners and morals in other ways.

The purpose of this chapter is not to work over the debris, but to get on to the issues posed for Christians by homosexuality as a fact in human life.

3

tart by noting the debris in order to avoid confusing it with
lf. In particular, we must give some attention to the factor
and the consequent guilt of society and church toward its

The Victimization of Homosexuals

Whatever our final judgment about homosexuality, there is something peculiarly unhealthy in the zeal of its persecutors. Ours is a culture that, by and large, tolerates much. We are not a people among whom "all hearts are open, all desires known, and from whom no secrets are hid." We permit and encourage considerable anonymity. The common life abounds in material for rumor and innuendo, and gossip is far from rare. Yet a noblesse oblige works to neutralize some insinuations and to protect their victims.

The exception is homosexuality. In high echelons of public life careers have been ruined by episodes of homosexuality. The hint of homosexual behavior is an absolute barrier to numerous public and private jobs. Blackmailers and extortionists fleece their victims with impunity.

An example makes the point. In 1966 the press disclosed the operations of a gang of racketeers who had squeezed millions of dollars out of more than a thousand reputed homosexual victims over roughly a decade. So bold were the operators that in one case two of them, masquerading as New York detectives, entered the Pentagon and led out a high military officer. They managed to mulct him for thousands of dollars before driving him to suicide.[1] One need not have a phobia about the Pentagon to surmise that the private lives of its thousands of denizens offer a good many occasions for possible disclosure and embarrassment. But only on the issue of homosexuality is a moral (or moralistic) passion so built into social institutions as to assure the success of organized blackmail.

Because defense against accusation is so hard and costly, there is no way of knowing how many people suffer severe penalties from their neighbors or from society on this issue. Anybody who writes or speaks publicly against the common cruelty to homosexual persons is likely to receive further evidence by mail—sometimes signed, sometimes anonymous—from victims or their friends and counselors.

The sources of the peculiar horror of homosexuality in our culture are obscure and complex. The Christian tradition, both on the formal and on the popular levels, has had something to do with the case. A very few verses of the Bible, often wrenched out of context and interpreted with doubtful accuracy, have had their influence. Before attributing too much to their power, anybody might ask about many other verses of scripture, more explicit and more emphatic in the original, that have *not* shaped our culture. Churches are showing increasing sensitivity to the harm done by intolerance toward sexual deviance. In Great Britain, after the Wolfenden Report advocated that homosexual relations between consenting adults no longer be considered a crime, the Church of England moved more quickly than Parliament to take up the cause. But the churches are still perplexed and embarrassed by the many issues related to homosexuality.

What I have said thus far presupposes no ethical evaluation of homosexuality itself. It assumes only that, whatever judgment may be made on homosexuality, church and society owe to human beings a concern for justice and a respect for dignity and privacy. Morality is not a valid pretext for cruelty.

Empirical and Theological Factors in Christian Judgment

Any attempt to get at the meaning of homosexuality demonstrates immediately one characteristic of all understanding of human behavior. Understanding comes out of a subtle interaction between two personal-social processes. One is comprised of those moral-aesthetic sensitivities about human nature and its possibilities, those purposes and valuations that influence any person's awareness of his world. The other is the acquisition of information empirically available or discoverable by scientific methods of inquiry. Both processes are essential; each is important but by itself is insufficient.

The reason is that meanings, including moral meanings, can never be imposed upon life without regard for the specific facts and circumstances that have meaning for people; hence understanding requires empirical evidence. On the other hand, sheer factual evidence is rarely if ever self-interpreting; it takes on meaning within the experience of persons and communities with their histories, their loyalties, and their purposes.

Human death, to take one of the most obvious of all facts, is never solely a fact; it enters human experience as fate or as accident, as tragedy or absurdity, as defeat or victory, as murder or manslaughter or simple error, as moral outrage or as natural necessity, as enemy or as friend. In any given case the meaning of a death is determined in part by the facts of the situation; it is determined also by the web of experience, beliefs, and commitments by which persons meet the death of themselves and of others.

Christian ethics is not unusual in bringing to any situation a constellation of experiences that contribute to the meanings that can be found in the situation. All ethical thinking does that. The distinctive quality of Christian ethics is that the experiences, the memories, and the expectations that it brings to all phenomena are related to the experience

rist. It does not expect any collection of unevaluated facts to
ignificant human meaning; it finds meaning as the awareness
rts persons to the possibilities and perils of life. Hence there
...theological factors at work in any Christian apprehension of empirical
situations.

Christian judgments on human conduct are subject to change. The
hastiest glance at history will show such change in judgments of
behavior—whether sexual, economic, military, racial, political, or almost
anything else. The Christian community, living in history, modifies its
judgments—both for better and for worse—in the light of new
experiences, new temptations, new insights. But it always—insofar as it is
true to its faith—brings to experience the awareness of Christ and of the
biblical history that tells it of Christ.

All this means that Christian ethics approaches a problematic situation
within a context of inquiry that in some important way is given. There is a
discipline of Christian inquiry. The Christian community does not ask
simply how men may have most fun or use up most consumer goods or
lead the most untroubled lives. It does not even ask how they may achieve
the fullest self-expression or happiness. It is concerned for the good of
man, not for abstract causes. But in searching for the good of man it sees a
cruciform pattern in life. "If any man would come after me, let him deny
himself and take up his cross and follow me. For whoever would save his
life will lose it, and whoever loses his life for my sake will find it" (Matt.
16:24-25).

Thus a paradox is built into the heart of Christian ethics. The paradox
has been misused. Christians have prescribed crosses for others while
exalting themselves. They have deceived themselves by cultivating trivial
forms of self-denial while indulging in frantic self-aggrandizement. They
have elaborated heresies that denied the joyful recognition of the good of
life, forgetting that their Lord came that men might "have life, and have it
abundantly" (John 10:10). But the recognition of a cruciform quality in
life, despite its history of distortions, is inherent in Christian ethics. It
distinguishes the Christian ethic from the most prevalent alternative in
Western culture, the ethic of self-realization that extends from Aristotle
to contemporary philosophy.

This ineradicably theological factor in Christian ethics does not of itself
provide many precise ethical judgments. Certainly it does not prescribe a
code of behavior for contemporary man. If anybody thinks that it does, he
might try to answer the simple question "Where?" He can hardly locate
the authoritative code in the teachings of Augustine, Thomas Aquinas, or
Calvin. If he proposes the Bible, again the question is "Where?" Does any
contemporary person take the book of Leviticus as an adequate guide for
the ethical perplexities of contemporary urban life? Or, to use a more

embarrassing example, does anyone so take the Sermon on the Mount? Certainly there is no automatic process by which a believer can lift out of biblical or historical tradition a moral commandment to meet a contemporary perplexity.

The theological component in Christian decision-making is a context of inquiry and a sensitivity of perception. It is a possibility of self-understanding and the understanding of others. It is an awareness of divine gifts and divine demands. It is a set of convictions, in some ways unassailable and in other ways not fully defined, about the good of man, about what is wrong with him, and about new possibilities for human life.

Among the Christian convictions about man are an awareness of the gift of freedom and unique personhood in each individual, a sensitivity to the needs and opportunities of life in community, an awareness of the sin that infects human life, and an openness to the possibilities of personal transformation. These convictions, although not codified, are not utterly vague. They have quite concrete meaning, even though the meaning cannot be readily prescribed.

A comparison with two other styles of ethics is possible. The ethic of self-realization, which I have already mentioned, says to the person: "Be yourself. Realize your possibilities." Against it stand the many ethics of imposed standards, which say: "Be the self that some authority (the church, the police force, the peer group, your parents, the popular culture) tells you to be." The Christian ethic differs from the first alternative because man, as he is, is not a good enough model for himself. It differs from the second because it (the second) asks the person to conform to the expectations of others. In contrast to both, the Christian ethic says: "Become the person that only you, in your created freedom and by God's grace, can become."

The theological factor, as I have described it, is experiential; but it belongs to the type of human experience associated with man's moral imagination, his human sensitivity, and his religious faith. In understanding the concrete decisions of life it must be joined with the kind of information that comes from empirical investigation of facts, both in the manner of practical everyday observation and in the manner of scientific investigation. Especially in the understanding of a topic like homosexuality, which has often been obscured by superstition and erroneous information, clarification of the facts can contribute to understanding of their meaning.

Thus the knowledge that men (and equally women, for that matter) are not divided into two opposite classifications, homosexual and heterosexual, but can be placed on a heterosexual-homosexual continuum, is significant for the understanding of human responses and behavior.[2] The information does not, of itself, dictate what behavior is to be encouraged or discouraged. But it enables persons to understand better themselves and their own approval or condemnation of others.

Similarly, information about the causes of homosexuality has some significance for an understanding of its human meaning. If, as some psychiatrists maintain, homosexuality is a matter of arrested psychosexual development, that bit of knowledge says something about its desirability. If, on the other hand, it is a frequent characteristic of persons who in every ascertainable respect are mature and healthy, that says something else about it. Presumably some progress in the resolution of such arguments is possible. In neither case does the evidence establish an incontrovertible ethical judgment—and in neither case could the evidence possibly justify the persecution of homosexuals that I have already criticized. But further information is likely to influence normative judgments.

Another question, subject to empirical inquiry, is the changeability of sexual responses, both emotional and behavioral. To the extent that a person is free to change himself and his personal characteristics, new possibilities are available to him. To the extent that he cannot change, he must learn to live with himself as he is. Again no ethical conclusion is dictated; the changeability of a person's character does not itself establish that he should change, nor does the unchangeability of it in some respects mean that it is in those respects admirable. But possibilities of change are evidence of freedom; and what a man does with his freedom, as contrasted with conditions he cannot change, is always an ethical issue.

Yet the subtlety of this issue forbids hasty conclusions. Suppose a man changes his sexual behavior by turning himself into a manipulated object. There are methods of treatment that, in some cases, can do just that. If a man is homosexually responsive and heterosexually unresponsive, behavioristic techniques of "therapy" may change him, by subjecting him to homosexual stimuli accompanied by pain (e.g., electric shock), then to heterosexual stimuli accompanied by pleasurable experiences. Thus he may be conditioned or directed toward heterosexuality. The troubling question is whether such treatment does not succeed in bringing the person to conformity with the dominant moral culture, while violating his own freedom and selfhood.

In one other area—the relation of homosexuality to other personal and cultural patterns—increasing knowledge can be illuminating. If, as appears to be the case in current experience, homosexual relationships are in general less stable and less genuinely interpersonal than heterosexual relationships, why is this so? Is homosexuality inherently instable, or do cultural patterns make it so? If homosexuals frequently live in a subculture with undesirable characteristics, is it homosexuality or is it the prejudice of the society that produces such a culture? What is cause and what is effect? Normal marriage, although vulnerable enough, is supported by many legal, moral, and economic institutions of society. Homosexual relations, without such support, are likely to find transitory, sub rosa expression. Information about the stability and truly personal quality of homosexual relations is incomplete. But enough knowledge is available to dispel some popular prejudices.

In all of these cases accurate information about homosexuality has some implications for understanding its meaning. The inadequacy of present knowledge is one reason why many judgments about homosexuality must be tentative. Even so, it remains the case that information alone does not establish meaning or dictate valuation. At the present time the conflicts over the meaning of homosexuality are as great among the scientists who have done research on the subject as among laymen. Such specialists as Albert Ellis, Daniel Cappon, Edmund Bergler, and Irving Bieber give the impression that homosexuality is a neurotic phenomenon, subject to correction by therapy; whereas Clara Thompson, Judd Marmor, Evelyn Hooker, and Wardell Pomeroy find data leading to friendlier judgments. Although most of these scholars are psychiatrically trained, they probably could not tell for themselves with any certainty to what extent their findings arise from hostility or friendliness to homosexual persons.

The Traditional Christian Normative Judgment

The Christian tradition over the centuries has affirmed the heterosexual, monogamous, faithful marital union as normative for the divinely given meaning of the intimate sexual relationship. Alongside this, it has recognized a valid vocation of celibacy for some persons.

Within this tradition Christians have sometimes contributed to, sometimes tried to correct, the peculiarly harsh judgments against homosexuality that have been prominent in our culture. Today there are determined efforts within the church to make amends for the severe judgmentalism and the isolation that the church often has inflicted, and frequently persists in inflicting, upon homosexual persons.

There is widespread Christian recognition today of the need for increased understanding that may lead to the revision of many traditional attitudes. But for the most part the renunciation of the ethic of condemnation has not led to an ethic of endorsement. Daniel Day Williams has summarized well, without necessarily stating as his own, a characteristic position in theological ethics today: "Homosexuality—whatever its genetic, cultural, and psychological aspects—involves modes of human experience which are in some way deviant from the fullest possibilities of sexual life which are realized only in heterosexual relationships."[3]

Certainly there are impressive biblical foundations for such a position.

The Bible, I have already insisted, does not deliver to the Christian a code of conduct for modern life. Hence there is something futile about the enterprise, occasionally pursued, of tracking down all the biblical texts referring to homosexuality and arguing from them to a set of norms for today. The battle of proof-texts goes on, but not to much avail. What the Bible communicates to the Christian is a revelation of divine love and the possibilities of responsive human love, including the meaning and possibilities of human sexuality. In that sense, rather than in any amassing of miscellaneous texts from a variety of historical contexts, there is a clear endorsement of heterosexuality.

It is most evident in Jesus' teaching on the fundamental meaning of sexuality, in which he quotes and makes his own certain statements from the first two chapters of Genesis: "But from the beginning of creation, 'God made them male and female.' 'For this reason a man shall leave his father and mother and be joined to his wife, and the two shall become one' " (Mark 10:6-8).

Christians have had long practice in misusing the words of Jesus. It is a misuse if a church, which has long tolerated deviations from almost all the teachings of Jesus, uses such a text to condemn those who deviate from it. It is a misuse if Christians violate the integrity of other men and women by imposing upon them the understanding of sex that most Christians derive from Christ, the Christian tradition, and their own experience. But it is not a misuse for Christians to testify that their faith has made them aware of the peculiar meaning of the one-flesh relationship between male and female under God.

Christians have usually believed that the ethical awareness given to them through Christ, although not necessarily demonstrable outside the community of faith, meets some similar intimations or signs of confirmation in wider human experience. They believe that the *Logos* made flesh in Christ is the same *Logos* through which the world was made. They do not expect the Christian faith and insight to be confirmed by unanimous agreement of all people, even all decent and idealistic people. But they do expect the fundamental Christian motifs to have some persuasiveness in general experience.

Such a persuasiveness is evident in the reasoning of Erich Fromm. (Fromm will not be offended to be identified as a non-Christian, since he would feel unjustly treated if we called him a Christian.)

> The male-female polarity is also the basis for interpersonal creativity. This is obvious biologically in the fact that the union of sperm and ovum is the basis for the birth of a child. But in the purely psychic realm it is not different; in the love between man and woman, each of them is reborn.[4]

It is important to examine exactly the reasoning involved here. The point is not to invoke the authority of Fromm (since other authorities take other positions), but to examine what he is saying. His argument is *not* that the purpose of heterosexual love is procreation—or that procreation is somehow necessary to justify sexual love. He is rather pointing to an analogy between biological and psychic creativity, an analogy that, as he goes on to say, is impossible in homosexuality. He also goes on to say that many heterosexual relations fail in this love. There is no ground here for the equation of heterosexual with good and homosexual with bad, but there is a clear affirmation of the meaning possible in authentic love between one man and one woman and impossible otherwise.[5]

If there is in Christian theology a clear emphasis on the normative place of heterosexual love, there is an equally clear awareness that no legalism is adequate to define authentic sexuality and sexual love. Although the Christian tradition endorses the monogamous, faithful, heterosexual marital union, such a marriage may still be joyless or exploitative.

Certainly there have been polygamous families with more love and mutual concern than many monogamous families. There have been promiscuous and adulterous liaisons with more personal concern than some technically faithful unions. There have been homosexual relationships with more mutual appreciation than some heterosexual marriages. Any legalistic definition of conditions that make sex "right" is a trap. Even so, it is still possible to maintain that there is a normative expression of sexual love, as Christian faith understands the meaning of such love.

To many honest representatives of homophile groups, this position will seem entirely inadequate. It will not help to add that there is no insinuation here that any given homosexual individual is morally inferior to any given heterosexual individual or to heterosexual people as a class. Nor will it be enough to continue that, in Christian terms, no person ever achieves righteousness or moral excellence, but the best of men are sinful and live by the mercy of God. All such talk, in the face of the history of moral condemnation of homosexuals, is likely to appear as pious prattle concealing an unbearable condescension.

In reply, all that can be said is that some Christians genuinely believe the position that has been set forth here and that they believe the consistent theme of Christian ethics requires the maintenance of moral apprehensions derived from Christ, together with a refusal to use those apprehensions to condemn those whom Christ did not condemn.

The Current Theological Discussion

The position I have sketched here is not a final verdict. In contemporary theological discussions there are at least three other distinguishable possibilities that deserve discussion.

One of these is the decisive reaffirmation of the biblical tradition as stated by Karl Barth. The central theme in all Barth's theology and ethics is the overwhelming grace of God. The ethic is thoroughly biblical. Barth is not interested in the many empirical questions I have raised in this discussion, and his ethic is far less tentative in its moral judgment than the position I have described above in the language of Daniel Day Williams. Barth believes that man's sexuality is inherent in his created nature and destiny, that men and women both know themselves only in relation to the other sex, that homosexuality is a rejection of creatureliness and an idolatry. It is a malady of "perversion, decadence, and decay." Thus far the judgment seems harsh. Yet, Barth is not interested in moral condemnation. Christ has conquered sin, and Barth perceives men as elected to redemption in Christ. So his message to every person, however perplexed or troubled by life's problems, is the message of exuberant confidence in God's love. The implication is that no one should try to defend or justify homosexuality; equally no one should condemn any person or despair over any sin.[6]

A second possibility appears in the thought of Helmut Thielicke, who is more interested in the empirical study of homosexuality than Barth, but no less concerned with its theological meaning. Thielicke plainly regards homosexuality as an abnormality, a distortion or depravation of the normal created order. But in a world where all men share in fallen and distorted existence, "there is not the slightest excuse for maligning the constitutional homosexual morally or theologically." When the homosexual can change to heterosexuality, he should seek treatment or healing. Where he cannot, he may find it possible to sublimate his homosexual desires. If not, he may seek "to structure the man-man relationship in an *ethically responsible* way." Such an effort is hazardous, given the patterns of society; and Thielicke does not want to change those patterns basically, except that he endorses the Wolfenden proposals for removing the criminal status of adult homosexual behavior and he opposes the judgmentalism of society. He would encourage the homosexual to make the best of his painful situation without pretending that it is normal.[7]

The third possibility is a full acceptance of homosexuality. The theme is stated in the well-known statement of the English Quakers: "One should no more deplore 'homosexuality' than left-handedness . . . Homosexual affection can be as selfless as heterosexual affection, and therefore we cannot see that it is in some way morally worse."[8] A similar position has been stated persuasively by some Christian pastors who have worked closely with homosexuals and homophile organizations.[9] Some have recommended that the church acknowledge homosexuality to the extent of providing a rite of homosexual marriage. This latter position marks an abrupt departure from theological and liturgical tradition, but it stems from a genuine concern for persons.

Christian ethics rarely prescribes final forms and institutions for human behavior. More specifically, this is not the time in history for final judgment on the meaning and ethical import of homosexuality. Information about the phenomena, the causes, and the possibilities of change is still inadequate. Meanwhile the three themes just described all have a justifiable place within the conversations of the Christian community as it seeks further wisdom on a troubling issue.

As Christians seek better understanding on this issue, they have a responsibility to remain open to any new sources of information and insight. They have a similar responsibility to remain faithful to the moral apprehensions of the Christian gospel. Among those apprehensions those that have been most neglected in the past practice of the church in this sphere are the sensitivities that warn against condemnation and that evoke compassion.

The Contemporary and Christian Contexts

Tom F. Driver

We may as well start with a few signs of the times.

1. Nineteen years ago [1954], students at Union Theological Seminary, where I teach, invited Robert W. Wood, author of *Christ and the Homosexual,* to speak. The then president of the school was out of town. When he returned to face the prospect of an outspoken gay contingent in his student body, he summoned his faculty into session extraordinary and demanded they endorse his proposal to expel all homosexuals unless they undertook therapy. The faculty refused.

2. In 1971 the now president of the same school quietly (though not without some urging) announced as policy that no faculty, student, nor staff member would be discriminated against in any way because of sexual preference.

3. In 1972 the editors of *Commonweal* send me for review *five* new books about gay liberation.* Later they ask me instead to write an article on "The Christian and the Homosexual." I wonder if they mean that the categories are mutually exclusive.

Homosexual: Oppression and Liberation, by Dennis Altman (Outerbridge & Dienstfrey, $6.95). *Dancing the Gay Lib Blues: A Year in the Homosexual Liberation Movement,* by Arthur Bell (Simon and Schuster, $5.95). *On Being Different: What it Means to be a Homosexual,* by Merle

14

4. On the day I begin to compose the article I receive in my mail an open letter to the Union Seminary Community:

> Metropolitan Community Church (MCC) of New York and its national parent body, the Universal Fellowship of Metropolitan Community Churches, are important manifestations of an emerging Christian spirit among members of the second largest minority in the nation, the hitherto-hidden gay community. Founded in Los Angeles in October 1968 by a young minister named Troy Perry, the "gay church" there quickly grew from twelve persons to a current average weekly attendance of well over 1,000. . . .

The writer, Howard R. Wells, Pastor of MCC New York, goes on to speak of "homosexuals embracing Christ's spirit without rejecting their God-given sexual identity." God-given? That's laying a lot on God, but it reminds me that many heterosexual males seem to regard their masculinity as a divine endowment. Maybe we need a theology of sexuality, not just sex.

5. In the municipal, state, and Congressional elections of 1970, the Gay Activists Alliance in New York City campaigned vigorously on behalf of candidates who publicly supported equal rights for homosexuals, or who responded favorably to a GAA questionnaire. Twenty-four out of thirty-six winners had GAA support, including the following who gave "particularly strong support": Bella Abzug, Edward Koch, Antonio Olivieri, Albert Blumenthal, Shirley Chisholm, and Stephen Solarez. Gay Activist Marc Rubin has further noted that "statistical analysis of the State Senatorial and State Assembly races produced an interesting fact: Where only one of the two major-party candidates supported us, he usually won his election. Seventy-four percent of such races were won by candidates who added their support of homosexual rights to their campaign policies. Political support for these rights was not, therefore, the kiss of death that many people thought it would be; it turned out to be an asset."

Until I read the books on gay liberation that *Commonweal* sent me, I had not realized the extent to which the social context for thinking about homosexuality has changed. All the writers agree that the movement came awake in the summer of 1969. On June 28, New York police raided the Stonewall Inn on Christopher Street, a bar catering to homosexuals. Such raids are expected from time to time. They are part of a charade in which the police pretend to uphold morality while also maintaining

---

Miller (Random House, $4.50). *Homosexual Liberation: A Personal View*, by John Murphy (Praeger, $5.95). *The Gay Militants*, by Donn Teal (Stein and Day, $7.95). I have also read at this time *Sexuality and Homosexuality: A New View*, by Arno Karlen (Norton, $15), and *The Christian Male Homosexual*, a series of three articles by John J. McNeill, S. J., published in 1971 in *The Homiletic and Pastoral Review*.

convenient arrangements with the underworld operators of gay bars. At the Stonewall that night, however, the customers fought back. Somehow or other they got the police to barricade themselves inside the place while the gays barraged it from outside with flying bottles, cans, bricks and what-not. In this act of rebellion the gay community surfaced politically and has not been the same since.

The Stonewall incident is a convenient peg, but it is far from being a cause of gay militancy. The Mattachine Society (begun in 1950) and the Daughters of Bilitis (founded 1955) were forerunners in somewhat the same sense as the Civil Rights Movement was a forerunner of Black militancy. Just as there is a division between those Blacks who favor the "civil" strategies of SCLC or NAACP and those who support the militancy of the Panthers, so the gay community is divided between old-liners like Mattachine and militants like Gay Liberation Front. In social terms it is best to say that the gay liberation movement represents an assertion of group identity through protest in much the same spirit of reckoning that has also given rise to Black Power and women's liberation. All, in turn, are indebted to the rise of Third World consciousness, and they share an antipathy to control of the world's resources and mores by the White (heterosexual) males of Europe and America.

Gay liberation, therefore, forces us to consider homosexuality not only as a psychological, moral and religious question but also as a political one. These four aspects, however, are not easily separable. If homosexuality is a psychological illness, society has reason to treat of it politically by strategies of containment and cure. If it is immoral (like murder or rape) society has the political right to punish it. And if it is a religious offense, the churches have a duty to withhold their sanction.

The apologists for gay liberation whom I have read are unanimous in their condemnation of psychoanalysts and religionists. They understand both groups to be moralistic and repressive—the analysts mainly because of Freud's doctrine that heterosexual genitality is the norm of sexual health in the adult, and the religionists because they use Scripture and dogma to forbid homosexual love. The analysts and the religionists are thus seen together as the *raisonneurs* of an oppressive society which systematically deprives the homosexual minority of its civil rights through harassment, ostracism, job discrimination, oppressive laws and imprisonment.

Recent liberal opinion has attempted to "neutralize" homosexuality in a political sense. It was Mrs. Patrick Campbell, I am told, who said of homosexuals, "I don't care what they do as long as they don't do it in the street and frighten the horses." The famous Quaker Study in 1962 affirmed that what was done in private by consenting adults was none of society's business, and this was also the burden of the Wolfenden Report, which led to the reform of English law on the matter.

However, so neat a distinction between public and private sexuality cannot long hold. It is theoretically weak because it violates the integrity of person, allowing in private a sentiment of which all public acknowledgment is forbidden. And it is pragmatically weak because it never knows where to draw the line.

The moral truth of the matter is that society cannot hold to a "positive" attitude toward heterosexualtiy (to be rewarded with legal and religious blessing in marriage) while simultaneously holding to a "neutral" attitude toward homosexuality (to be denied social sanction yet tolerated by non-prosecution). If it tries to do so, it denies the homosexual all social identity; and this, as is now fully recognized by gay spokesmen, is tantamount to social prosecution, even if the police do not harass and the law does not condemn. If you deprive my sexual life of social recognition, you force me to a life of shame. No heterosexual faces such ignominy. It were better to prosecute the homosexual than to tell him that his sexuality, if he hides it, is of no matter.

If a person's sexual identity is denied social sanction, he will appeal elsewhere—to nature, God, or the Devil. But the human being is never simply this or that. The appeal to nature, God, or Devil is futile because none (of itself) takes proper account of freedom, which pertains to sexuality as much as to any other human quality. The domain of human freedom (always related to responsibility) is society. The human question of sexuality is the question of sex in social life. Anything we say about sex in nature or sex in the eyes of God lacks human significance until it is placed in the context of "life together." When gay liberation makes homosexuality a *political* matter, it makes it also a properly human and theological one.

American society seems to be moving away from the prosecution of homosexuality. Illinois and a few other states have eliminated laws forbidding homosexual practice among consenting adults, and New York City has, under pressure from organized gays, ceased entrapment by the police and most other forms of harassment. This trend will probably continue, along with the general sexual permissiveness, unless there occurs a puritanical backlash; and this is not likely except as part of a rightwing political move. Gay liberationists are correct in thinking that the treatment of homosexuals is an index of the degree of liberty in the country.*

This being so, the attitude of the churches is important. A backlash of moral indignation against homosexuals would require the endorsement of religious spokesmen. This it would surely get unless the churches and their leaders move now, while they can, to remove from homosexuality

---

*For this reason, Blacks, women and other liberationist groups ought not to scorn it, a point Huey Newton has seen and Eldridge Cleaver has not.

the religious condemnation under which it has for so long lived. The question is: can the Christian affirm homosexuality as a valid behavior and way of life?

In raising this question, I am not asking about all the things that often go along with homosexuality, no more than an apologia for heterosexuality need defend everything that is associated with it. I do not speak here of sado-masochism, "camp" style, the ambience of gay bars and porno movie houses, child molestation, etc., etc. All these have their heterosexual parallels. I speak only of the human and theological validity of the sexual love of a person for another of the same sex.

The fear that homosexuality, were it condoned, would spread through the population like an epidemic is probably not well grounded. It were a curious anthropology to think that sexual appetite is mainly directed toward the same sex and has to be channeled toward the opposite by social and religious pressure. Without a social taboo against it, homosexuality would, in my guess, manifest a temporary rise and then a marked decline. Meanwhile, we would probably see and hear a good deal of bisexual imagination and behavior. This is the opinion of Dennis Altman in *Homosexual,* the best written and best argued of the recent books I have read.

Bisexuality, I would further guess, is the church's deepest sexual fear, the possibility that is most threatening to the church's ancient sexual negativity. The reasoning, if spelled out, would run as follows:

"The best of all sex is sublimated sex (celibacy). But in order to preserve the race there exists a tolerable sexuality (hetero) in marriage. So say Paul, Augustine, most of the Fathers, and the tradition. Of this suitable and divinely sanctioned sex there exists a perversion, the love of men for men and women for women. It is as cursed as the other is blessed, and in condemning it we bear testimony to the estate of marriage which Our Lord blessed at Cana. Thus we can see that good and evil are symmetrical.

"Now there come those saying that the sexual loves of people are not clear but confused. Men may love men, women may love women *and* the same men and women may love each other. This is as much as to say that all sexual love is good, and that its form does not matter. When homosexuals proclaimed that their love was best, we understood them, for they were but devils calling the worst best. But now profligates arise and say there is no best, that all is allowed to whosoever loves. This strikes at our doctrine of celibacy, for within its chastity we *do* say that all love is good, but these are saying the same from the vantage point of unchastity. If we agreed with them, we should have to admit that sexual lust is not bad, that the sublimation of sex is not ideal, that love is free to find its own way. What would happen to marriage? What evil thoughts would fill our picture of Heaven? We must defend ourselves against this most awful persuasion of sexual anarchy."

Had I written on homosexuality three or more years ago, I should not, in fact, have thought that the issue *is* the sanctity of marriage in its traditional regard. Today, however, both gay and women's liberation have arisen to say that marriage either is or has become a repressive institution. The Catholic church, in unwitting irony, agrees with this in forbidding its priests and nuns to marry, thus maintaining a witness to a "love" that is more free than marriage, less bound to temporal obligation.

So the old questions come round again, and we find ourselves having to think once more about sexual lust in relation to marriage. Augustine taught that lust should be avoided even between husband and wife, sex being of procreation, not pleasure. Vatican II attempted to recognize the validity of sexual pleasure in the cementing of the marriage bond. But the taint of evil remains, the deep, lingering conviction that sexual desire contradicts the love of God.

The moral posture of Christianity, then, is not merely to prevent sexual behavior that is harmful but to regulate it *en tout,* as if it were a disease to be kept under control. This leads to a hierarchy of sexual forms, a scale of perversions, which does achieve the desired effect—to inhibit the spontaneity of desire. Today the conflict between spontaneity and marriage is very great, and marriage is the loser.

I do not think we are being asked by either the gay or the women's movement to give up marriage. I think we are being asked to do three things, one compatible with tradition and two not:

1. We are being asked to think of marriage as a special vocation, thus not a natural, a religious, nor a social fate. This means that marriage should be chosen, not stumbled into, nor contracted because it is the expected thing. There are also other ways to live. This is what marriage has, in principle, meant all along. It is the sense behind the venerable doctrine (which the church took over from ancient Roman law) that the essence of marriage is the willing consent of the partners. We ought not to grumble at having to relearn this basic principle from radicals.

2. Life outside marriage is not necessarily or even normally virginal. I doubt if it ever has been for most people, but there would have to have been a Kinsey in every age to prove it. In any case, to prove the opposite—that marriage means the moral right to have intercourse—is no easier. Here again we are being asked to consider marriage as the choice of a life together, not primarily or exclusively as a sexual arrangement.

3. Life inside marriage is not to be construed as forbidding sexual relations with other persons. If this seems to strike at the very foundation of marriage, that is because we have insisted on viewing marriage as a sexual contract, with the result that we do not care what sacrifices of personhood it requires, or else (more often) wink at the "indiscretions" that accompany it.

I do not call into question the teaching that marriage is a lifetime commitment, that its nature is exclusive, and that it is based upon fidelity. I wish only to question whether these concepts are rightly understood when they are taken to refer primarily and necessarily to sexual congress. Is it not instead the case, both in theory and in practice, that the validity of a marriage is judged by the intent and consent of the partners? What counselor, when hearing a case of adultery, would judge by the act committed rather than by the agent's testimony of love, concern and willingness to preserve the married relation? In these matters, to be sure, there is an important aspect known as "injury"; but this is not an absolute standard unless the "injured party" is of an absolutist persuasion. Wise counselors learn that the greatest threat to marriage is, in fact, absolutism.

Far more important to marriage than adherence to rule is open communication between the partners, which implies trust, mutual respect and the partner's welfare as the highest good. To be sure, there can be little trust where the partners play by different rules. This leads us to see that the essence of rule (standard, law, norm, etc.) is its expression of a mutual understanding, its character as the terms of a faithful relation. Do the terms define the relation, or does the relation define the terms?

In a Christian frame of reference, it cannot be that terms, rules, or law define a relation. To think so is to confine gospel within law, whereas the good news of God in Christ is precisely deliverance from such a stage of bondage. From this good news regarding "the law" two possibilities flow: 1) The law is "dead." The consequence drawn is antinomianism. There is some warrant for this conclusion in Christian tradition, but I do not follow it. There are several reasons why not, but the strongest is Jesus' own apparent respect for law. 2) Law has a valid place in human (and divine) life, but that place is relative. That is, the law serves a higher good; and when it does not, it alienates man from God.

"The Sabbath was made for man, not man for the Sabbath" is the most radical of all Jesus' ethical sayings. Transposing, we should say that marriage is made for men and women, not they for marriage. This is precisely the message of our friends in gay and women's liberation, and if we refuse that message we risk refusing it also from their brother in Christ.

My words, I realize, may be taken to offer license to all kinds of random behavior. While that is not my intention, I assume the risk. It is worth taking in order to rescue marriage from the legalism that has latterly beset it, for which we are paying the price of letting the divorce courts and not the church determine the essence, meaning, and purpose of marriage. In order to preserve this "holy estate" we must rediscover what is holy about it. That is to be found in its mutual love and not in its parallels with the laws of property.

The rise of homosexuality and bisexuality in society exerts a pressure on marriage that causes us to re-appropriate its meaning. If this is done, we are freed to recognize that the forms of sexual love do not matter when compared to the dignity of persons and their capacity for trust.

The gay liberation movement raises homosexuality to political consciousness. It prevents our regarding the topic as merely a "psychological problem" or a matter of "private morality." It forces us to consider policy. The movement should have our thanks if it causes us to reconsider the policies of marriage, and most of all if it helps us to see that sexual plurality is the very scene and stage upon which are played out the dramas of love.

Catholic
Homosexuals

Gregory Baum

How does Catholic theology today look upon homosexual men and women?

The traditional position is only too well known. Homosexuality has always been rejected as an unnatural vice. In patriarchal communities such as Israel, homosexuality among men was vehemently repudiated as undermining the dignity of the male and the very structure of society. Jesus was silent about homosexuality, but the Apostle Paul followed the teaching of the Hebrew tradition. While there had been a certain practice of pederasty in Greek society, the Christian Church repudiated homosexuality in any form as in direct opposition to the natural and social order. Homosexuality was regarded as a sin against nature and as such abhorrent. This has been the voice of tradition.

In recent years, however, the argument from nature has become somewhat problematic in Catholic theology. The reason for this is not the influence of existentialism or what is sometimes called situation ethics—this represents too individualistic an emphasis to fit into the Catholic tradition—but, rather, the realization, derived from the analysis of culture and society, that what is called human nature has a history and is, in part at least, created by people, their interaction and their symbolic language. Human nature is not simply a given. It is a given for the individual born into a specific environment, but looked upon historically and collectively, human nature has been created by the actions of people bound together by institutions and a common set of symbols.

22

For this reason, theologians hold that what is called human nature in various cultures must be looked at critically. Since it has been produced over a long period of time, it may include elements that are dehumanizing. Since a culture usually calls 'human nature' the self-understanding of the dominant class and since this usage then greatly extends the ideals and the power of this class, the theologian must try to discern in the inherited, historically constituted human nature the possible structures of oppression, legitimating various forms of what Hegel has called master-slave relationships. Thus, the Catholic theologian dealing with the relationship of men and women has become suspicious of the old arguments from nature. Is not much talk about the nature of men and women a legitimation of the superior power men hold in our culture?

God's judgment, enabling us to discern the structures of evil in this world, rests even on man's historically constituted nature. Christians believe, of course, that divine grace and the divine call are also operative in man's making of man in the various cultural traditions: but theologians wish to be equally aware of the dehumanizing elements woven into our cultural ideals and institutions. In other words, human nature as it is at present is not normative for theologians: they want to detect in it possible reflections of the master-slave relationship. What is normative for normal life is the human nature to which we are divinely summoned, which is defined in terms of mutuality. This, at least, is the promise of biblical religion.

Are we certain that homosexuality in men and women is against nature? Is the prohibition against homosexuality, constant in our cultural and religious heritage, a protection of the good and holy in human life? Or is it a legitimation of the inherited social structure which assigns men and women definitive and unequal places? Since human nature is historical, since, in other words, people over the centuries have participated in the creation of human nature through the institutionalization and symbolization of their lives, the old argument against homosexuality based on human nature will have to be re-examined.

The recent discovery that symbols and institutions enter into people's historical self-contribution affects theological reflection on homosexuality from another point of view. Studying the effects of society on consciousness, we have become keenly aware that the radical rejection of homosexuality and the taboos surrounding it in religious and secular culture inflict unspeakable burdens on the men and women who discover themselves as homosexuals. People who are held in contempt by society, marginalized by custom, vilified by a vulgar or subtle language of exclusion, and judged as sick, as immoral, as perverts, will in one way or another internalize these judgments in the form of self-rejection and self-hatred. Homosexual men and women belong to the most oppressed of all groups in society. For while other groups exposed to contempt and rejection can find in their own tradition sources of pride and self-respect, homosexuals are led to believe in the perversity of their own nature and deprived of the very ground of their self-respect. Seeing a collective crime of such proportions and the violence inflicted on homosexual men and women, the theologian begins to suspect that the traditional arguments against homosexuality were not so much based on a sound concept of nature as summonded forth by God's call, as on a refusal to take a look at the foundations of our culture.

Let me add that these reflections on the power of society to create consciousness also put a question mark behind a good deal of psychological research done on homosexuality. For who knows whether the behavior patterns of homosexuals in our society, especially their inner conflicts, their hang-ups, their debilitating fears, are due to the special nature of homosexuality or, rather, to the wounds inflicted on them by a hostile society? Could it be that the psychological problems of homosexual men and women tell us more about the exclusion patterns of society than about the nature of the homo-erotic orientation?

What, then, do we know about homosexuality? The psychological literature does not provide us with many answers regarding the nature and origin of homosexuality. In his book, *Leonardo da Vinci*, Sigmund Freud proposes a theory relating the origin of the homo-erotic orienation to certain experiences and conflicts in early childhood; he adds, however, that this theory may be applicable to some homosexuals only and that what goes under the common name of homosexuality may in fact refer to a complex human phenomenon that cannot be reduced to a single origin. It is interesting, moreover, that while in this book Freud adopts a theory that regards homosexuality as a defective personal development induced by traumatic childhood experiences, he strongly insists that Leonado da Vinci, the homosexual, was non-neurotic and creative. Most psychiatrists turn to their patients for a knowledge of homosexuality: Freud preferred to study this sexual orientation in a genius capable of transcending the pressure of society and thus arrived at a distinction, usually neglected in the Freudian school, between neurotic and non-neurotic homosexuality. This distinction, we note, is obscured by the psychiatrists who like to call homosexuality a sickness.

Despite the different theories regarding the origin of homosexuality, there is wide agreement among psychiatrists and psychologists of various schools that it is possible to distinguish *two modes* of homosexual orientation, a *phase* to be passed through and a *constant* to be lived with. In some people homosexual interest and activity appear as a temporary phenomenon, either as regression to an earlier stage of personal development or as a special response to heterosexual deprivation and other pressures. In other people, men and women, the homosexual orientation appears deeply rooted in their personality structure. In the first case, homosexuality is a phase disguising the more basic sexual orientation of the human person; in the second, homosexuality is a constitutive element of the personality.

If this distinction is justified, it is the task of men and women who discover a homosexual inclination in themselves to discern whether they are caught in a phase which prevents them from fulfilling their real possibilities, or whether homosexuality is a constitutive element of their personality structure. It may often be difficult to make this distinction. Gay people easily turn to psychiatrists and psychologists to come to such self-discovery, but only too often do their counselors disagree among themselves. I suppose that eventually the homosexual community itself will produce tests and therapeutic insights that enable people to come to greater self-knowledge and discover whether they are constitutively homosexual.

What is the moral task of people who discover that they are basically homosexually oriented? May they affirm this inclination within themselves? In the past, we used to say that because of the unnatural direction of their drive, these people must suppress their inclination as much as possible. But since the notion of human nature, especially when applied to the relation of men and women, has become problematic, we hesitate to draw the same conclusion today. The important question, according to the reflection made above, is whether homosexuality is open to mutuality. Is the homosexual orientation capable of grounding friendship that enables the partners to grow and become more truly human? This is the crucial question. For the structure of redeemed human life is mutuality. There are gravely damaged sexual inclinations, e.g., sadism, masochism, and paedophilia, which may not be acknowledged without a struggle: for they exclude mutuality. They bind the participants in a cruel game of possessor and possessed. The important question, therefore, is whether homosexuality is open to mutuality. Can it be integrated into the kind of human life to which God summons us?

Some psychiatrists and psychologists give a negative reply to this question. Their patients have convinced them that homosexual relations give rise only to torment and unstable passions. However, we have today the witness of homosexual men and women who have struggled for self-knowledge and transcended the weight society has put on them and who tell us that their lives are based on mutuality. More specifically, we have the religious witness of Christians and Catholics that homosexuality grounds responsible—sharing and sustained friendship. The theologian must take this witness seriously and may conclude that persons who are constitutively homosexual must accept their orientation and live accordingly. Homosexual love, then, is not contrary to the human nature, defined in terms of mutuality, toward which mankind is summoned.

If it is true that some people are constitutively homosexual and that homosexual relations allow for mutuality, then, from the viewpoint of Christian theology, it is the task of homosexuals to acknowledge themselves as such before God, accept their sexual inclination as their calling, and explore the meaning of this inclination for the Christian life. This is the position adopted by Dignity. Dignity holds that it is the call of Catholic homosexuals to affirm their sexual orientation in faith, to regard themselves as equal members of the believing community, and to express their sexuality in a manner consonant with Christ's teaching of love.

This theological position, I wish to add, is quite independent of any particular theory about the origin of homosexuality! For even if one wishes, following Freud, to regard homosexuality as a defective personal development, as a loss or lack of completeness (like having one leg or being born blind), it is still necessary for a believing homosexual to affirm himself or herself before God in faith, to be accepting without regrets and self-pity, to reject the self-depreciation which the world imposes on him/her, and to seek a good and full life in keeping with basic self powers.

It is necessary to add at this point that homosexual men and women are in greater need of self-knowledge and personal wisdom than other people. In our culture gay people are often gravely wounded and must wrestle with themselves before the freedom to love and to forget themselves becomes accessible to them. This can be affirmed quite apart from the unsolved question about the origin of homosexuality. For even if one denies the Freudian theory that homosexuality is caused by infantile traumata and thus accompanied by conflicts that have to be faced in later life, it is beyond dispute that society places enormous burdens on homosexuals and that it is almost impossible for persons with a homosexual orientation to grow up without being exposed to the threats and pressures of a cruel world. Wounds there are, whatever their origin. But where can gay people turn for wisdom? Who teaches them self-knowledge? The psychiatric profession and many psychologists tend to regard homosexuals as medical cases. Other psychologists adopt a permissive attitude without leading their clients to critical self-understanding. The churches have looked upon homosexuals as sinners. If gay people will ever find guidelines to free themselves from the wounds that lead to hostility and self-hatred, it will be a wisdom generated within the homosexual community itself.

While the arguments examined in these pages may have a good deal of persuasive force, it is not likely that the Catholic Church is about to change its traditional teaching. Since the organizational center of the Catholic

Church is situated in a country with social and cultural conditions that differ greatly from those of North America, official Catholic teaching is often less concerned than are some other churches with the problems that emerge in our society. Thus the strict views on birth control and on remarriage after a broken union still prevail in the official teaching.

From Machismo to Mutuality

Rosemary Radford Ruether

Rosemary Radford Ruether is Georgia Harkness Professor at Garrett Theological Seminary, Evanston, Illinois, having previously taught at Howard University, Washington, D.C., and Yale Divinity School, New Haven, Connecticut. She is the author of several important works, including: The Radical Kingdom, Faith and Patricide, *and* New Woman, New Earth. *She has also edited the feminist anthology,* Religion and Sexism: Images of Women in the Judaeo-Christian Tradition, *as well as co-authoring with Eugene C. Bianchi the work,* From Machismo to Mutuality, *from which this excerpt is taken.*

In this article, "The Personalization of Sex," she asks the question, "why is it that cultures, especially those that regard themselves as refined, have tended to depersonalize and brutalize sexuality?" and suggests that the solution may be found in the "personalization of sex," a concept which "challenges both the traditional Christian doctrine that sex be limited to procreation and also the libertine view that reduces sex to physiological relief without depth of communication and relationship."

Another corollary of this notion is that it "throws into question the norm of heterosexuality as the sole norm of healthy sexual relations," founded as it is on the premise that "sexual union by nature must be a union of two opposite sexes, each the complementary counterpart of the other"—a viewpoint represented in the present volume in the selections taken from Karl Barth's Church Dogmatics, *and from*

Ruth Tiffany Barnhouse's Homosexuality: A Symbolic Confusion, *which Ruether then proceeds to evaluate and critique in the following passage.*

The personalization of sexuality must also throw into question the norm of heterosexuality as the sole norm of healthy sexual relations. The view that made heterosexuality the only legitimate expression of sex/love depended on two assumptions, both of which are challenged by personalized sexuality and the growth of women to autonomy and personhood. The first presupposition is that sexuality is primarily for procreation. Sexual relations must be "oriented to the possibility of procreation," even if every act is not procreative. Sexual communion cannot be viewed as good in itself detached from this procreative end. Hence homosexual love, which is inherently nonprocreative, cannot be either "natural" or "good."

A second more subtle argument against homosexuality lies on the level of what are presumed to be the psychic natures of men and women created by their distinct biologies rather than simply an argument confined to biological procreation. This argument assumes a doctrine of "complementarity." Those traits traditionally called masculine and those called feminine are presumed to define the unchangeable natures of men and women. Men are actors, thinkers, doers who protect and act upon others. Women are passive, dependent, weak in their ability to take care of themselves, emotional, lacking full rationality, perhaps more "spiritual" and "intuitive." Sexuality to be whole must unite these two halves of the human psychophysical essence. Sexual union by nature must be a union of the two opposite sexes, each the complementary counterpart of the other. Only when the two sexes, masculine and feminine, are united does sexual relation signify completion or communion. Sexual love therefore must be heterosexual. Homosexual love is intrinsically narcissistic or incomplete. The homosexual loves only himself (herself) in reflection and not the "other." Eugene Bianchi, especially in his essay on "The Super-Bowl Culture of Male Violence," has described the fears of effeminacy that are typical of a masculinist society and the way in which the rejection of homosexuality is related to the repression of the gentle side of men.

Such a concept of complementarity depends on a sadomasochistic concept of male and female relations. It covertly demands the continued dependency and underdevelopment of women in order to validate the thesis that two kinds of personalities exist by nature in males and females and which are each partial expressions of some larger whole. Such a view can allow neither men nor women to be whole persons who can develop both their active and their affective sides. Once women reject this psychology of dependency and that repression of their active and intellectual traits that is implied by the ideology of femininity, the myth of complementarity is overthrown. This concept of complementarity must be recognized as a false biologism that attempts to totalize on the level of the whole human existence a limited functional complementarity that exists on the level of procreative systems. Procreative systems—vagina and penis, sperm and ovum—might seem like two opposite sides of a process that only together become a whole, a new person. But even complementarity on this level has traditionally created false myths about women by denying that women had an ovum that was equally a seed to the male sperm (Aristotle) and attempting to repress the active orgasmic drive of women located in the clitoris (Freud and his ancestors back to primitive times).

When sex ceases to be limited to this procreative function and becomes a total bodily possibility of two persons this notion of opposites necessary to make a whole disappears. On the level of total organisms men and women both equally have all the organs of thinking, feeling, and relating. It is meaningless to say that men are more active and women more receptive. The maintenance of this false biological analogy on the level of total psychophysical organisms depends on an elaborate conditioning of women to passivity and males to aggressiveness. The mind and the five senses are the organs of thinking and feeling in total organic existence, not penises and vaginas. Men and women are equally well-equipped with the psychophysical organs of thinking and feeling, action and receptivity. Only a distorted psychic conditioning of the two sexes into opposite personalities, formed by power relations of domination and subjugation, makes them appear to be psychic opposites of each other, analogous to the superficial contraries of genitals.

Once sex is no longer confined to procreative genital acts and masculinity and femininity are exposed as social ideologies, then it is no longer possible to argue that sex/love between two persons of the same sex cannot be a valid embrace of bodily selves expressing love. If sex/love is centered primarily on communion between two persons rather than on biologistic concepts of procreative complementarity, then the love of two persons of the same sex need be no less than that of two persons of the opposite sex. Nor need their experience of ecstatic bodily communion be less valuable.

Both the woman's movement and the gay movement are moving from the psychology of complementarity to the psychology of androgyny. Although the term itself retains all too clearly its dualistic origins, what it means is that both males and females contain the total human psychic essence. Men are just as capable of being receptive and intuitive as women; women are just as capable of being thinkers and decisive actors as men. Such a view of persons as androgynous is not antibiological as some have claimed. It is a correction to the false biology presupposed by the doctrine of complementarity. It is a simple recognition that people hear with their ears, feel with their bodies and think with their brains. People don't hear with their vaginas and think with their penises. Men and women equally have the organs of psychic activity and receptivity. Psychically men and women are not complementary but "mutual."

Authentic mutuality means not only that men speak and women hear, but that women also speak and men hear. It means that men and women cease to be half personalities. Both must grow to unite the many sides of themselves through multiple relationships with other people. The strong active side of one can be complementary to the receptive side of another, but the receptive side can be nurtured by the emotive, receptive side of another in a way that is equally important for full human development. Head can nurture head, and heart can nurture heart. Men can nurture women in both intellectuality and aggressiveness and also in emotionality and receptiveness. And women can do the same for men. In still different ways men can nurture and challenge each other, and women can nurture and challenge each other. In androgynously developed persons it is not possible to rule out sex/love relations between women or between men. This also means that heterosexual and homosexual relations cease to be ideological contraries. Straight and gay can cease to occupy different worlds, the heterosexual world dominating the legitimate universe and the gay subculture lurking in the shadows. The politicization of the demand that a person be exclusively heterosexual or exclusively homosexual can be surpassed. Each person seeks his or her full soul by nurturing human wholeness in a plural (but not infinite) community of persons. Relations center upon personal respect and mutual development.

The unification of sexuality and in-depth interpersonal communication and commitment cannot be determined either by law or by gimmicks of instant encounter. Neither the legalistic approach that demands that two persons, once having been officially yoked, stick it out to the death even when their relationship has become primarily one of mutual destruction, nor that narcissistic promiscuity that would have us hopping endlessly from bed to bed corresponds to authentic intimacy. There is a need for covenants of commitment for better or for worse as long as even the "for worse" belongs to a growth relationship. But such commitments cannot rule out other sex/love friendships entirely even if our present proprietary traditions of sexuality make it very difficult to develop such plurality in a mature way, without elements of jealousy and hurt. There may also be a need for the techniques of the encounter movement that help to break down our body alienation and open us up to our untapped potential for total psychophysical ecstasy and self-disclosure. But instant turn-on's are not committed friendships.

Real intimacy must be a profound creation. Its guides are those of personal friendship and commitment to mutual growth. This cannot be done by a technological concept of psychic or sexual functions. Nor can it be tied to exclusivistic marriages when friendship is irreparably blocked or when sexuality and subsistence are exchanged only on superficial or brutalized levels. Intimacy is a creative activity whereby over some period of time of sharing, growth and exploration we find ways to open ourselves to the beloved other person on deepening levels. We learn slowly to create our body-selves as the sacrament of personal communication, restoring to our sexuality that power of grace that we usually relegate to a docetic spirituality. This takes place only between people who share their deepest selves, who risk bad moments as well as good ones with each other. It takes place between people who are seeking truthfulness, who are engaged in a project of mutual growth, who can support each other's development even in directions that may take a part of the person away into other communities of work and relationship. This is hardly possible when woman is domesticated and man's work goes on in a sphere alienated from "woman's place." It is possible only when women are freed from underdevelopment and dependency and men from a false self-sufficiency. It is possible only when people are colleagues as well as lovers who share life and work in a quest to give birth to each other's fullest selves. This is the mystery that has been pointed out and promised when we speak of love. But it is a threatening and morally exacting task that we usually avoid and deny in our sexist and atrophied marriages, our hasty sexuality and our narcissistic demand for instant intimacy.

Must Homosexuals Be Jewish Outcasts?

(Sh'ma *does not normally print anonymous articles. We would like the Jewish Community to be a place where any serious statement and its maker would be welcome. This emphatically not being true of homosexuals today, we hereby make an exception to our practice.—E.B.Borowitz*)

As a Jew whose commitment to Jewish survival and values is demonstrated in almost everything I do, I find myself in an extreme dilemma. The cause of my dilemma is that I have recently decided to stop denying and repressing my homosexuality and have made contact with the homophile community, the homophile subculture. The act has been liberating and I have a new sense of freedom in being honest with myself and selected others, which has resulted in a kind of euphoria.

The joy of openness, the pain of concealment.

I have told a few friends, chosen very carefully on the basis of their liberatedness, life experience, non-judgmental attitudes, and their love for me, and they were well chosen indeed. They did not reject me, they did not tell me I am sick or urge me to see a psychiatrist, they did not judge me. In fact, they assured me that I'm still me and nothing has changed except perhaps that our friendships will deepen because as a happier, more fulfilled person I have more to bring to our friendship, and also sharing this part of me with them has served only to strengthen the bonds of friendship. I am relieved. I don't have to lie to them anymore.

I have other dear friends whom I simply cannot tell but wish I could.

They don't seem quite ready for it. It's too heavy for them. I feel they would judge me even if they wouldn't reject me. They would urge me to see a psychiatrist to get rid of this sickness. (As a matter of fact I am seeing a therapist who is supporting me and helping me deal with my newly acknowledged feelings). I feel that my friends whom I cannot tell are victims of the many myths and misconceptions which society at large has about homosexuals, basing their misinformation on the miniscule number of homosexuals who may appear freaky and also upon the secrecy which surrounds the subject.

Perhaps the most mind-blowing aspect of my recent entry into the homophile community is the number of Jews I am finding, seemingly far out of proportion to the general population of homophiles. This may be because it's New York. There is an especially large number of young men and women in their teens and twenties, a significant number of *Our Jewish Youth*—the youth we are always talking about trying to reach. Which brings me to why I am writing for this particular journal, a journal of responsibility, controversy and openness.

I want to reach into the minds of Jewish intellectuals, scholars, rabbis, those people I look to with respect, sometimes awe, and with whom I feel a close affinity.

Jewish homosexuals: forced to hide, to dissemble

A large number of Jewish homosexuals with whom I am coming into contact are not happy about the fact that they, as total human beings, are not accepted into the bosom of Judaism. Some continue to have contact, but they are living a lie. These are not freaky people. They are ordinary men and women (often extraordinary) with whom many of you may come into contact and are never aware of their secret. The secret is kept because of the effect it will have upon you, certainly not because they are ashamed of anything. These are mostly proud, intelligent, often creative and talented people who would like nothing more than to be honest and open—accepted by the general society for the people they are and all that makes them different is their sexual preference which is, after all, a private matter.

You may ask then, if it is a private matter, why bring it up at all? It is because we are forced in so many ways to lie. We lie when we attend family or public Jewish functions either alone or with a "date" of the opposite sex, rather than with the partners of our choice, the persons we love, the persons to whom we have commitments no less than the commitments between husbands and wives. You are always trying to marry us off, wanting to introduce us to eligible single men or women and we maintain the lie either by accepting, or by telling some other lie. We lie when we laugh at your misinformed and often cruel references or jokes about homosexuals, hoping to throw you off course. We lie when we introduce a lover to you as a friend, relative or roommate. But mostly we lie when we don't correct your myths that homosexuals are sick, depraved, over-sexed, preying upon innocent children, that gay men are always on the make, that gay women cannot be trusted in the presence of straight women for fear of seduction, that sex is always present and that all there is to it is sex. The only time we don't lie is when we are with each other, other homophiles, or with straight friends with whom we've shared our secret—and that is when we are the best of what we are. It is too bad you can't really know us as we really are; it is your loss.

I am finding out that many young Jewish men and women want to be part of Jewish life, but have dropped out because they are morally opposed and constitutionally unable to engage in these lies. We make various attempts to set up gay synagogues, conduct gay seders, involve ourselves in a Jewish subculture where access to Jewish excellence, authenticity, scholarship and just plain Jewish knowledge and contact is limited at best.

Is there really no room for us in judaism?

Some—and this pains me—have turned to attending church services in their quest for spiritual expression. There are some churches which welcome homosexuals as homosexuals and where they don't have to lie. At any rate, there is an awareness and openness in dealing with the issue among many priests and ministers. Would that it were so among rabbis as well!

You may say that there is no room in Judaism for the expression of homophile feelings, that the *Torah* and rabbis and *chochmei Talmud* (sages) through the ages have condemned it, if they dealt with it at all. But who among us practices *halacha* in all its rulings? Who among us abides by all of our tradition's historic precedents? Who among us does not justify for ourselves our own departures from *halacha*? Are some departures worse than others? Is an expression of love, if not within a narrow definition, really among the worst of departures?

We accept ourselves as more fulfilled people because we are not repressing something which is only beautiful and life-giving to us. "Choose Life," we are told. Love is a positive force in the human condition, not a negative one and we do not want—we cannot—choose whom we love. Love is a mystery, as God is a mystery. We will not deny or be told we must repress or feel anything but joy and goodness in our honest expression of this love. But we do not want to be secretive or have to lie to you.

We must strive for dialogue and interaction

Ultimately, we would like for you to accept us for what we are. This is a long-range goal and myths will have to be replaced by information and knowledge. In the meantime, I am asking for the opportunity of a dialog, a recognition within Judaism that this phenomenon exists and that there are many Jews in the homophile sub-culture, more than you can imagine. I hope my writing this article will open up the possibility of a serious, intelligent discussion. I would like a confrontation on this issue as it relates to Judaism. Let's bring it out into the open. Let's talk and listen to each other. I want to tell you what it means to be a homophile in this society. I want you to tell me what this means in Jewish terms, whether I can still be a good Jew and continue to be actively involved in the Jewish community with the difference that I won't have to lie to you anymore. I want us together to explore new possibilities of honest integration of homophile Jews into heterophile Jewish life.

The alternative is that we will be forced to remain outside of our people, or to remain in it dishonestly. There is a great reservoir of intelligence, creativity and talent among us, eager to be channeled through Jewish streams.

IIa
Homosexual Acts are Intrinsically Evil
(The 'Traditionalist' School)

Saint Thomas Aquinas
Karl Barth
Robert Gordis

Summa Theologica

Saint Thomas Aquinas

Question 153, 2
Second Article
Whether No Venereal Act Can Be Without Sin

Let us move to the second article.[1]

OBJECTION I It would seem that no venereal act can be sinless. For nothing but sin hinders virtue and every venereal act is a very definite hindrance to virtue. To quote Augustine, *"I do not consider anything more capable of sending a man's mind plummeting from its lofty heights than a woman's charm and the touch of their bodies."*[2] Therefore it seems that no venereal act is sinless.

OBJECTION II Furthermore any excess that makes one forsake the good of reason is sinful. For we know from the *Ethics* of Aristotle that there are two ways of destroying virtue—excess and deficiency.[3] Now in every sexual act there is an excess of pleasure which so absorbs the mind that it is impossible to think about anything else as Aristotle has noted.[4] Or as St. Jerome says, while engaged in sex the prophets are out of the reach of every prophetic impulse.[5] Therefore no venereal act can be sinless.

OBJECTION III The cause is more powerful than its effect. Now original sin is transmitted to children by concupiscence, without which no venereal act is possible as Augustine points out.[6] Therefore no venereal act is sinless.

But on the other hand Augustine also states, *"This is an adequate rebuttal to heretics, if they can grasp it, that anything which does not violate nature, customs or law is not sinful."*[7] And he says this in reference to the polygamy practices by the patriarchs. Therefore not every sexual act is a sin.

RESPONSE—In the realm of human actions, those which we properly call sins are the ones which violate the priorities of reason (d) which arranges everything according to its proper end. Wherefore if the end is good and if what is done is in keeping with that end, and in harmony with it, then no sin is present. Now just as the preservation of a single human life is obviously good, how much greater is it to preserve the whole human race and just as the use of food is directed to the preservation of the life of the individual, so is the use of venereal acts ordered to the survival of the race. Hence Augustine says: *"What food is to man's well being, such is sexual intercourse to the well being of the race."*[8] Wherefore just as the use of food can be without sin if it be taken in due manner and order as is required for the welfare of the body, so also the use of venereal acts can be without sin if they are performed in the proper manner and ordered to the preservation of the race.

REPLY

1 To the first objection it must be said that it is possible to hinder virtue in two ways, one by opposing it at a basic level which necessarily involves sin, and the other by hindering the highest expression of it by some action that is not a sin but merely a lesser good. And in this way sexual intercourse may send the mind plummeting not from virtue, but from virtue's highest expression. Hence Augustine says, *"Martha was doing good when she concerned herself with serving the holy men but Mary was doing a greater good by listening to the work of God. So too we praise the worth of Susanna's conjugal chastity but prefer the worth of the widow Anna and still more that of the Virgin Mary."*[9]

2 To the second objection as stated above the balance of virtue is not attained by the yardstick of quantity but by the degree it is in harmony with the best dictates of reason.[10] And therefore the exceeding pleasure experienced in the sex act, so long as it is in harmony with reason, does not destroy the balance of virtue. Furthermore virtue is not concerned with the amount of pleasure experienced by the external senses, as this depends on the disposition of the body; what matters is how much the interior appetite is affected by that pleasure. (e) Nor must we conclude from the fact that reason cannot attend to spiritual things while experiencing venereal pleasure that the act itself is opposed to virtue any more that it would be safe to assume that any reasonable interruption of the activity of reason goes against virtue—otherwise it would be immoral to fall asleep. However this much is true, that sexual desire and pleasure are not subject to the sway and moderation of reason as a result of original sin; inasmuch as the reason for rebelling against God deserves to have its body rebel against it, as Augustine says.[11]

3 To the third objection Augustine says, *"a child is born shackled by original sin as a daughter of sin from the concupiscence of the flesh which in the new-born*

is not imputed to them as sins."[12] Hence it does not follow that the act in question is a sin but that it contains something penal derived from original sin.

Third Article
Whether the Lust That Surrounds the Sexual Act Is Sinful

Let us proceed to the third article.[13] It would seem that the lust which surrounds the sexual act is not sinful. For through the sexual act semen is discharged which is an excess by-product of food according to Aristotle.[14] But there is no sin in the emission of other superfluous substances. Therefore, neither can be anything sinful concerning the sexual acts.

2   Furthermore everyone can lawfully use what is lawfully his own. But in the sexual act what is a man using except that which is his own except perhaps in the case of adultery or rape. Therefore there can be no sin in sexual activity and therefore lust would not be a sin.

3   Besides all sin has a vice which opposites it. But lust does not seem to have an opposite vice. Therefore lust is not a sin. On the other hand the cause is greater than its effect. But wine is forbidden by the Apostle Paul on account of lust, *"Do not allow yourselves to become drunk with wine wherein there is lust."*[15] Therefore lust is prohibited.

Besides in Galatians it is enumerated among the works of the flesh.[16] RESPONSE—It must be said that the more a thing is necessary the more crucial it is that it be regulated by reason and consequently the greater the evil if that order of reason is violated. However as we have already stated sexual acts are very necessary for the common good which is the survival of the race. Therefore concerning them the greatest attention must be paid to the ordering of reason. Consequently if anything is done in connection with them against the order of reason it is a sin. And so without any doubt lust is sin.

REPLY

1   To the first objection it must be said that according to Aristotle in the same book[17] *semen is a surplus* which is necessary, he says it is a surplus insofar as it is a residue of the action of the nutrient power yet it is necessary regarding the generative power. The other waste-products of the body are not necessary and therefore it does not matter how they are disposed of provided the decencies of social life are observed. But it is different with the emission of semen which must be done in the way befitting the end for which it is needed.

To the second objection Paul speaks against lust, *"You were brought at a great price. Give glory and carry God in your bodies."*[18] It follows from this that anyone who uses his body in an inordinate way because of lust offends God who is the Supreme Lord of our Bodies. Hence Augustine says that

"God who governs his servants to their own advantage commands them not to defile the temple of their bodies by illicit pleasures."[19]

To the third objection we reply that the opposite of lust is not frequently encountered since men are very prone to pleasure. Nevertheless, it is a vice that comes under the heading of insensibility and occurs in one who dislikes the sex relation so much that he doesn't even give his wife her conjugal rights.

Question 154
Whether We Can Aptly Classify Sins Of Lust Under Six Species

THE FIRST POINT[20]—It would seem to be inappropriate to divide lust into six categories, simple fornication, adultery, incest, seduction, rape and unnatural sin.[21] For diversity of material does not make for diverse species. But the aforementioned division is made on the basis of diversity of material, according to whether the act is committed by a woman who is married or unmarried or of some other circumstance. Therefore it would seem that the species of lust are not distinguishable on this basis.

2   Furthermore one species of vice should not be differentiated on the basis of something proper to another type of vice. But adultery differs from fornication only by the fact that some takes to himself a woman who belongs to someone else and commits an injustice and so adultery should not be classified as a special or different type of lechery.

3   Again, just as it can happen that a man have relations with a woman who is bound to another man by marriage, so too he might have relationships with a woman who is bound to God by vow. Thus if adultery is considered a species of lust so too sacrilege should also be a species of lust.

4   Furthermore someone who is married not only sins if he goes to another woman but even if he uses his own wife inordinately. But this sin comes under the category of lechery and should therefore be counted as one of the types of lechery.

5   Furthermore Paul wrote, *"May God not humiliate me a second time when I come to you and bewail the fact that many of those who had sinned before still do not repent of the uncleanness, fornication and lewdness they have committed."*[22] It seems therefore that uncleanness and lewdness must be considered species of lust just as fornication.

6   Furthermore one does not further separate a subject from the things it is divided into. Now we have mentioned the divisions of lechery, but Paul in Galatians says, *"The works of the flesh are manifest, they are fornication,*

uncleanness, impurity and lechery."[23] It would therefore seem inappropriate to make fornication a species of lechery.

On the other hand, this six-fold division was adopted in the *Decretum.*[24]

RESPONSE—It should be mentioned, as we have already mentioned, that the sin of lechery consists in this—that a person engages in venereal pleasure not in accordance with right reason.[25] This can happen in two ways: one is respect to the substance of the act in which the pleasure is sought. The other in which the act is proper but other conditions are not met. And because the circumstances of such an act do not determine the species of a moral act. But its species is only determined by its object which is the material of the act we must therefore assign separate species of these acts solely on the basis of material or objective.

Now it may conflict with right reason in two ways. One because it is repugnant to the purpose of the venereal act and thus, insofar as it impedes the generation of children, it is a vice against nature which is any venereal act from which generation cannot follow. However insofar as the necessary education and advancement of the offspring is impeded we have simple fornication between unmarried people.

The other way in which the sexual act is exercised against right reason arises from a comparison to other human beings and this can happen in two ways. First on the part of the woman herself with whom someone has relations because the respect due her is not given. Thus we have the sin of incest which consists in the abuse of a woman by one related by blood or affinity. The second way is on the part of the one who is in charge of her; if it be her husband, it is adultery; if her father, it is seduction (if force is not used) and rape if she is taken by force.

Notice however that these species of lechery differ more from considering the woman's role than the man's. Because in the sex act she is the passive one and for that reason the material element whereas the man is the agent.[26] And as we mention, the different species are assigned on the basis of material differences.

1   To the first objection it must be said that the aforementioned diversity of material has a corresponding specific difference of objectives understood as the different ways it violates right reason.[27]

2   To the second objection we reply that nothing prevents the several ugliness of various vices from occurring together in the same act[28] and in this way adultery comes under the heading of both lust and injustice. Nor is injustice entirely incidental to injustice for lust becomes worse when following concupiscense it leads to injustices.

3   To the third we reply that because a woman who has vowed continence enters into a kind of Spiritual Marriage with God, sacrilege which is committed by violating such a woman is a type of spiritual adultery and

similarly other kinds of sacrilege that involve lusting can be reduced to some type of lechery or other.

4   To the fourth objection we reply the sins of husbands with their wives are sin not because of improper material but because of attending circumstances and so, as was said, they do not constitute a specific kind of moral act.[29]

5   To the fifth let me say that as the gloss says that uncleanness stands for lust against nature, while lewdness pertains to corruption of the young which is a form of seduction.[30] Or we can also say that lewdness pertains to those various acts surrounding the sex-act such as kissing, caressing and the like.

6   Finally to the sixth we respond that lust according to the dictionary includes any kind of excess.[31]

Eleventh Article
Whether the Unnatural Vice Is a Species Of Lechery

Let us proceed to the eleventh article.[32]

1   It would seem that vices against nature are not a type of lechery because in the aforementioned list there is no mention made of vice against nature.[33] Therefore they are not a species of lechery.

2   Furthermore, lechery is opposed to the virtuous and is therefore a kind of wickedness. But unnatural vice is not a kind of human wickedness but a type of bestiality as Aristotle makes clear in his Ethics. Therefore a vice against nature is not human lust.[34]

3   Besides lechery concerns activity that serves human generation. Unnatural sin is an act from which generation cannot follow. And therefore is not a kind of lechery.

On the other hand Second Corinthians numbers it among other types of lust. *"And they have done penance for the uncleanness and fornication and lasciviousness,"*[35] where the gloss says *"lasciviousness is unnatural lust."*[36]

I answer that as stated above[37] wherever there occurs a special kind of deformity whereby the venereal act is rendered unbecoming, there is a determinate species of lust. This may occur in two ways, by being contrary to right reason and this is common to all types of lust. Secondly, because in addition it is contrary to the natural order of the venereal act as befits human species and this is why it is called the unnatural vice. It can happen in various ways. First by having orgasm outside of intercourse for the sake of venereal pleasure which pertains to the sin of uncleanness which some call effeminacy.[38] Secondly by copulating with another species which is called bestiality. Thirdly by copulating with the wrong sex, male with male or female with female as St. Paul states[39] (Rom. 1: 27) and this is the vice of sodomy. Fourthly, by not observing the natural manner of copulation either as to not using the proper organ or as to other monstrous and bestial manners of copulation.

1   We reply to the first by saying, that there we were enumerating the species of lust that were not against human nature; wherefore the unnatural vices were omitted.

2   Bestiality goes beyond human wickedness for the latter is opposed to human virtue by a certain excess in regards to the same field and therefore can be reduced to the same genus.

3   The lustful man intends not human generation but venereal pleasure. It is possible without those acts from which human generation follow: and it is this which is sought in unnatural acts.

Twelfth Article
Whether the Unnatural Vice Is the Greatest Sin Among the Species Of Lust?

We proceed thus to the Twelfth Article:[40]

OBJECTION I   It seems that the unnatural vice is not the greatest sin among the species of lust. For the more a sin is contrary to charity the graver it is. Now adultery, seduction and rape which are injurious to our neighbor are seemingly more contrary to the love of our neighbor, than unnatural sins, by which no other person is injured. Therefore the unnatural sin is not the greatest among the species of lust.

OBJECTION II   Further, sins committed against God would seem to be the most grievous. Now sacrilege is committed directly against God, since it is injurious to the Divine worship. Therefore sacrilege is a graver sin than the unnatural vice.

OBJECTION III   Further, seemingly, a sin is all the more grievous according as we owe a greater love to the person against whom that sin is committed. Now the order of charity requires that a man love more those persons who are united to him—and such are those whom he defiles by incest,—than persons who are not connected with him, and whom in certain cases he defiles by the unnatural vice. Therefore, incest is a graver sin than the unnatural vice.

OBJECTION IV   Further, if the unnatural vice is the most grievous, the more it is against nature the graver it would seem to be. Now the sin of uncleanness or effeminacy would seem to be most contrary to nature, since it would seem especially in accord with nature that agent and that which he acts upon should be distinct from one another. Hence it would follow that uncleanness is the gravest of unnatural vices. But this is not true. Therefore unnatural vices are not the most grievous among the sins of lust.

On the contrary, Augustine says *(De adult. conjug.)*[41] that of all these vices (belonging, namely, to lust) that which is against nature is the worst.

I answer that, in every genus, worst of all is the corruption of the principle on which the rest depend. Now the principles of reason are those things that are according to nature because reason presupposes things as determined by nature, before disposing of other things as it is fitting. This may be observed both in speculative and in practical matters. Wherefore just as in speculative matters the most grievous and shameful error is that which is about things the knowledge of which is naturally bestowed on man, so in matters of action it is most grave and shameful to act against things as determined by nature. Therefore, since by the unnatural vices man transgresses that which has been determined by nature with regard to the use of venereal actions, it follows that in this matter this sin is gravest of sins. After which comes incest which, as has been said, offends against the natural respect we should have for those who are related to us.

Other kinds of lechery only pertain to rules arrived at by reason from principles of nature. For instance it is more repugnant to reason to have intercourse not only in a manner which not only harms the offspring but also injures the other person. Therefore, simple fornication which is committed without injuring the partner is the least among the sins of lechery. Furthermore, it is a greater sin to abuse married women than it is to abuse a woman who is under a guardian's care and therefore adultery is worse than seduction and if violence is also a factor the sin is worse, so it follows that raping a virgin is worse than seducing her and raping a wife is worse than adultery. All of these as we said above are made more serious offenses if sacrilege is also involved.

REPLY

1   To the first objection we reply that men can fashion patterns of thought but God Himself arranged the natural orders. And so a sin against nature in which the natural order itself is violated is a sin against God who is the creator of that order. Augustine writes, *"Offenses against nature should be abhorred and punished always and in every case. Such as those committed by the people of Sodom which if every nation committed them they would be held just as guilty by the same divine law which never intended that men treat one another in such a fashion. For the fellowship which should exist between God and man would be destroyed when nature which is God's handiwork is made foul by the perversity of lust."*[42]

2   To the second, it must be said that the sins against nature are against God himself, and in fact they are worse than sacrilege since the order of nature is more basic and stable than the laws which are derived from nature by reason.

3   To the third it will be said that the individual is more bound to the nature of species than he is to other individual members of that species and therefore the sin which attacks nature itself is more grievous.

4   Finally, sins of abuse are more serious than sins of omission. And so among the unnatural sins, masturbation holds the lowest because it omits the involvement of another person. The gravest, however is bestiality which does not even involve the same species. Thus on the text found in Genesis, *"He accused his brothers of the worst sin."*[43] The commentary interprets this as meaning "they copulated with cattle."[44] After bestiality, sodomy is the worst because the wrong sex is involved. After sodomy comes the sins of lechery which invole improper manners of intercourse and this is worse if it is not effected in the proper vessel than if the perversion of the sex act is done in some other way.

Church Dogmatics

Karl Barth

The Jew is a Jew in the Lord only, but precisely, to the extent that he confronts and is confronted by the Greek. The free man is free in the Lord only, but precisely, to the extent that the slave is associated with him and he with the slave. Similarly the male is a male in the Lord only, but precisely, to the extent that he is with the female, and the female likewise. That they are one in the Lord holds them together. It allows and commands them to be together. And it is the basis of their distinction, which is rooted in the fact that they have their essence in the fact that they are directed to be in fellowship. Because their freedom is that which they have from and before and for God, therefore it can take shape only in their fellowship with each other, and their humanity can consist concretely only in the fact that they live in fellow-humanity, male with female, and female with male. Every right of man and woman stands or falls with the observance and maintenance of this rule, and every wrong consists in its contravention.

This rule is from this standpoint the command of God. If we are to be obedient to the divine command we cannot regard ourselves as dispensed from its observance. It is clear that in it we have to do with the fundamental law of love and marriage in so far as it must be in particular the law of the being and attitude of a particular man in relation to a particular woman and *vice versa*. But the woman is the partner of the single man too, not woman in general, not an idea of woman, certainly not the Virgin Mary, but the concrete and definite form of woman encountering him in a particular way. She does actually encounter him too, being unmistakably present for him at varying distances and in many different ways, even though she does not come into question as a companion in love or marriage. She is woman for him too, whether as mother, sister, acquaintance, friend or fellow-worker, just as she is also present in all these and other forms—and always as woman—for the man who is bound by love and marriage. Similarly, the man is undoubted partner of the single woman, not (it is to be hoped not!) as an epitome or ideal form of manhood, as the heavenly bridegroom and such like, but as the real man who encounters her in concrete and definite form, not as a companion in love and marriage, but no less truly as a man in kinship, acquaintance, friendship and vocation than he is in relation to the woman to whom he is specially and individually bound. That the man is and should be with the woman, and the woman with the man, applies to the whole sphere of relationships now under consideration, and in this regard the primary and fundamental formulation of the relevant command should be as follows—that whether in love and marriage or outside this bond, every woman and every man should realise that he is committed to live consciously and willingly in this interrelationship, not regarding his being abstractly as his own but as being in fellowship, and shaping it accordingly.

As against this, everything which points in the direction of male or female seclusion, or of religious or secular orders or communities, or of male or female segregation—if it is undertaken in principle and not consciously and temporarily as an emergency measure—is obviously disobedience. All due respect to the comradeship of a company of soldiers! But neither men nor women can seriously wish to be alone, as in clubs and ladies' circles. Who commands or permits them to run away from each other? That such an attitude is all wrong is shown symptomatically in the fact that every artificially induced and maintained isolation of the sexes tends as such—usually very quickly and certainly morosely and blindly—to become philistinish in the case of men and precious in that of women, and in both cases more or less inhuman. It is well to pay heed even to the first steps in this direction.

These first steps may well be symptoms of the malady called homosexuality. This is the physical, psychological and social sickness, the phenomenon of perversion, decadence and decay, which can emerge when man refuses to admit the validity of the divine command in the sense in which we are now considering it. In Rom. 1 Paul connected it with idolatry, with changing the truth of God into a lie, with the adoration of the creature instead of the Creator (v. 25). "For this cause God gave them up unto vile affections: for even their women did change the natural use into that which is against nature: and likewise also the men, leaving the natural use of the woman, burned in their lust one toward another; men with men working that which is unseemly, and receiving in themselves the recompence of their error which was meet" (vv. 26-27) From the refusal to recognise God there follows the failure to appreciate man, and thus humanity without the fellow-man (*C.D.* III, 2, p. 229ff). And since humanity as fellow-humanity is to be understood in its root as the togetherness of man and woman, as the root of this inhumanity there follows the ideal of a masculinity free from woman and a femininity free from man. And because nature or the Creator of nature will not be trifled with, because the despised fellow-man is still there, because the natural orientation on him is still in force, there follows the corrupt, emotional and finally physical desire in which—in a sexual union which is not and cannot be genuine—man thinks that he must seek and can find in man, and woman in woman, a substitute for the despised partner. But there is no sense in reminding man of the command of God only when he is face to face with this ultimate consequence, or pointing to the fact of human disobedience only when this malady breaks out openly in these unnatural courses. Naturally the command of God is opposed to these courses. This is almost too obvious to need stating. It is to be hoped that, in awareness of God's command as also of His forgiving grace, the doctor, the pastor trained in psychotherapy, and the legislator and judge—for the protection of threatened youth—will put forth their best efforts. But the decisive word of Christian ethics must consist in a warning against entering upon the whole way of life which can only end in the tragedy of concrete homosexuality. We know that in its early stages it may have an appearance of particular beauty and spirituality, and even be redolent of sanctity. Often it has not been the worst people who have discovered and to some extent practised it as a sort of wonderful esoteric of personal life. Nor does this malady always manifest itself openly, or, when it does so, in obvious or indictable forms. Fear of ultimate consequences can give as little protection in this case, and condemnation may be as feeble a deterrent, as the thought of painful consequences in the case of fornication. What is needed is that the recognition of the divine command should cut sharply across the attractive beginnings. The real perversion takes place, the original decadence and disintegration begins, where man will not see his partner of the opposite sex and therefore the primal form of fellow-man, refusing to hear his question and to make a responsible answer, but trying to be human in himself as sovereign man or woman, rejoicing in himself in self-satisfaction and self-sufficiency. The command of God is opposed to the wonderful esoteric of this *beata solitudo*. For in this supposed discovery of the genuinely human man and woman give themselves up to the worship of a false god. It is here, therefore, that for himself and then in relation to others each must be brought to fear, recollection and understanding. This is the place for protest, warning and conversion. The command of God shows him irrefutably—in clear contradiction to his own theories—that as a man he can only be genuinely human with woman, or as a woman with man. In proportion as he accepts this insight, homosexuality can have no place in his life, whether in its more refined or cruder forms.

Homosexuality and the Homosexual

Robert Gordis

Nowhere else is the confrontation between the classical religious tradition and emerging contemporary attitudes sharper than with regard to homosexuality. Biblical law and biblical life are completely at one in condemning the practice. The sexual codes in the Torah describe male homosexuality as an "abomination" punishable with death like other major infractions of the moral code, such as incest and sexual contact with animals (Lev. 18:22; 20:13).

The practice is clearly regarded as worse than rape, as is evident from an incident narrated in Chapter 19 of Genesis. Two strangers, who are actually angels sent by the Lord to survey the sinful city of Sodom, are given hospitality by Lot, Abraham's nephew. When the townsmen hear of the strangers in their midst, they besiege Lot's house and demand that he turn the wayfarers over to them for homosexual abuse. Horrified at this breach of the ancient custom of hospitality, Lot offers instead to send out his two virgin daughters to the mob to do with as they wish. When the mob refuses the offer and tries to storm the door of Lot's house, it becomes clear that the city is beyond hope, and its destruction is decreed by God.

A similar tragic incident, going back to an early, lawless period shortly after the conquest of the land, is reported in Chapter 19 of the Book of Judges. A traveler passing through the town of Gibeah in Benjamin is denied hospitality by the townspeople. Only one old man gives lodging and food to the stranger, his concubine, and his animals. When the Benjaminites learn that the stranger is being housed among them, they gather and demand that he be handed over to them for sexual purposes. The host remonstrates with them in vain, offering to turn over his daughter and his guest's concubine to satisfy their lust. When the mob does not desist, the guest takes his concubine and pushes her out of doors. They rape her and abuse her all night and leave her lifeless body on the threshold. The book of Judges goes on to narrate the punishment visited upon the Benjaminites, leading to the virtual extinction of that tribe from the household of Israel.

There are many instances where rabbinic law has modifed biblical attitudes in the direction of greater leniency, but this is not true of homosexuality.[1] Here the attitude remains strongly negative, though the practice receives relatively little attention in the Talmud, probably because the rabbis believed that "Jews are not suspected of committing homosexuality and buggery."[2]

This persistent feeling of revulsion toward homosexuality was nourished by a variety of historical causes. During the biblical period, the fertility cults that were widespread throughout the Middle East included intercourse with sacred male prostitutes at the pagan temples. From the Canaanites these practices, along with idolatry in general, penetrated into the religious practices of the Hebrews during the early days of the Davidic kingdom. These functionaries were finally banished from the precincts of the Temple, but only after repeated and determined efforts by several Judean kings, Asa, Jehoshaphat, and Josiah.[3]

During the Greco-Roman era and beyond, the opposition to homosexuality by Jewish rabbinic leadership was a reaction to its widespread presence in the ancient world, where it was furthered and encouraged by pagan society and religion. Homosexual liaisons played a significant role in the social and cultural life of the ancient Greeks and Romans. Indirect evidence of the strong hold that homosexuality had on the Greco-Roman world is to be found in Paul's Epistle to the Romans. In the strongest of terms he castigates homosexuality as "dishonorable" and "unnatural." That he places homosexuality at the head of a list of offenses would suggest that the practice was widespread. It is also noteworthy that he first levels his attack against the women and only then turns to the men as "likewise" engaging in these "shameless acts." (1:26, 27)

This negative attitude toward homosexuality has been maintained by Jewish tradition to the present time. It regards homosexuals as flouting the will of the Creator, who fashioned men and women with different anatomical endowments and with correspondingly distinct roles to play in the sexual process.

All these objections to homosexuality in Judaism were intensified in Christianity because of several additional factors. Most of the converts to the early Christian Church were former pagans who had been exposed to the presence of homosexual practices in their previous environment. Paul, as well as the Church after him, therefore felt it incumbent to attack the practice with all the power at his command. Moreover, as we have seen, classical Christianity was basically unhappy with the sexual component of human nature in general. It had to concede that sexual contact was legitimate, first because the instinct cannot be successfully suppressed by most men and women and, second, because it is essential for procreation. Since this last factor is obviously lacking in homosexual activity, there is no justification for yielding to "unnatural lust."

In sum, both Judaism and Christianity, in spite of differences in their approach to sex, have regarded homosexuality as a violation of God's will and a perversion of nature.

The subsequent weakening of religion and the growth of secularism in the Western world did little to reduce the sense of hostility toward homosexuality. The new emphasis on the cultivation of the body and the development of athletics in the modern period underscored the goal that men should be men. Nowhere is masculinity revealed more unmistakably than in sexual potency. Psychoanalytic theory, particularly in its classical Freudian formulation, saw male and female sexuality as the fundamental element in the human personality, which, when diverted from "normal" channels, becomes the source of psychological and physical trauma. In this respect as well, homosexuality ran counter to the values of the age. As a result of all these factors, as well as vestiges of the religious approach, homosexuality continued to engender feelings of revulsion going beyond the bonds of rational response.

Perhaps the most sensational manifestation of this reaction came at the end of the nineteenth century. In 1895, the brilliant and gifted English dramatist and poet Oscar Wilde was prosecuted by the Crown for having homosexual relations with Lord Alfred Douglas. Wilde was convicted, imprisoned for two years, and emerged from this experience a man physically broken and creatively ruined.

Wilde is by no means the only example of talent or genius to be found among homosexuals. More or less plausibly, many distinguished figures of the past and the present have been described as homosexuals. It is likely that lesbianism is as common as male homosexuality, but it is felt to be less offensive because its manifestations seem less blatant.

The hostility of society to homosexuals is reflected in the statute books. Homosexual behavior is treated as a crime in China and the Soviet Union; in the United States, homosexual soliciting is a criminal act. To be sure, such laws have often not been enforced in this country, particularly in the recent past.

By and large, the penalties accorded to homosexuals have been social and economic rather than legal.[4] Homosexuals have been driven underground and have had to suffer all the psychological traumas associated with a closet existence. They have been forced to deny their desires and to pretend to interests and feelings not their own. Always there is the human propensity to cruelty, of which the twentieth century has made us painfully aware. Add to it the negative attitude toward homosexuals in the religious tradition and in secular law and you have a moral base for flagrant discrimination and hostility toward homosexuals in housing and employment.

The alleged effeminacy in dress and demeanor of homosexuals has been the butt of ridicule and scorn in public and in private, on the printed page, the radio, television, the screen, and the stage. This in spite of the alleged high percentage of homosexuals in the artistic, literary, and entertainment worlds.

Only within the past two decades has the public attitude begun to change. The general weakening of traditional religion has diminished the influence of biblical and post-biblical teaching on the subject. In addition, sexual experience without regard to procreation has increasingly been accepted and glorified as a good in itself, if not as the *summum bonum* of existence. Hence, homosexuality has lost some of the horror it conjured up in earlier generations. Above all, in our age, the drive for new and exciting experiences, however untried and even dangerous they may be, has led to new patterns of sexual conduct, like sexual communes and wife-swapping, not to speak of various forms of perversion. Advocates of homosexuality have, therefore, felt free to argue that they are simply practicing an equally legitimate life style, a variant pattern to the dominant heterosexuality of our culture. Some have maintained that 10 percent of the population are homosexual, a figure that can neither be demonstrated nor disproved.

Substantial success has already crowned the efforts of the various organizations in the gay liberation movement to remove disabilities in employment and housing from homosexuals in the United States. In France, Italy, Sweden, Denmark, Switzerland, Mexico, and Uruguay, the practice has long been decriminalized. Great Britain took the same step in 1967 and Canada in 1969.[5]

What approach toward homosexuality should modern religion sanction and modern society adopt? No excuse can or should be offered for the cruelty that traditional attitudes toward the practice have engendered in the past. Nevertheless, the classical viewpoint of Judaism and Christianity, that homosexual conduct is "unnatural," cannot be dismissed out of hand.

Here a brief theological digression is called for. That the goal of the universe and, by that token, the purpose of existence are veiled from man has been the conviction of thinkers in every age. Koheleth in the Bible and the medieval philosopher Maimonides are at one with the Hasidic teacher Rabbi Bunam of Pshysha, who found his beloved disciple Enoch in tears. The rabbi asked him, "Why are you weeping?" and Enoch answered, "Am I not a creature of this world, and am I not made with eyes and heart and all limbs, and yet I do not know for what purpose I was created and what good I am in the world." "Fool!" said Rabbi Bunam. "I also go around thus."

Nevertheless, we may perhaps catch a slight glimpse of the purpose of the Creator, or, if secular terms be preferred, the direction and goal of the life process in the universe.[6] The lowest creatures in the evolutionary ladder, the single-cell organisms, multiply by fission, the splitting of the cell into two equal parts. As a result, each of the two new beings possesses exactly the same attributes as the parent, no more, no less, no change. Only with the emergence of multicellular organisms does bisexuality appear on the evolutionary ladder. Fission is now replaced by bisexual reproduction, which becomes the universal pattern. This fundamental change seems to indicate that the Author of life has intended the life process to be not a perpetually static repetition of the old but a dynamic adventure, with new combinations of attributes constantly emerging through the interaction of a male and a female producing a new organism different from both its parents. It therefore follows that, in purely secular biological terms, homosexuality is an aberration from the norm, a violation of the law of nature.

It may be objected that since man is not merely a creature of nature and is free to modify his environment and perhaps even his heredity, what is natural is not the sole touchstone of what is right for man. There is, however, good reason for believing that homosexuality is a violation not only of nature but of human nature as well. No attribute is more characteristic of humanity than the gift of speech. Language is probably the greatest intellectual achievement of primitive man. Imbedded in the structure of all languages is gender, a recognition of bisexuality, which, by extension, is applied to every object in the real world. Gender remains basic to language and to thought for the most sophisticated of moderns.

For later stages of human development, it may be noted that no society has made homosexuality its basic or even its preferred pattern of sexual conduct. This is true even of predatory groups that could have replenished their ranks through captives taken in war.

Transposed into theological language, heterosexuality is the will of God. It therefore follows that homosexuality is a violation of His will, for which the traditional term is "sin." The concept of sin in general may seem outmoded to modern ears and, in any event, too harsh a term to apply to homosexuality. But the etymology of the Hebrew word *het*, like its Greek counterpart, *hamartia*, is derived from marksmanship and means "missing the mark," as has already been noted. Sin means a turning aside from the right path that can and should be followed. Consequently the Hebrews *teshubbah,* generally translated as "repentance," means "returning" to the right road.

Judgments and attitudes aside, what are the facts about homosexuality? In spite of the vast interest in the phenomenon, very little is really known about its origin and nature or any possible treatment. Modern psychologists may be correct in believing that latent homosexual tendencies are to be found in most people. If this is true, it would seem that homosexual patterns of behavior become dominant for some men and women because they are stimulated by personal contact with homosexuals. If, therefore, homosexuality is culturally induced, it would be a flagrant example of a conscious and often conscienceless distortion of normal human nature.

On the other hand, homosexuality may be the product of a genetic disturbance. In this case, it must be regarded as a biological abnormality. Whether the practice is the result of heredity or of environment, or of both, intensive research is needed to discover the etiology of homosexuality and then to search for a remedy, or at least for methods of treatment.

For centuries, society, abetted by religion, has been guilty of condemning as a sin and punishing as a crime what should have been recognized as an illness. In fact, physical illness in general was regarded as a Divine visitation, a punishment for sins for which the sufferer himself was responsible. This attitude is not altogether dead today. Recently, the president of a mammoth bank in New York demonstrated that he is obviously afflicted with massive spiritual myopia. He declared that physical illness is a crime against society committed by those who are ill, and that therefore society has no obligation to provide medical care and other social services to the sick poor.

If homosexuality is an abnormality or an illness, as has been maintained, a parallel to our problem in several respects may be found in alcoholism. So long as the alcoholic was regarded as an incorrigible sinner, little progress was made in curing this major malady. It is only in our day, when alcoholism is being recognized as a disease, probably genetic in origin though socially stimulated, that genuine progress has begun to be made overcoming it.

The analogy is helpful in another respect as well. Experts are agreed that the will to recover, as expressed in total abstinence, which is encouraged by such programs as Alcoholics Anonymous, plays an indispensable role in the treatment of alcohol addiction. It is also known that only a fraction of all alcoholics, somewhere between one third and one half of all patients who undergo treatment, recover fully or substantially.[7]

At the present level of our knowledge, the percentage of homosexuals who can be "rehabilitated" is almost surely lower than that of alcoholics. To a substantial degree, this is due to the varying attitudes of contemporary society toward two phenomena. While alcoholism is universally recognized as a liability, homosexuality is often defended as a normal life style, a legitimate alternate pattern to heterosexuality. The gay liberation movement has vigorously opposed the older traditional view of homosexuality as a sin. It is not more kindly disposed to the more modern concept of homosexuality as an illness. It uses every available means to propagate the idea that homosexuality is an entirely proper life style.

Nevertheless, if we are not to fall prey to the old prejudice or to succumb to the new fashion, we must insist that homosexuality is not normal. To the extent that men and women cannot control their homosexual desires, they are suffering from an illness like any other physical disability. To the degree that they can hold the impulse in rein and fail to do so, they are committing a sin, a violation of the will of God or, in secular terms, an aberration from the norm.

However, a basic caution is in order. Ignorant as we are of the etiology of the disorder, we are in no position to determine to which category a given act belongs. Hence, homosexual activity, when carried on by adults in private and violating no one's wishes and desires, should be decriminalized on the statute books. The practice belongs to the rabbinic category of an act that is "free from legal punishment (by human agency), but forbidden."[8] The homosexual in contemporary society has a just claim to be free from legal penalties and social disabilities.

Yet there are some critical areas where blanket removal of all restrictions against homosexuals may be unwise. Such a decision should be reached without panic or prejudice, on the basis of a careful investigation of all the relevant factors. Sensing the widespread erosion of conventional moral standards everywhere, homosexual groups are pressing for much more than freedom from discrimination and harassment. They are demanding that homosexuality be recognized as a legitimate and normal alternative to heterosexuality.[9]

Some Christian theologians, troubled by the tragic and undeniable fact that Western society has been grievously lacking in compassion for homosexuals, have attempted to give a Christian justification for homosexuality. One Catholic writer explains away the biblical condemnations of homosexual practices as "Old Testament legalism."[10] A Protestant theologian takes his point of departure from the Christian doctrine that salvation is directed to all mankind, so that all human beings are equally sinful in the eyes of God. He, therefore, leaps to the non sequitur that "no absolute or ultimate distinction can be made between homosexuality and heterosexuality." He goes even further and declares that "no human condition or life style is intrinsically *justified* or righteous—neither heterosexuality nor homosexuality, closed nor open marriage, celibacy nor profligacy." He proceeds to express doubts as to whether the family centeredness of contemporary Christianity can be justified theologically, since both Jesus and Paul were suspicious of family ties! He concludes that there are three life styles open to men and women intrinsically equal in moral validity: marriage, celibacy, and homosexuality.[11]

The lengths to which sympathetic souls may be led are evident in the secular sphere as well. In fact, like the generous Irishman who was asked, "Isn't one man as good as another?" and answered, "Sure, and a whole lot better, too," some advocates have argued that homosexuality is not merely as good as heterosexuality but better, since it avoids the possibility of increasing the population! The same logic would lead to the conclusion that sterility is healthier and more beneficial than fecundity.

It is perhaps a sign of the times that a recent radio broadcast referred to a sado-masochist liberation movement, which calls itself the Til Eulenspiegel Society. This group, whose size was not indicated, demands "equal rights" for the practice of sexual perversion, including such forms as flagellation and sodomy, which, they insist, are also legitimate alternatives.

Having mastered the modern art of lobbying, homosexuals carried on a campaign among the members of the American Psychological Association and, in 1974, succeeded in having homosexuality removed from the list of abnormal patterns of behavior. An effort is being made in some quarters to reverse the ruling of the American Psychological Association. The argument advanced by gay liberation groups is that homosexuals are basically healthy, well-adjusted individuals who do not seek medical or psychiatric treatment because they do not need it. Spokesmen for homosexuality, aware of the widespread frustration and unhappiness with conventional marriages, have urged the claim. In a growing number of cases, homosexuals have asked the clergy to officiate at homosexual "marriages." No comparative study is available of either the permanence of homosexual unions or of the quality of life of homosexual couples.

On the other hand, testimony has been advanced to show that the self-acceptance and satisfaction with life expressed by many homosexuals is often only a facade for resignation and despair, all the more hopeless because it cannot find channels of expression. In their youth, it has been maintained, homosexuals have suffered from rejection and unhappiness, which are integral to their condition. In adult life, they continue to experience conflict, anguish, and pain which they deny even to themselves. It has also been argued that the growing militant assertion of "gay pride," coupled with the A.P.A. declaration that homosexuality is normal human behavior on the one hand and the generally negative attitude of society on the other, has intensified their unhappiness. That there is so much heat and so little light demonstrates only how slight is the authentic scientific knowledge available on this important issue.

There have been some specifically religious aspects to the campaign for equal rights for homosexuals. In 1976, the Episcopal Bishop of New York ordained a woman to the priesthood who stated publicly that she was a lesbian. The act raised considerable protest among many communicants and clergy. Some time ago, on the West Coast, a group of Jewish homosexuals organized themselves into a congregation and were admitted into membership in the Union of American Hebrew Congregations. In the East, a "Gay Synagogue" holds Friday evening services in New York City that are announced by *The New York Times* each Friday.

How should the Jewish community react to a call for special worship facilities for homosexuals? The answer would not be difficult to reach were the issue not beclouded by so much passion on both sides of the barricade. Men and women suffering various disabilities do not organize special synagogues. The only exceptions are facilities for worship for the blind and the deaf, dictated by the necessity of finding alternate modes of communication. Jewish male and female homosexuals are Jews and should always be made welcome among their people. In the discussion engendered by the West Coast group, it was explained that homosexuals wish to be able to kiss one another publicly after the conclusion of Sabbath services. Evidently, they believe that this type of greeting is a law of Moses from Sinai. But missing a kiss in public hardly justifies founding a synagogue. Undoubtedly, other and weightier motives play their part as well.

As is so frequently the case, truth and justice in this troubled area lie, not with the extremes, but with the center position. We can no longer accept the traditional religious reaction to homosexuality as a horror and an abomination. On the other hand, the fashionable doctrine being propagated in our time—that it is an alternate life style of equal value and legitimacy—must be decisively rejected. Homosexuality is an abnormality, an illness which, like any other, varies in intensity with different individuals. Until more efficacious means are discovered for dealing with their problem, homosexuals deserve the same inalienable rights as do all their fellow human beings—freedom from harassment and discrimination before the law and in society.

There can be no question that homosexuals are entitled to more than justice before the law. It is not enough merely to remove the various kinds of legal disability and overt hostility to which they have long been subjected. Whatever evaluation is placed upon their condition, be it moral, medical, or psychological, they are human beings, our brothers and sisters, who deserve compassion and love from their fellow men and, above all, from their brothers in kinship and in faith.[12]

IIb
Homosexual Acts are Intrinsically Evil

(The 'Neo-Traditionalist' School)

John Giles Milhaven
William Muehl
Ruth Tiffany Barnhouse

Homosexuality and Love

John Giles Milhaven

A couple of years ago, ninety Episcopal priests of the New York metropolitan area expressed agreement that the church should classify homosexual acts between consenting adults as "morally neutral" and acknowledge that in some cases such acts may even be a good thing.[1] Public discussion of the morality of homosexuality was flaring up at the time, and was reflected in popular periodicals and TV panels.[2] Eventually the public excitement subsided, but Americans and Christians continue to question what their fathers felt was unquestionable. One form of their question is: "If a Christian has strong impulses to homosexual behavior, what should he or she do? What does Christian morality say about it?"

First of all, "Christian morality" does not say anything about homosexuality or anything else, because there is no such person named "Christian morality." At least not that I know of. There is nobody named "Christian morality": there are just Christians, we who are the Church, are Christ's Body, are God's people, us. How, then, do Christians answer the question: "What should the Christian do who has strong impulses to homosexual behavior?" Nowadays, Christians go about answering the question in different ways.

Some Christians turn to the Bible. They read, "No homosexual will inherit the Kingdom of God." For some Christians no more need be said. God's Word condemns all homosexual behavior. No Christian, therefore, may ever act homosexually. Among the Christians who answer the question in this way, simply by reading the Bible by themselves, there are, I believe, more Protestants than Catholics.

Other Christians turn to natural law. They look for God's creative purpose as inscribed in the nature of things. One purpose of God that some Christians find inalienably inscribed in man's sexual nature is that every single sexual act be ordered to bring new life into the world. God, through nature, forbids that a man ever act sexually in such a manner as to render impossible the procreative purpose. For some Christians, no more need be said. God's Law condemns all homosexual behavior. No Christian may ever act homosexually. Among the Christians who answer the question in this way, simply by reading in nature God's precise purpose for every sexual act of man, there are, I believe, more Catholics than Protestants.

But there are Christians today who cannot adopt either of the two approaches. The approaches go toward the right sources, of course. The Christian, facing an ethical decision, must turn to God's Word as recorded in the Bible, and he must turn to God's purpose as manifested in the realities He created. They are *the* two sources of light in which a Christian lives. But the two approaches we have described do not go far enough. To listen to God's Word, it is not enough to read sentences out of the Bible, especially if we understand them without a twentieth century mentality and take them as direct answers to our twentieth century questions. If nothing else, the Christian biblical scholars of our time would tell us this.

And—as far as the second approach goes—to be able to discern the general purpose God has for the realities He created does not mean we can discern a fixed, specific purpose He has for a particular kind of act, a precise purpose which must be respected every time the act is performed. The Christian philosophers, thinking in the mode of the philosophy of our time, would say that we cannot.

To the ethical question concerning homosexual behavior, therefore, some Christians employ an approach that is different from the two we have been discussing. People have come to label the approach "the new morality." The term means something general: a certain way of thinking about ethical questions, a way of thinking which is widespread among Christians trying to lead examined lives. The new morality offers an answer for at least certain forms of homosexual behavior. But before considering the answer, let it be clear what the new morality is and is not.

Suppose I face a decision to make in my life concerning homosexual behavior. Suppose I say to myself, "I don't recognize any absolute moral law of God prohibiting this behavior. Therefore I'm free to do as I please." I may have different reasons for saying that no absolute moral law, no divine prohibition, applies here. Perhaps I do not think that God has laid down any moral laws at all. Or perhaps I just do not think it is clear and certain that He prohibited all homosexual behavior. In either case, my reasoning runs the same: "I hold the new morality. I do not admit that

God has absolutely prohibited homosexual behavior. Therefore I may do as I please."

Except that this is not the new morality. It does not accept the principle I am going on, namely that where no absolute prohibitions apply, one is free to do as one pleases. It would consider my way of thinking to be a childish form of legalism. All that matters is what Daddy and Mommy say. But they didn't say that *every day* I should stay away from the cookie jar. So, to the cookie jar I go. I don't have to worry about what the cookies may do to my stomach. I don't have to worry how much will be left for my brothers and sisters. I'm not old enough for that.

The Christians who live according to the new morality do not, it is true, base their moral judgments on any absolute, specific prohibitions laid down by God. But neither do they feel free to do as they please. They base all their moral judgments and their lives on something else, something positive, though general: the absolute, Divine, command to love. Facing the question of homosexual behavior, they would say: God has laid down no specific and absolute prohibitions against homosexual behavior. But He and I do want absolutely one thing: that I live a life of love.

Here again one could misunderstand the new morality. One could claim to be living according to the new morality and not be doing so at all. It depends on what I mean by "love." Suppose what I mean by "love" comes down to affectionate impulse and nothing more. By "love" I mean I have a genuine fondness and affection for another person, a deep and strong feeling for him or her. The affection makes me want to express it physically, sexually. I appeal to the new morality: love is the only absolute. This is love. I go ahead.

Except that the Christians who live according to the new morality would not call that "love." The impulse of feeling is often part of love, but love is always more than that. Here a man's experience comes in. If a man is honest with himself, his experience shows him that some of his affectionate impulses lead to actions which, in the long run, badly hurt the person he loves. For example, he may recognize that some of his impulses towards his teenage son lead him to overprotect him, run his life for him, keep him from exercising responsibility. He concludes that these are not impulses of love. He is coming to realize, as most of us human beings do, what we really mean by love. It lies deeper than feeling. It must include the free determination, commitment, of a man or woman to further the good of a certain person.

There is nothing new about such an understanding of love. The situationist, Joseph Fletcher, defines "love" this way.[3] But exegetes like Spicq and Dodd testify to the same sense of the word ($\dot{\alpha}\gamma\dot{\alpha}\pi\eta$) in the New Testament.[4] Christians of the new and old morality can agree that love, as the promotion of human good, is what makes Christian ethics. As Thomas

Aquinas puts it, a man offends God only inasmuch as he acts against the human good of himself or another man.[5]

But here, I believe, the Christian of the new morality adds something new. Or at least introduces a new emphasis. To understand what is good for a person, he, a man of the twentieth century, relies exclusively on experience. For him, love knows no *a priori* laws, sees only the ones loved and what experience shows is happening or likely to happen to them. Love is, therefore, pragmatic, hard-headed, often unromantic. It is pitiless for all that experience shows will oppose the good of the person loved, whether the opposition comes from within the lover or without. Moreover, love's view, looking to experience, is long-range. It, therefore, is tough, puts up with all things, holds out, goes for distance. A man's love for the woman he marries and the children he begets, is judged authentic—to really be love—only after the test of the years and of the problems and burdens and dangers life brings down on his family one after another. There is no other test for anyone else. Love has to be as mighty as death, as strong as hell. Let the buyer beware.

Christ emboldens the Christian to buy love. The Christian sees in Jesus Christ how great a thing love is. God's forgiving love, communicated through Christ to the Christian, gives him the confidence and strength to love. But only if he undersands what love is, and only if he has bought love, taken it on, and is trying to live it, only then has he the right, according to the new morality, to come to a question like that of homosexual behavior with love as his sole norm. Only then can he, with the love of a twentieth century man, turn simply to experience for an answer to his question: "Would homosexual behavior really be good or bad for myself and the other person?"

One man's experience of homosexual behavior is extremely limited. The man of the new morality must turn to the experience of the community. Most of the community have little or no experience with homosexual behavior. They must turn to those who have extensive, critical experience, pre-eminently the psychologists, psychiatrists and analysts. Dr. Isadore Rubin, in a "Discussion Guide" for SIECUS (Sex Information and Education Council of the U. S.), reports that though there is no unanimity among specialists, the most commonly held opinion is that all homosexuals are mentally ill or neurotic.[6] Moreover, many psychiatrists who would not judge homosexuality so negatively, if considered abstractly in itself, do believe "that homosexual behavior could not be maintained in the face of a hostile and punitive environment [i.e., present day society] unless strong neurotic fears blocked the path to heterosexual adaptation."[7] Furthermore, according to prevailing psycho-analytic opinion, says Dr. Rubin, homosexuality represents a fixation at, or regression to, an immature state of development.

The word "homosexual" has, of course, a spectrum of meanings. But what the specialists have defined as the kind of person they are discussing is, in fact, a kind of person who poses acutely ethical and pastoral problems for the Christian. By "homosexuals" are not meant here those who at one time or other have indulged in sexual behavior with members of their own sex, nor those who often feel sexual attraction toward their own sex, but, generally speaking, feel a stronger attraction toward those of the opposite sex. What is meant here is rather "those individuals who more or less chronically feel an urgent sexual desire towards, and a sexual responsiveness to, members of their own sex, and who seek gratification of this desire predominantly with members of their own sex."[8] Such persistent, preferential emotional and physical attraction to members of the same sex, a committee of the Group for the Advancement of Psychiatry declares, without qualification, to be "a severe emotional disorder."[9] As the understanding of the various psychological causal factors of homosexuality has increased, it appears more and more evident that the homosexual is an emotionally immature individual who has not acquired a normal capacity to develop satisfying heterosexual relationships, which will eventuate in marriage and parenthood."[10]

In other words, homosexuality is not just a physical oddity like colorblindness or being left-handed. Its roots go deep and spread wide in the personality. Like all our basic sexual attitudes and patterns of sexual behavior, it is psychosexual, organically expressing an attitude and stage of growth of one's very person. What homosexuality expresses, as Dr. Philip Heersema puts it, writing in the *Journal of the American Medical Association*, is "an arrest of personality growth," "stunted development and disturbed personality."[11]

These conclusions of the community's experience are not certain. There are psychologists who dissent, seeing little cause for alarm in many cases of homosexual behavior. Unquestionably, there is need for more quantity and analysis of data. New evidence suggests a nuancing or even a revision of the above conclusions. Nevertheless, the conclusions, as they stand, represent the most reliable experience in our community at the present time. Most generalizations distilled from the community's experience, including those refined by scientific analysis, are far from certain when applied to individual situations. Even relatively reliable principles, e.g., concerning safe and unsafe ways of autodriving or courses of physical illnesses, will turn out often enough to be unverified. Less certain are the applications of the community's experience in obscure areas such as economic inflation, population growth, air pollution, adolescence, etc. A lack of certainty can be critical for an ethic based on law. But not for a morality of love. One who loves does not demand certainty before deciding how to help the one he loves. He uses the best evidence at hand. A man will arrange an operation medically indicated for his wife simply because it is less likely that she will die with it than without it.

A man with genuine love for himself and others will refrain, in his behavior, from expressing and deepening particular feelings when the evidence on hand indicates strongly, if not with certainty, that the feelings are profoundly immature and disordered. Thus a Christian moving in the spirit of the new morality condemns homosexual behavior more severely than one using traditional arguments. According to a traditional argument, homosexual behavior is wrong in that it frustrates a faculty of man. According to the Christian who is moved only by love and relies on the experience of the community, homosexual behavior is wrong in that it frustrates the man himself. It fixates him at a stage far short of the full emotional and sexual development of the "living man" who is "God's glory."

In other words, a Christian for whom love is the only absolute understands that love is free, strong, open. (One might think of the analyses of Erich Fromm.) If I act in a particular way basically because I am afraid to look a woman in the eye, to relate with her independently as one grown person to another, if, for example, the affection I am seeking by my homosexual actions—though I may not realize it, but as psychological analysis finds—is Mommy's love for her little boy, then I must say to myself that I am not acting out of love. I am fleeing from love. Which is the greatest sin and the greatest failure for any man and, in a special way, for any Christian.

To have impulses in this direction is neither a sin nor a failure. According to Dr. Heersema, evidence of the universality of homosexuality can be found to some degree in every individual.[12] He adds that there is a brief period, usually at the onset of puberty, that may properly be called a normal "homosexual" stage. In fact, all of us adults have strong, recurrent impulses that correspond to "an immature stage of development" or "an arrest of personality growth." In other words, we all have childish impulses. They draw us from the free, strong, open love that we want to have. The impulses may have nothing to do with sex. I may have strong impulses to self-pity. Or to vindictiveness. Or to fear and anxiety. My impulses may be more childish, more opposed to love than the feelings leading this other man to homosexual behavior.

The point for every man is: how do I react to the childish feelings? He has to ask the question over and over again. Do I go along with them, confirm and strengthen them, express them in action and live according to them? Or do I choose to love? Do I free myself, inasmuch as I can, from childish feelings and choose to do only what expresses and furthers a mature lover within myself and others? In real life, it is a hard choice. If I am a Christian, Christ helps me choose.

Recently, evidence has been shown that for certain individuals the choice of homosexual behavior has been the kind just described.[13] There are active homosexuals whose emotional life seems to be no less mature and healthy than the average heterosexual. Insofar as I can judge, the evidence is still too fragmentary to unseat the prevailing scientific appraisal of homosexuality as the living-out of sick and stunted emotions. The odds are still high that the average individual who chooses homosexual behavior will be choosing a sick, immature way of life. The odds should determine the ethical decision, it seems to me, at least for the individual for whom professional analysis has confirmed his emotional sickness or whose personal experience has offered no grounds to believe that he is an exception to the general rule.[14]

In one sense, therefore, the Christian of the new morality condemns homosexual behavior more severely than a Christian of the old. He sees its evil not in the abuse of a human faculty, but in the refusal to love., i.e., to live and let live a full human life. But this is only an ethical answer to an ethical question. It says what one ought to do. It says nothing about sin or guilt and responsibility or Church membership or civil laws. It is one thing for me to say that to be an alcoholic or a shrewish wife is wrong, in open contradiction to the life and love Christ calls us to. That is an ethical statement a Christian can make. It is another thing for me to say that alcoholics and shrews are great sinners, that all alcoholics and shrews are guilty and responsible for what they do because they are free to do otherwise, that all alcoholics and shrews should be excluded from Church membership, that alcoholism and shrewishness should be made a criminal offense, punishable by law. The four statements are, at best, unlikely. But that alcoholism and shrewishness—and homosexual behavior—are wrong and unChristian is, I submit, true.

I would like to allude to a second and older way a Christian can answer the ethical question of homosexual behavior. When he believes in Jesus Christ, he does not believe in a person who only lived on earth 2000 years ago and now is in heaven. He believes in a person still present here today in His body and in His community, the Church.

> For he has given us some men as apostles, some as prophets, some as missionaries, some as pastors and teachers, in order to fit his people for the work of service, for building the body of Christ, until we attain unity in faith, and in the knowledge of the Son of God, and reach mature manhood, and that full measure of development found in Christ. We must not be babies any longer, blown about and swung around by every wind of doctrine through the trickery of men with their ingenuity in inventing error. We must lovingly hold to the truth and grow up into perfect union with him who is the head—Christ himself.[15]

I read this, not simply as a sentence out of the Bible, but as a word understood and lived by Christian communities from the beginning until now, whether they be Roman Catholic or Lutheran or Greek Orthodox or any other. In different ways, but always in some way, the man who believes in Christ, as he faces concrete questions of living such as that of homosexuality, know that the "pastors and teachers" of Christ's Body play their part in helping him "hold lovingly to the truth." The Church has always set limits to the role of pastors and teachers. But to limit is not to deny. For many Christians, heeding the words of their pastors and teachers is a wiser and, therefore, more loving response to the question of homosexual behavior than reading the evidence of the psychiatrists and psychologists of our secular city.

Some Words of Caution

William Muehl

We know very little about the causes and nature of homosexuality. Some psychotherapists treat it as an illness. Others refuse to do so. There appear to be people who are born into a physiological sexual ambiguity. And there are obviously many who adopt it either in response to abnormal social isolation such as imprisonment, or to provide outré thrills and stimulate a jaded appetite. There are homosexuals who long to become heterosexuals, while others profess to be quite content with their lot. As a psychological phenomenon homosexuality still seems to be a profound mystery.

There is nothing unclear, however, about the attitide of the Christian community toward sexual relations between persons of the same gender. They have been consistently proscribed and their practitioners often cruelly persecuted by ecclesiastical authorities. Both Old and New Testaments condemn homosexuality. Any effort to make a case to the contrary involves the kind of torturing of Scripture by which racists seek to defend segregation, and martial spirits to justify preemptive strikes. Whether the motives of those who want to blur the hard edges of the truth are compassionate or self-serving, the facts of history cannot be disputed. Genital homosexuality has been regarded as immoral by responsible Christians. Any discussion of the subject which begins with another basic assumption is doomed to futility.

To make the statements I have just made about the past and present attitude of Christians, even to propose that this attitude is right and ought to be perpetuated within the community of faith, does not imply any justification for the way in which homosexual people are treated by secular society today. Our society has encouraged the most flagrant exploitation of sexuality. It has allowed our appetites to be titillated in a great variety of ways by experts in the business; and the relevant moral standards of the past are being abandoned with shouts of liberation by those who first reflect and then shape the prevailing mood of Western society.

Statesmen and politicians are only mildly embarrassed when they are reported accurately to be womanizers. Business enterprises use commercial lovemaking to lure customers and clinch deals. Colleges virtually subsidize fornication by their dormitory arrangements. And those newspaper columnists who have become the arbiters of ethics urge prudent parents to put their teen-age daughters on the pill.

It is both hypocritical and grossly unjust, therefore, for secular institutions to persecute and prosecute those whose sexual irresponsibility is somewhat more adventurous than average. A society cannot make free sex the national hobby and then penalize those who show creative imagination in the way they play the game.

It seems clear to me, as to many others, that when they act as citizens, Christians have a serious obligation to support basic civil rights for homosexuals. It is unthinkable that men and women should lose jobs, be denied housing, and suffer police harassment for refusing to be bound by rules which most of their neighbors have for all practical purposes abandoned long since. If we argue that what happens in bedrooms is not the public business, we cannot in good conscience keep peeking through keyholes. If we hold that what happens in bedrooms *is* the public business, we have far more pressing problems to solve than those presented by Gay Liberation.

Does the logic of this position require that Christians abandon their historic stand on homosexuality and declare to be good what they have in the past condemned? Obviously not. What is required is a firm reassertion of the time-honored distinction between toleration on the one hand and approval on the other. Or to put it in more familiar religious terms, adherence to the principle that one must love the sinner while hating the sin.

The appropriate Christian answer to the increase of sexual irresponsibility in society is neither to adopt that irresponsibility as its own mode of behavior nor to expel from its midst those who fall victim to it. It is, rather, to see all abuses of human sexuality as manifestations of that sinfulness which plagues our common existence; and to define homosexuality as one more symptom of a general problem rather than the outward and visible sign of a special depravity.

This is not an easy thing to do; partly because homosexuality has been so consistently condemned by religion that it has come to be regarded with special distaste. But more important for this discussion is the fact that homosexuals themselves show so little interest in being tolerated and seem determined to equate *acceptance* of themselves as persons with *approval* of their peculiar life style. As one informed colleague puts it, "The gays really don't want the right to privacy in their sexual activities. They want to act out their fantasies in public and force the rest of us to applaud."

The demand of militant homosexuals today is for social and religious endorsement of gay relationships, the recognition of same-gender sex as an appropriate expression of Christian love, the accrediting of gay persons as instructors, interpreters, and exemplars of the faith, and the solemnization of their unions by the church. They are asking, in short, that the religious community reverse its strongly held position on genital homosexuality and declare it to be fully consistent with a viable Christian commitment. And when anyone presumes to suggest that this proposal requires careful examination and the review of a number of substantive theological issues, he or she is very likely to be accused of loveless bigotry and charged with causing great pain to some very sensitive people.

A central feature of Gay Liberation strategy in the churches is to call attention to the unhappiness of homosexual men and women in our society and to demand that, as an expression of acceptance and love, compassionate Christians redefine homosexuality and call it good. You cannot really love us, they argue, unless you love our sexual preferences. And they have had an amazing success in getting otherwise intelligent human beings to accept this fallacy.

Yet if anything is central to Christian ethics it is the need always to distinguish between the doer and the deed. One need not embrace Marxism in order to acknowledge the humanity of Communists or adopt the social statics of Herbert Spencer out of regard for Republicans. If an alcoholic were to declare that we could not accept him as a person unless we endorsed alcoholism as a desirable life style, we should suppose him to be well into his cups. When the Christian community is faithful to its calling, its doors and hearts will be open to all people. But it cannot be expected to deny its convictions and consecrate what it has steadfastly condemned in order to make any of us sinners feel more at home in the pews.

In a recent panel discussion of this topic I used the analogy with alcoholism and was immediately and angrily pounced upon by one of the other panelists. "What a cheap shot," he declared, "to compare homosexuality with alcoholism. Alcoholism prevents one from functioning as a viable human being. Homosexuality doesn't."

Well, that is precisely the issue involved in the Christian consideration of homosexuality, is it not? Does genital homosexuality impair one's ability to function in truly human fashion? Obviously it does not interfere with basic physical activity, any more than most alcoholism does. Thousands of alcoholics perform their daily jobs adequately, even impressively, then go home and drink themselves into a stupor. Undoubtedly an equal number of gay persons, perhaps many more, play out their economic and social roles efficiently all around us from nine to five.

The viability with which the Christian must be concerned, however, has far deeper and more complex dimensions than can be measured by a well-earned pay check. It is with this profound viability that moral statements are intended to deal. The panelist who wanted to make a qualitative distinction between homosexuality and alcoholism was guilty of a classic form of question-begging. He *defined* the gay life as "viable," and therefore good, and he casually brushed aside the great weight of Christian opinion to the contrary.

This is a problem which cannot be solved by definition. One must bore in relentlessly in a search for some responsible answer to the question which my fellow panelist sought to beg. Do homosexual relationships harm the persons involved in them?

Those who reply in the negative tend to rely on relatively gross standards in measuring the damage done to human beings by particular modes of behavior. (And they delight in finding damaging contrasts between the position of the church on homosexuality on the one hand and war on the other.) Homosexual activity does not kill, cripple, or shed blood; it probably causes no more incidental pain than heterosexual coupling. Ergo, it does no damage to those who participate in it.

There is only a superficial plausibility to such reasoning. And in any other area of debate those who champion the gay cause would be among the first to point this out. The human psyche is a very fragile thing and can be wounded in ways that leave no obvious scars. There is something called "dignity" that can wither and die without ever uttering a cry of pain or shedding a drop of blood. Why do Christians oppose the treatment of criminals by brain surgery or electrode implants? Surely such remedies are more humane than life-long imprisonment. Why do we waste the bodies of our dead on cemetery grass when their decaying flesh could be used as fertilizer to ease the world food shortage? They are beyond the reach of pain and embarrassment, and the living would be greatly served by such a policy. Why do we prevent people from exposing themselves in school playgrounds? There is some reason to suppose that the kiddies find the performance highly amusing.

The answer to such questions cannot be given in measurable units of harm to personality. We can only affirm that there are ways of hurting people which break no bones and may even provide the victim with a moment of pleasure. And there seems to have been a clear consensus among Christian thinkers over the ages that genital homosexuality assaults human dignity in some such subtle fashion. That view may be in error. But it cannot be defined away or refuted by the absence of scars on homosexual partners.

Even if one were to grant the unsubstantiated premise that gay relationships do no damage to those individuals most immediately engaged in them, questions inevitably arise about the social consequences of giving religious sanction to genital homosexuality. What will happen to the concept of the Christian family in a society which *endorses* same-gender sexual coupling? Will the painful sexual ambivalences of adolescence be made more difficult and more likely to be resolved in favor of a homosexual orientation if the local rectory is occupied by the pastor and his or her "lover?" Can the battered institution of Christian marriage stand the sight of gay unions being solemnized at the altar? What will be the effect upon all sexual relationships of the consecration of what are essentially sterile unions characterized by a very high degree of instability?

It is the multitude of such legitimate questions and the scarcity of persuasive answers which argues strongly that the Christian attitude toward gay relationships be one of toleration rather than approval. Centuries of ruthless repression—one indication of how strongly the traditional opinion has been held—have forced gay people to live their lives furtively and have made it almost impossible even for sophisticated analysts to evaluate the impact of homosexuality upon persons and society. It is altogether possible that much of what seems essentially destructive in the gay life style is really the neurotic consequence of a hostile environment. Once legal bans on same-gender sex have been removed and its practitioners allowed to live without harassment, we shall be in a far better position to see the implications and consequences of any change in the basic positions of the churches on this difficult subject.

I wish it were possible to stop at this point and assume that I have made the case for great caution in responding to the demands of gay militants for full approval of their way of life by the Christian community. Some experience in this area, however, has convinced me that those who wish to give serious thoughts to the place of homosexuals in the churches will find themselves under considerable pressure to throw caution to the winds in the name of something loosely called "love."

"God is love"—so runs the argument. Anything that is an expression of love is good. Since same-gender sex is an expression of love, it should be blessed by the church. This is another classic example of question-begging, an effort to define homosexuality into a state of grace. As such it needs very careful examination.

One of the most popular errors in the realm of Christian ethics has been the effort to make love an omnipotent spiritual quality which has the power to sanctify anything that is done in its name. The Inquisition tortured people's bodies in order to save their souls and sought to justify this action in the name of love. For centuries white Christians imposed patterns of paternalism upon blacks as an expression of their love for the sons of Ham. Employers once professed to love their employees too much to let them fall into the evil clutches of labor organizers. Parents tend to dominate their children's lives in the name of this same love. And generations of male chauvinists have counseled their sisters, wives, and daughters to eschew power and find their dignity and security in the love of their menfolk.

It is fashionable to interpret all such claims as sheer hypocrisy, as many of them were. But far more often than we care to admit, acts of exploitation and even brutality have been committed by people who honestly believed they were expressing disinterested love for their victims. It was the recognition of this hard fact of life which led Reinhold Niebuhr to say that we human beings are "never as dangerous as when we act in love." When we are motivated by anger or aggression, he pointed out, we arm our own consciences, alert our critics, and put our intended victims on their guard. But when we act in love, we disarm conscience, critic, and victim in one act and can do our worst unimpeded.

This was Niebuhr's characteristically dramatic way of saying that love does not empower anyone to transcend fully the structures of responsibility in human relating, and must always be expressed in ways that are appropriate to particular historical contexts and specific human associations. Love does not hallow the inquisitor's cruelty; the white's oppression; the employer's, parent's, and male's domination of others. It condemns such inhumanity and bids it cease. Love establishes the modes of interpersonal relating. It does not simply consecrate those that we find pleasant or profitable.

Thus, love does not always justify sexual union. It frequently makes it clear that sexual union is grossly inappropriate to a relationship. It is wrong for fathers to act out their love for their daughters in coition, for mothers to take their sons to bed, for brothers and sisters to copulate. Only the sickest minds would hold otherwise. And once we have established that fact the argument that homosexual union is good simply because it is motivated by love falls of its own weight. It is every bit as likely that the love of man for man or woman for woman bids them refrain from sexual intercourse as that it urges them into it.

For the purpose of making such statements about the argument that same-gender sex is an expression, however inappropriate, of love, I have assumed that some form of affection is, indeed, the driving force in gay relationships. This is by no means incontrovertibly established. A number of authorities in the field argue that the dynamic of homosexuality is not love for the same sex but hatred of the opposite sex. Men who take other men to bed, they suggest, may be less interested in expressing affection for their partners than in displaying contempt for women. And the same would be true, *mutatis mutandis*, for lesbians.

Still other psychologists hold that homosexuality is the result of a less sexually focused anger and reflects a more general aggression against people of both sexes. And there are obviously additional interpretations of the phenomenon for which there is no space here. While I am not qualified to evaluate such analyses, their net effect is to cast even more doubts upon the proposition that Christians ought to reverse their historic position against genital homosexuality and accept it as a manifestation of interpersonal affection. One needs to be very cautious about sacramentalizing what may well be a ritual of hatred or aggression.

In all discussions of this topic it seems crucially important to insist upon adequate time for full consideration of what is at stake. Too rapid a rate of change in critical areas of human relating can be dehumanizing in itself. But the Christian community has an understandably uneasy conscience on this point. It has often dragged its feet when it should have been leading the parade. And in consequence its leadership is somewhat inclined to suppose that in any proposal for change the burden of proof rests upon those supporting the status quo.

Some of the more militant gay leaders have been quick to seize the opportunity which this guilt syndrome offers. No more delays!—they cry. And link their cause with crusades on behalf of blacks, poor people, antiwar programs, and women. But there is a very important distinction between the proposals of Gay Liberation and such other appeals for changes in the attitudes of Christian churches. Most of the confrontations with which Christians are being called upon to deal these days reflect the demand that they bring their practice into line with their principles, that they more fully live up to what they have long been preaching.

The appeals of Gay Liberation, on the other hand, represent a proposal that the churches reverse their position on a moral issue of great importance to both themselves and society. This is not a question of bringing practice up to the level of principle but of revising principle in order to accommodate a particular and somewhat exotic practice. It is critical that Christians bear this distinction in mind and not allow their guilt feelings to push them into premature and ill-advised responses toward homosexuality. To allow themselves to be stampeded on this issue by emotional appeals and the fear of hurting someone's feelings will set a precedent which cannot help returning to haunt the churches often in the years ahead.

Let us end where we began. Homosexuality ought not to be treated as the manifestation of some special depravity whose practitioners should be driven from the chuch and harassed at law. But neither can it be defined as an appropriate expression of Christian love in interpersonal terms. The gay relationship is one form of sexual irresponsibility among many and no more reprehensible than most. Those involved in it have as much place in the pews as all the rest of us sinners. And as long as they recognize it as a problem and are prepared to seek help in dealing with it, there should be no arbitrary limits placed upon their full participation as leaders in the Christian fellowship.

When gay people claim, however, that their way of life is a morally healthy one, insist upon their intention to affirm it publicly, and ask that it be consecrated in some way by the church, they put themselves in contempt of Christian conscience. Under such circumstances it is not only the right but the duty of other Christians to express grave misgivings about the seriousness of their faith and to challenge the wisdom of admitting homosexuals to positions of leadership in the churches.

Homosexuality: A Symbolic Confusion

Ruth Tiffany Barnhouse

It is unquestionably time for society to stop oppressing homosexuals by abrogating their civil rights and labelling their behavior criminal. (I do not speak here of those who molest children or attempt to seduce minors, or engage in violence. Such behavior is in a different category, not related to homosexuality as such, since heterosexuals commit similar offenses.) Furthermore, they must not be oppressed by those misuses of the concept of illness which perpetuate their second-class citizenship. But it is also time for homosexuals to stop shouting "Oppressor!" at anyone who dares to say that homosexuality is less than normal.

I believe the underlying problematic issue is that of responsibility. The average educated person today, brought up in an intellectual climate permeated by popularized and diluted versions of Freudian theory, believes that psychoanalysis states that people are not responsible for their neuroses because they are caused by unconscious complexes, the result of infantile or childhood trauma over which they have no control.

This oversimplification, while it contains some truth, does violence to a

79

central aspect of Freud's theory. There is a crucial distinction between *trauma* and *conflict.* In a brilliant article discussing the impact of modern sex research on psychoanalytic thought, Dr. Robert Stoller, a distinguished professor of psychiatry who has specialized in the study and treatment of sexual deviation, explains the difference. Trauma may be in the form of internal sensations, such as hunger or pain; or it may be in the form of external events, such as physical violence or the death of a parent. Such trauma may only cause reaction or change. The affected infant or child may, with more or less pain, automatically adapt to the new circumstances. Dr. Stoller goes on to say that "Not all (traumas) produce conflict; conflict implies intrapsychic struggle to *choose* among possibilities." [1] It is conflict, not trauma, which produces an internal fork in the developmental road. The reason this is so important is that neuroses, including perversion of sexual development, do not result simply from trauma, but from particular resolutions of conflict in this technical sense of that word. As a result of conflict the individual chooses, however primitively and unconsciously, one solution over another. It seems to be this element of choice which is so antagonistic to the modern consciousness and which most modern sex research opposes. Dr. Stoller describes this as follows:

> The new research seems aimed unanimously at tearing down the conflict theory; no other aspect of Freud's system has created such resistance, perhaps because Freud believed perversion is *motivated,* i.e., that a person is somehow, in his depths, in part responsible for his perversion. The deviant act, Freud felt, is the product of the great human capacity for choice and so ultimately has a moral quality (even if one's responsibility is mitigated because the choice is unconscious and was arrived at because of unsought threatening circumstances in childhood).[2]

The attack on the conflict theory has taken four forms, each of which attempts to substitute a morally neutral explanation of behavior. All four of these explanations are being used in the specific case of homosexuality, and homosexual apologists draw heavily on them in their presentations. The Church, which has more than a little reason to have collective guilt feelings because of its contribution to the climate of persecution which homosexuals have had to endure, may be peculiarly vulnerable to the argument of cultural relativity. Dr. Stoller's interpretation of the significance of all of these views is this:

> . . . the author uses the research of others to support his position for sexual freedom. This is especially the case with activists banded together to relieve the guilt and social degradation traditionally laid upon them . . . [Here the four attacks on conflict theory are summarized.] . . . Crucial for each of these

defenses is the relief of guilt; since one's self did not choose it, one is not responsible for it, and besides the condition is not shameful.[3]

He concludes this discussion with the following extremely significant observation: "We may not solve these moral issues, which masquerade as scientific ones, as easily as either side hopes." Human behavior unavoidably stands between *what is* and *what ought* to be, and any examination of it must therefore involve us not only in scientific but also moral reflection. To try to avoid such issues merely compounds problems into the future and is therefore irresponsible. As Dr. Stoller says, these questions cannot be answered easily. Nevertheless, the effort to address them must be made; perhaps that difficult task can be eased by attempting to separate the moral from the scientific components.

It has been conclusively demonstrated that there is a usual progression from infancy to maturity which involves many different steps of psycho-sexual development. The principal ways in which the homosexual adapts, involve a failure to take one or more of these steps. In this sense, homosexuality is immature. I have tried unsuccessfully to find some word other than *immature* because this, too, has a "bad" connotation. And therein lies the question: should the failure to take all possible maturational steps be assigned a moral value?

The placement of the sexual thread in culture's web has always been dependent upon the answers to three questions. What is sex for? Who may engage in it, and with whom? What sexual acts are permissible and under what circumstances?

I believe that it is demonstrable that the answers to the second and third of these questions have always been contingent upon the answer to the first. It is true that at various times in history—and by no means only Christian history—some have tried to claim that sex was only for reproduction. From the purely religious point of view, such a claim is a grave heresy, from the psychiatric point of view it is demonstrably false. That sex is pleasurable has always been known, and for the most part, thoroughly appreciated. Sometimes the pleasure has been seen as dangerous, tending to precipitate people into the temptations of lust. Others have seen the pleasure as providing a most necessary cement to the otherwise fragile covenant of marriage. Still others have perceived sexual pleasure as an essential precondition of the responsible business of reproduction, for without such enticement people would probably never do anything so ludicrous and peculiar! Throughout the many variations of these and other themes, nobody until the present century ever seriously questioned that the primary answer to the question "What is sex for?" was the reproduction of the human species.

One set of answers to the second and third questions is obviously contingent on this fact. The restriction of sexual partnership to those situations providing for the orderly devolution of lineage and property, assuring the nurture and training of children, and protecting the species against perils of inbreeding, clearly supports the reproductive purpose. Promiscuity, incest and homosexuality could be understandably proscribed for this reason alone; even within marriage, non-coital acts engaged in as a substitute for (rather than as a prelude to) coitus and the practice of birth control have also been prohibited on these same grounds. These marital prohibitions can be shown to rest on too narrow an interpretation of reproductive purpose, but are, nevertheless, indissolubly connected with it.

Now in the last quarter of the twentieth century we have reached a new point in human history. Not only do we realize that it is no longer desirable that reproduction should be the primary goal of sex, but we have also developed a reliable methods of birth control so that, for the first time, it is possible to avoid reproduction safely without resorting to sexual abstinence. The full impact of these changes has yet to be appreciated. I know of no congress of theologians or secular ethicists which has gathered for serious debate of the new question: if the primary goal and consequence of sex is no longer reproduction, what is it?

The failure of responsible professionals to engage this issue directly has left a vacuum in our culture and the result has been a rapid removal of sex from the area of ethical and moral concern.

A culture which prides itself on its devotion to knowledge cannot afford to continue to deal with so crucial an issue as sex in a shallow way which currently prevails. Nothing we know from history, anthropology, or any other discipline supports the idea of sex as only a pleasurable activity, any more than as only a reproductive one. Sex is not just a technique for "getting closer to those you love," for instance. Who is to say that getting closer, however pleasurable, is always a desideratum? Or that the means do not matter? Or that one way is as loving as another?

These questions must be examined seriously. It must be ascertained whether there are any goals to human sexuality beyond the physical ones of reproduction and pleasure. If sex is found to have some serious symbolic significance, the nature of this might well have a bearing on the moral implications of homosexuality.

Thus, an important question emerges, one which is ultimately theological, not scientific. Should the failure to take all possible maturational steps be assigned a moral value? If so, how can religious people decide the application of this principle to homosexuality? Odd as it might at first appear, I believe that the wholesale rejection of Christianity which we see in the rising forces of secularization is due to exactly the same reason that there is a strong current attack on classic psychoanalytic theory. It consists in the rejection of real personal responsibility. Dr. Stoller's discussion of Freudian conflict theory pointed out that the reason the theory is under such intense attack is because it insists that all conduct, even when the motivations are unconscious, is the result of choice, and that therefore people are ultimately responsible in their depths. In fact, upon closer examination it is clear that were not this true, psychotherapy could not possibly work. People cannot change that which is entirely beyond their control. The process of psychotherapy entails a large element of helping sufferers to understand that they are not victims of something beyond themselves, but that choices made in the past, however unconsciously, can be reviewed and new decisions taken.

Freedom and responsibility go hand in hand and come in roughly equal increments. The attempt to enjoy one without the other always leads to trouble. It is possible to describe the Victorian era as one which laid too much stress on responsibility at the expense of freedom, and a corrective move toward liberation from that strain was inevitable. In our time, the pendulum has swung dangerously far in the other direction. Systems of dealing with human suffering which do not go beyond the attempt to substitute pleasure for pain both illustrate and contribute toward this pendulum swing. This is because freedom without responsibility makes people prisoners of impulse and restricts their range of activity accordingly.

What troubled people need, through the appropriate application of religious and psychiatric categories, either singly or in combination, is to learn to take serious responsibility for their attitudes, behavior and circumstances. Included in this process must be not only those issues which are contemporary and conscious. As the twig is bent, so grows the tree. Wrong choices made in the past prevent healthy development and therefore contribute to present problems.

Viewed in these terms, every failure to take a possible maturational step has moral significance and falls under the rubric of original sin, that doctrine which accounts for the fact human beings are simply incapable of always choosing wisely and require constant help, love and guidance to learn to do better. We have also seen that this is true even if the person's responsibility is mitigated by the process having taken place unconsciously. It is impossible for homosexuality not to be included in this category. By the same token, all failures of maturation are to be viewed similarly, and there is no reason to single out homosexuality for cruel and unusual punishment.

Homosexuality then cannot be viewed as a perfectly normal alternate lifestyle. It comes in many varieties, not all of which are accompanied by obvious failures of personality development or adjustment, or by other unacceptable or socially undesirable behavior. If one speaks of homosexual acts taking place between two consenting adults in private in the context of an ongoing relationship between the partners, even though the homosexual disposition itself constitutes an immaturity, it surely ranks well below other immaturities in the amount of social or moral harm which is done.

It seems to me that the Church is involved in a gradual, important and long overdue change. Instead of dealing with sexual aberrations almost exclusively through the harsh processes of judgment and condemnation, it is learning to deal with them in the penitential mode, through compassion and forgiveness extended to those who are doing their best to take responsibility for their lives. With respect to such things as divorce and illegitimacy, the change is nearly complete. With respect to adultery and abortion, it is well underway. With respect to homosexuality, it is just beginning. I believe that homosexuals who try to claim that their condition is normal are in danger of impeding this necessary change.

The true religious goal of human sexuality can be seen not as satisfaction but as completeness.[4] Without this goal of completeness, satisfaction pursued as an end in itself deteriorates into lust. It is the dualist error in a subtle form: the body is used as an instrument in the service of a self-centered aim. It matters little whether that self-centered aim is the pleasurable release of physical orgasm, the reproductive pride of producing an heir, or the community pride of living "respectably." These are all, in the end, lusts. The problem with sex is that no other phenomenon of human existence can symbolize the vision of the sacramental universe in which all things are harmoniously connected, and at the same time manifest the tragic discontinuities which were inflicted on us and our world through the Fall. No other human activity lends itself to subtle, as well as obvious, exploitation both of self and of others.

We have forgotten far too long that the image of God, in which the sacred myth tells us that humanity was created, includes both man and woman. As we try to move forward toward a less exploitative, more conscious, more responsible understanding of sexuality, we must keep that fact in the forefront of our deliberations. Homosexuality constitutes a rejection, either partial or total, of the possibility of union with the other sex. Very clearly, the wholeness of the sacred order is neither symbolized nor approximated by sexual practices which are thus grounded in the denial of half of the image of God. Some measure of physical or partial emotional satisfaction may be achieved, but the Christian goal of completeness is not. John Dixon describes the failure of homosexuality in these words:

> It is not a valid mode or model of sexuality for it affirms the incompleteness. I cannot affirm my wholeness except in the other who is truly other. It is

probably true that any love is better than no love in a loveless world. But love is not a single, lone act isolated from other acts. It is a part of a whole, the ordering of relation. It communicates a sense of the structure, of the forming of paradigms . . . Fulfillment must be found outside the self if it is to affect the self. But in sexual matters fulfillment is completeness, the coming together of differences.[5]

In the recent Vatican statement, *Declaration on Certain Questions Concerning Sexual Ethics*, which reiterated the Church's traditional position with regard to the "disordered" quality of all sexual acts outside of marriage, homosexuality was condemned in these words: "For according to the objective moral order, homosexual relations are acts which lack an essential and indispensable finality."[6] The finality which is meant is that of the possibility of procreation as an essential ingredient of a morally acceptable sexual act. This formulation fails to engage the question of the symbolic significance of the sexual act, which gives it its sacramental character. I do not believe that it is any longer possible, in the present state of the world's history, to defend the once appropriate idea that the mysteries of sexuality are all contained in the physical act of procreation. On the contrary, I believe that procreation itself is a symbol of still deeper rich mysteries which we are only beginning to glimpse.

As Christians we must eschew selfish and hedonistic goals, not only for sexuality but for everything else as well. The serious Christian examination of what these goals may be has only just begun. If we accept the view of sexuality as symbolic, and I think the evidence for that is incontrovertible, then it is no doubt true that we will never exhaust the meanings, no matter how long we may continue to consider them. By its nature, a living symbol is a bottomless well. But I have no doubt that Dixon's formulation of the mystery of completeness to be achieved only by encountering the truly other will stand as among the most important, the best, and most enduring of these meanings.

Homosexuality is, in the end, a symbolic confusion.

III

Homosexual Acts are Essentially Imperfect

Charles Curran
Helmut Thielicke
H. Kimball Jones
Hershel Matt

Homosexuality and Moral Theology: Methodological and Substantive Considerations

Charles E. Curran

Dialogue With the Homophile Movement: The Morality of Homosexuality

The discipline of moral theology or Christian ethics is in a state of transition today. The changing self-understanding of the Roman Catholic Church has affected moral theology. Moral theology also reflects the contemporary emphases in religious and philosophical ethics as well as the changing mores and life styles of our contemporary world.

An area of ethical concern receiving wide attention in the last few years is homosexuality. The militant homophile movement strives to bring the question to the fore and argues for equality for homosexuals in all spheres of life.[1] No longer can society at large or the Christian Church ignore the existence of homosexuality or the homophile community. How will the Church, specifically the Roman Catholic Church, respond to these demands? What should be the attitude of the law to homosexuality? The scope of this essay is more narrow: a discussion of the morality of homosexuality and the methodological approaches employed in this consideration. This study should, however, furnish a basis for forming a proper pastoral approach to the homosexual and the homophile community and also indicate an approach to the question of the law and homosexuality. A proper pastoral approach should develop in the light of moral theology, although a Dutch symposium on homosexuality almost ten years ago tried to develop a pastoral approach prescinding from moral theology because they obviously feared the rigidity of moral theology.[2]

A discussion of homosexuality from the viewpoint of moral theology necessarily raises methodological questions for moral theology itself. Christian ethicists have employed different methodological approaches even though they may have arrived at the same conclusion. In considering the morality of homosexual acts this essay will also evaluate the different methodologies employed and also raise specific methodological questions which concern the particular topic of homosexuality as well as the entire gamut of topics considered by moral theology.

Two important methodological questions for the discipline of moral theology come to the fore in the discussion of homosexuality—the use and place of the Scriptures in moral theology and the role of the empirical sciences in the moral judgment. The present paper will illuminate these general considerations in the light of the particular question of homosexuality.

Methodology and Biblical Data

Christian ethics reflects on human reality within the context of Christian revelation, but there have been differences about the exact role and function of Scripture in the discipline of moral theology. In general, Roman Catholic moral theology has approached concrete ethical questions in the light of a natural law methodology which tended to downplay the role of Scripture. The theological manual written by Noldin-Schmitt, for example, discusses homosexuality very briefly according to the principles of the natural law and merely refers to three scriptural texts in a footnote.[3] Very often the general approach to Roman Catholic theology included a few proof texts from the Scriptures which were employed to prove the point which had been founded on natural law reasoning.[4]

Protestant theology methodologically gives more importance to the place of the Scriptures in ethical methodology, but a fundamentalistic Protestant approach errs by again using the Scriptures in a proof text fashion without any further consideration. The mainstream of Protestant theology benefiting from the impressive biblical studies begun in the nineteenth century realizes the cultural and historical limitations inherent in the scriptures themselves.[5] The renewal in Roman Catholic moral theology emphasized the need for a more biblically oriented approach. During and after Vatican II Catholic theology has, at times, gone to the opposite extreme and become almost exclusively biblical to the detriment of its historical self-understanding that the Christian shares much ethical wisdom and knowledge with all men.[6]

Today Protestant and Catholic ethicians share a general convergence in their understanding of the place and function of the Scriptures in moral theology. The Scriptures do not have a monopoly on ethical wisdom and thus do not constitute the sole way into the ethical problem for the Christian ethicist.[7] Obviously the Christian ethicist derives his general orientation from a scriptural base and realizes the importance of particular attitudes and ways of life which are contained in the Scriptures. However, in the case of specific conclusions about specific actions Christian theologians realize the impossibility of any methodological approach which would develop its argument only in terms of individual biblical texts taken out of their context.[8]

In the question of homosexuality the biblical data has been interpreted differently, and possibly erroneous interpretations seem to have overemphasized the heinousness of homosexual acts. Although scriptural data forms only one part of theological data, the moral theologian must have an adequate understanding of that data. Christians generally interpret the famous story of the town of Sodom related in Genesis 19: 4–11 as the destruction of the city by God because of its great sinfulness as shown in homosexuality. Recently, D. S. Bailey has revived and revised an interpretation which maintains that the Sodom story does not refer to homosexuality or homosexual acts.[9] The word "to know" does not necessarily involve a sexual connotation but rather could be interpreted as a violation of hospitality. D. S. Bailey points out that the first explicit references involving the "traditional opinion" that the Sodomites were annihilated because of their homosexuality appeared in Palestine only during the second century B. C. Six Old Testament references (Genesis 13:13; 18:20; Jer. 23:14; Ex. 16:49–50; Wisdom 10:8; 19:8; Ecclus. 16:8) mention the sinfulness of the Sodomites because of which they were punished, but these texts do not identify the sin as homosexuality.

Most contemporary exegetes do not agree with Bailey's position that a new and dfferent interpretation identifying the sin of Sodom as homosexuality only arose in the second century. Perhaps these exegetes are not aware of the in-depth study made by Bailey. *The Jerome Biblical Commentary*, the *Jerusalem Bible*, *Genesis* in the Anchor Bible edition, all indicate that homosexuality is the sin of the people of Sodom because of which their city was destroyed.[10] Although Bailey does not find homosexuality in the sin of the people of Sodom, he still accepts a general condemnation of homosexuality (without the significant heinousness attached to the Sodom story) in the Old Testament as found in two references in the "Holiness Code" (Leviticus 18:22; 20:13). Homosexual acts between men were considered like many other acts to be major crimes punishable by death.[11]

The New Testament contains three direct references to homosexuality—Romans 1:27; 1 Cor. 6:9–10; 1 Tim. 1:9–10. Paul obviously regards homosexual acts as wrong and a perversion of the meaning of human existence willed by God. Helmut Thielicke, although accepting such a condemnation by Paul, emphasizes that Paul's condemnation of homosexuality does not justify the excessive severity which the Christian tradition has attached to such acts. Thielicke's hermeneutical interpretation points out that Paul's consideration of homosexuality appears only in the context of the more central theological affirmation that disorder in the vertical dimension of man's relationship with God is matched by disorder on the horizontal level. Homosexuality illustrates this disorder on the level of man's relationship with his fellow man. Despite the fact that Paul's understanding of homosexuality would have been colored by its acceptance in the Greek intellectual world, the Apostle considers it not in itself but only as illustrative of the central theological point that man's relation with God affects all his other relationships.[12]

Thus the biblical data indicates that the biblical authors in their cultural and historical circumstances deemed homosexual acts wrong and attached a generic gravity to such acts, but there appears to be no reason for attaching a special heinousness or gravity to these acts.

Methodology and Empirical Data

A second important methodological and substantive question concerns the empirical data about homosexuality. The substantive question seeks to discover the meaning of homosexuality in terms of the behavioral sciences such as psychology, sociology, psychiatry, anthropology, etc. The methodological question for moral theology centers on the way in which such data are incorporated into the moral judgment.

Different Christian ethicists exhibit different methodological approaches to the use of empirical data in determining the morality of homosexual acts. The behavioral sciences themselves only furnish data for the final human judgment which, in a sense, relativizes all the judgments of the particular sciences. Ethics can never make the mistake of absolutizing any one of the empirical sciences, such as psychology or psychiatry. These scientific disciplines have a particular perspective which can never be totally identified with the human perspective.

The question of homosexuality illustrates the hermeneutic problem within the confines of just one science when the practitioners themselves are divided on a particular point. Thus the individual theologian or person about to make a decision is faced with a dilemma which he is not equipped to solve. If the experts in psychology and psychiatry are divided, how can someone without that particular expertise make a competent judgment? The ethicist cannot merely follow the majority opinion, for history constantly reminds us that majority opinions are not necessarily true.

What is the psychological and psychiatric data about homosexuality? A first question concerns the etiology of homosexuality. An older, and minority, opinion would make genetic factors the determining element. The more generally accepted theory attributes homosexuality to circumstances in the developing life of the child and person, although there can be a certain conditioning because of genetic factors. Most recently some scientists have revived the theory that attributes homosexuality to hormonal imbalance.[13]

The theologian is not competent to judge between the conflicting opinions of the various scientists within their own disciplines. However, a review of the literature plus personal experience would seem to indicate that homosexuality does not necessarily make every individual a neurotic or emotionally disturbed person. Some homosexuals do seem to live comparatively well-adapted lives in society. The theological ethician must be in constant dialogue with these sciences, but he realizes that even the well-adjusted person can have proclivities and perform acts which are "abnormal" and/or morally wrong. Likewise, the ethician realizes that wrong actions or tendencies do not necessarily point to mental disturbances on the part of the whole personality. The conflicting evidence of these sciences must be viewed in a wider context.

The Theory of Compromise

The theory of compromise tries to add a new dimension to the theoretical solution. Catholic theology has neglected the reality of sin in its moral teaching based on the natural law.[14] Precisely because sin forms a part of objective reality, our moral judgments must give more importance to sin. The presence of sin means that at times one might not be able to do what would be done if there were no sin present. In the theory of compromise, the particular action in one sense is not objectively wrong because in the presence of sin it remains the only viable alternative for the individual. However, in another sense the action is wrong and manifests the power of sin. If possible, man must try to overcome sin, but the Christian knows that the struggle against sin is never totally successful in this world.[15]

Homosexual behavior well illustrates the theory of compromise. In general, I accept the experiential data proposed by the other mediating positions. The homosexual is generally not responsible for his condition. Heterosexual marital relations remains the ideal. Therapy, as an attempt to make the homosexual into a heterosexual, does not offer great promise for most homosexuals. Celibacy and sublimation are not always possible or even desirable for the homosexual. There are many somewhat stable homosexual unions which afford their partners some human fulfillment and contentment. Obviously such unions are better than homosexual promiscuity.

In many ways homosexuality exists as a result of sin. Those who accept an etiology of homosexuality in terms of relationships and environment can easily see the reality of sin in those poor relationships which contribute to this condition in the individual. In this situation, which reflects the human sinfulness in which all participate in differing ways, the individual homosexual may morally come to the conclusion that a somewhat permanent homosexual union is the best, and sometimes the only, way for him to achieve some humanity. Homosexuality can never become an ideal. Attempts should be made to overcome this condition if possible; however, at times one may reluctantly accept homosexual unions as the only way in which some people can find a satisfying degree of humanity in their lives.

The principle or theory of compromise differs from the other mediating positions. A position based on the distinction between formal and material sin or even the principle or choosing the lesser of two evils still admits a distinction between the objective and subjective orders. One might interpret such approaches as limiting the influence of sin to the subjective order. The theory of compromise is more radical in the sense that it sees sin as affecting also the "objective" order and thus does not rest on the distinction between the objective and subjective orders.

The theory of compromise differs from the mediating position implied in Thielicke and explained by Kimball Jones, for sin does not totally destroy God's work of creation and redemption. Sin affects this present order but does not do away with all the moral distinctions which are based on both creation and redemption. Thus the argument in the case of homosexuality never does away with the distinction between heterosexuality and homosexuality, even though not all heterosexual relationships are moral and good. The basic meaning or "structure" of human sexuality remains, even though some individuals may not be able to live in accord with it because of the infecting power of sin.

Are there any limits to the principle of compromise? Such a question does not assume great importance in the particular discussion of homosexuality, but the question remains. Theoretically there are limits to the theory of compromise based on the implied understanding of the effect of sin. Sin does not completely destroy moral meaning or do away with moral distinctions. The effect of sin itself is limited. Notice that the same question of the limits also exists for the principle of counseling the lesser of two evils. In general, such limits are the rights of other innocent persons or the rights of society, but even these values may be somewhat infringed upon for the sake of the values preserved through the compromise.

One can object that such a view still relegates the homosexual to second class citizenship.[16] Perhaps many proponents of Gay Liberation are making the same mistake today that theologians and churchmen made in the past. Both groups tend to identify the person with his homosexuality, but a sound anthropology argues against any such identification. One can still love and respect the person even though one believes his homosexual behavior falls short of the full meaning of human sexuality. In many other areas of life I can judge a person's behavior as being wrong or less than the ideal and still respect him as a person. The Christian humbly admits that sinfulness also touches him in one way or another and that he can make no claims to being perfectly moral, human, or Christian. Ironically, the Gay Liberation Movement seems to be making the same mistake that the Christian Churches made by making homosexuality almost the equivalent of personhood.

The Theologicoethical Aspect of Homosexuality

Helmut Thielicke

According to the Protestant principle of Scripture, the theological interpretation of homosexuality cannot ignore the relevant statements of the Bible. However, we would not be satisfying this principle of Scripture if we merely cited the Holy Scriptures instead of interpreting the quotations in accord with the kerygmatic purpose. A merely legalistic citation of Scripture which did not inquire into its significance would lead—by no means only in the subject under discussion—to the most fantastic combination of heterogeneous elements. This is demonstrated by the jungle of doctrines produced by the sectarians, all of whom appeal quite positively and unreflectively to the Bible.

As far as the Old Testament is concerned, it is uncertain whether the passages concerning sodomy, which have been traditionally authoritative, actually refer to homosexual acts at all. In any case, Isaiah 1:10, 3:3, Ezekiel 16:49, and Jeremiah 23:14 characterize the sins that were responsible for the downfall of Sodom quite differently.[1] Apart from this there can be no doubt that the Old Testament regarded homosexuality and pederasty as crimes punishable by death (Lev. 18:22, 20:13). Whether direct injunctions are to be derived from this for Christians must remain a matter of discussion, at least insofar as behind this prohibition there lies the concept of cultic defilement and thus the question is raised whether and to what extent the Old Testament cultic law can be binding upon those who are under the Gospel and to what extent it places them on a wholly new level and frees them from the Law. Here the problems of theological principle which are referred to in technical terminology under the subject of "Law and Gospel" become acute. Even the nontheologian can see the scope of this problem when it is realized that in the Old Testament the prohibition of divination, the drinking of blood, sexual intercourse with a menstruating woman, and many other things are put on the same level with the capital offense of homosexuality. It would never occur to anyone to wrench these laws of cultic purification from their concrete situation and give them the kind of normative authority that the Decalogue, for example, has.

In the New Testament homosexuality is again listed in catalogue fashion with other forms of disobedience, such as idolatry, fornication, adultery, greed, drunkenness, thievery (I Cor. 6:9–10; cf. I Tim. 1:9–10). Accordingly, there can be no doubt that Paul regards homosexuality as a sin and a perversion of the order of human existence willed by God, even though within this catalogue of vices it is not accented as being especially horrible, as many moral theologies would make it appear.[2] The listing of homosexuality with heterosexual offenses like adultery and fornication would rather suggest the problem of whether, along with the total rejection of homosexuality, we must not also consider the question to what extent this refers to the libido-conditioned disregard for one's neighbor, in other words, a particular way of homosexual behavior (possibly analogous with adultery, polygamy, etc.). In any case, it is worthy of note that, according to the Synoptics (in which the subject of homosexuality does not appear), Jesus dealt with the sensual sinners incomparably more leniently than he did with the sinners who committed the sins of the spirit and cupidity.

For the theological evaluation of the Pauline statements concerning homosexuality it is especially important to note the way it is dealt with in the most familiar passage about it: Romans 1:26 f. And here we cannot dispense with a number of hermeneutical comments.

This section deals with the question of why it is that the natural man, the "heathen," does not know God, even though the Creator is manifest in his creation. The answer given to this question is that man refuses to accept his creatureliness, that he does not acknowledge God and therefore does not know him. The natural man is not *in* in the truth and therefore he does not recognize or know the truth.[3] The wrath of God over his hubris expresses itself in God's giving man over, abandoning him (*paredoken*) to the consequences of this his fundamental attitude, leaving him, as it were, to the autonomy of the existence which he himself has entered upon. In consequence of this autonomy of judgment, then, religious confusion also leads to ethical chaos. It consists in confusion of the eternal with the temporal. That is to say, finite entities are vested with the sovereignty of God and men worship idols (Rom. 1:23). Because the lower and the higher, the creature and the Creator, are exchanged (perverted), the result is a perverse supremacy of the inferior desires over the spirit. And in this context the sexual perversions are mentioned as further marks of this fundamental perversion (Rom 1:26 f.).[4]

What is theologically noteworthy and kerygmatically "binding" in this exposition of Paul's is the statement that disorder in the vertical dimension (in the God-man relationship) is matched by a perversion on the horizontal level, not only within man himself (spirit-flesh relationship) but also in his interhuman contacts. One of the fundamental lines that runs through the Bible is that the analogy between the vertical and the horizontal relations is maintained and given theological foundation. An outstanding example of this two-dimensional view is the story of the Tower of Babel (Gen. 11:1 ff.) in which man's rebellion against the Creator (vertical movement) brings with it the dispersion, that is, the destruction of human community and thus the perversion of the fellow-human relationship along with the confusion of tongues (horizontal movement).[5]

The point of the Pauline statement lies precisely in this correspondence between the two dimensions. The individual demonstrative references, including the reference to sexual perversion, are simply illustrations of this point. They come from the stock of the tradition with which Paul was surrounded, above all the Stoic catalogues of vices and their Jewish counterparts, such as the "wisdom of Solomon," Philo, Josephus, and the Sibylline Oracles.[6]

There can be no question that Paul is here rejecting homosexuality, otherwise he would not characterize it in this passage (even more sharply and more incriminatingly than in I Corinthians) as a symptom of original sin. Nevertheless, as far as the relative theological emphasis is concerned, it is significant that it is not made the subject of separate theological statement, but that it appears only in the context of another, theologically fundamental, statement and as an illustration of it. This cannot be without significance for the interpretation of it. For we must reckon with the fact that Paul's conception of homosexuality was one which was affected by the intellectual atmosphere surrounding the struggle with Greek paganism. For the thinkers and especially the moral philosophers of late antiquity (and by no means only for the Christians living at that time), pederasty, however, was regarded as a sign of depravity and a decadent culture.

The fact that this status of homosexuality as an illustration within the context of a completely different statement is not irrelevant may become evident in another instance in which Paul employs an illustration to set forth a fundamental statement. In I Corinthians 11:2 ff. his concern is to argue against the putting of the sexes on the same level, or stated positively, to provide a Christological basis for the man's position as the head of the woman. This he illustrates by the fact that the man as the "image of God" (v. 7) should keep his head uncovered at worship, whereas the woman should wear a head covering or else her hair should be cut off. Here again the essential intention must be distinguished from the illustration. His essential intention is to combat the idea that there is no difference between the sexes, argued erroneously on the basis of the solidarity of all men before God, regardless of sex; the illustration is taken from the contemporary regulations for dress. And these in turn were probably so firmly bound up in Paul's "conception" with his idea of the difference between the sexes that he himself was not capable of realizing the difference in quality between the intention of statement (which is related to these differences) and the means employed in his statement (the symbol of the difference in dress). But the moment when men who are no longer bound to that contemporary situation (as we are not today) ask what is the kerygmatic bindingness of such statements, this difference in quality becomes highly important. The point is that the differentiation between the sexes, which is the point that Paul is here stating, is just as important for us today as it was then. It would never occur to us, however, that when we accept these statements of difference between the sexes we must also take over the dress regulations which had symbolical force at that time. We have the freedom to choose other symbols of this difference which come from our own time and situation.

Obviously, the statements concerning dress and those concerning homosexuality are different in importance; this is immediately clear from the text. And yet the fact that homosexuality here appears in the context of the symbolical and illustrative statements and thus is a means of statement and not the object of the statement of intention itself, gives us a certain freedom to rethink the subject. This freedom should be used to reflect upon the question of how homosexuality must be interpreted theologically if it is to be the independent subject of a statement (as it is not in Paul). In view of the difficulty of the problem and the fact that most of the traditional statements are not applicable, we have been obliged to go through these methodological considerations in order to gain a proper approach to our question.

In this area of legitimate inquiry thus opened up the first thing that must be said is that for biblical thinking and the Christian thinking which follows biblical thought, it is impossible to think of homosexuality as having no ethical significance, as being a mere vagary or sport of nature. The fundamental order of creation and the created determination of the two sexes make it appear justifiable to speak of homosexuality as a perversion—in any case, if we begin with the understanding that this term implies no moral depreciation whatsoever and that it is used purely theologically in the sense that homosexuality is in every case not in accord with the order of creation. (Therefore in ordinary usage Giese's term "abnormal" would in fact, be appropriate.) In this sense homosexuality falls on the same level with abnormal personality structure (= psychopathy), disease, suffering, and pain, which likewise are generally understood in the Bible as being contrary to God's will in creation. This points, then, to the hidden connections between the Fall as a disordering of creation and the pathological changes in existence in the world as a whole. In this sense the miracles of Jesus are understood to be a kind of reminder of what God originally intended the creation to be in a world in which his creation has been disordered. In the same sense, the eschatological statements concerning a coming world in which there will be no more suffering or crying or death are to be understood as allusions to the restoration and continuation of the original intentions of the Creator.

The disturbed original status of the world, however, must be strictly separated from its actualization, just as original sin (*peccatum originale*) is distinguished from the concrete sin (*peccatum actuale*). Applied to the case of homosexuality, this means that theologically one dare not put an endogenous homosexuality, which is a kind of symptomatic participation in the fate of the fallen world, on the same level with concrete acts of libidinous excess, no matter whether these acts are the result of the actualization of this inherited constitution or of infection by a diseased environment in the form of an induced or a merely meretriciously misused homosexuality. The predisposition itself, the homosexual potentiality as such, dare not be any more strongly depreciated than the status of existence which we all share as men in the disordered creation that exists since the Fall (*post lapsum*).

Consequently, there is not the slightest excuse for maligning the constitutional homosexual morally or theologically. We are all under the same condemnation and each of us has received his "share" of it. In any case, from this point of view the homosexual share of that condemnation has no greater gravity which would justify any Pharisaic feelings of self-righteousness and integrity on the part of us "normal" persons.

For the disorder of creation which manifests itself here we must point out the promise that lies in making use of the possibilities of relative healing inherent in creation. In this sense medical treatment is, from the theological point of view, symbolically significant of the preservative will of the Creator which still continues to be in force in the created world (Gen. 8:21 f., 9:13-16); and at the same time the healer may think of himself as one who carries out this will and as one whose vocation it is to serve his neighbor.

Applied to our particular subject, this means that homosexuality cannot simply be put on the same level with the normal created order of the sexes, but that it is rather a habitual or actual distortion or depravation of it. It follows from this that the homosexual is called upon not to affirm his status a priori or to idealize it (on this point Karl Barth is quite correct)—any more than any other pathological disorder can be affirmed a priori—but rather regard and recognize his condition as something that is questionable. (This does not rule out the possibility that it can become the vehicle of a blessing and a creative challenge.) The homosexual must therefore be willing to be treated or healed so far as this is possible; he must, as it were, be willing to be brought back into the "order." Since sexuality has an affinity to the totality of man, this would mean not only the willingness to consult the physician but also to be receptive to pastoral care.

But now experience shows that constitutional homosexuality at any rate is largely unsusceptible to medical or psychotherapeutic treatment, at least so far as achieving the desired goal of a fundamental conversion to normality is concerned. Thus it becomes properly a theological and ethical problem. Since, contrary to certain popular opinions which are frequently accepted by theologians, the great majority of homosexuals belong in this classification and their number is considerable, the church is here confronted with a grave problem in the area both of fundamental reflection and practical pastoral care.

The first thing that must be said about it is that here our attitude toward an ailment that is recognized as incurable changes. That is to say, we must accept it—which is different from the attitude which we described above, in which illness is declared to be contrary to creation and is attacked with the will to heal and be healed. What, then, does "acceptance" mean here? It can mean to accept the burden of this predisposition to homosexuality only as a divine dispensation and see it as a task to be wrestled with, indeed—paradoxical as it may sound—to think of it as a talent that is to be invested (Luke 19:13 f.).

Does this acceptance mean, then, that a person thus constituted may act in accord with his constitution, that this fateful *habitus* may be actualized? This is the most ticklish question of all. It can be discussed at all only in the framework of that freedom which is given to us by the insight that even the New Testament does not provide us with an evident, normative dictum with regard to this question. Even the kind of question which we have arrived at, namely, the problem which is posed by the "endogenous *habitus*" of homosexuality, must for purely historical reasons be alien to the New Testament. In the light of the findings of medical research to which we owe our understanding of the inseparable interinvolvement of the total personality structure (urges, character, disposition, etc.), the question must necessarily be faced afresh—in exactly the same way as in the age of the democracies, for example, the problem of the "governing authorities" must be rethought and cannot be settled by recourse to a timeless dictum of the New Testament concerning the state (concerning the necessarily contemporary state and its contemporary structure).

Perhaps the best way to formulate the ethical problem of the constitutional homosexual, who because of his vitality is not able to practice abstinence, is to ask whether within the co-ordinating system of his constitution he is willing to structure the man-man relationship in an ethically responsible way. Thus the ethical question meets him on the basis, which he did not enter intentionally, but which is where he actually finds himself, into which, as Heidegger would say, he has been thrown. A certain analogy with this situation may be seen in the Old Testament chapter concerning the Noachic covenant (Gen. 9:1 ff.). Here what has erupted in the world is attributed to the sinful disordering of creation which works itself out in the structure of society. But now God in the way in which he deals with the fallen world places himself on the basis of the disordered world: from henceforth force will be combated with force, or better, illegal force will be opposed with legal force. It is in this principle that penal law finds its theological foundation.[7]

In accordance with this conception we may assume that the homosexual has to realize his optimal ethical potentialities on the basis of his irreversible situation. Here one must seriously ask whether in this situation—naturally only in the case of adults!—the same norms must not apply as in the normal relationship of the sexes. This is the question with which the "sympathetic" pastor is confronted. It is the question of how the homosexual in his actual situation can achieve the optimal ethical potential of sexual self-realization. To deny this would in any case mean a degree of harshness and rigor which one would never think of demanding of a "normal" person. Celibacy cannot be used as a counterargument, because celibacy is based upon a special calling and, moreover, is an act of free will. That such a homoerotic self-realization can take place only among those who are similarly constituted and that, besides, it cannot be an open and public thing, because it falls outside the bounds of the order of creation, hardly needs to be pointed out.

Anybody who is willing as a Christian theologian to concede the idea that it is possible to achieve ethical realization on this questionable but noneliminable basis will be able to carry out this venture—for this is what it will always be, since there are never any "patent" solutions for the borderline cases[8]—only if at the same time he persistently addresses himself to the pastoral problem involved in this ethical realization. On this the following may be said. Even though it be true that the "normal" basis of the created order of sex relationship is fraught with hazards and temptations to go contrary to the order (cf. the Pauline catalogues of vices!), it is not difficult to see that the homosexual is exposed to even greater dangers, which in many cases where the help of the physician and pastor is lacking simply cause him to succumb to certain temptations. We mention only a few symptoms of this threatening descent.

1. The homosexual does not have the benefit of living within a supporting order that is informed by a traditional ethos such as that of the institution of marriage. Instead of having at his disposal a set of prefabricated decisions which are made for him by the tradition and make it easier for him to find his way about, he is to an unimaginably greater degree thrown back upon himself. Since he generally begins only gradually to recognize his disposition, he goes through phases of terrible loneliness and stages of groping and uncertain improvisations.

2. Otherwise than in the "normal" sphere, the noningrained normative attitude easily produces a propensity toward the excessive, toward rapidly changing partnerships (promiscuity) and thus a sabotage of even that relative "order" which the homosexual could achieve even on his basis.

3. The ostracism the homosexual suffers through the criminal law and the defensive instinct of society leads him to frequent very dubious circles. He cannot risk any public attempt to make advances. Whereas the "normal" person is permitted to regard a representative of the other sex as a potential partner and is exposed only to the possibility of being refused (without thereby being socially or morally compromised), the homosexual runs the danger of encountering a "normal" person, with all the consequences that this may involve. This search for a partner of his own kind in the shady areas of society means an extraodinarily heavy spiritual burden and, what is more, a dangerous temptation especially for the person who really wants to live an ethically responsible life.

4. The same burden and temptation result from the fact that the homosexual must wear a mask and act like a hypocrite before friends, acquaintances, and as a rule even in his own family, but nevertheless live in constant fear of discovery and its consequent compromise of character.[9] Thus he is thrown into a situation of permanent conflict.

From all this it follows that the homosexual in a very special way needs intellectual and spiritual guidance or at least care, which will give him a constantly renewed stability on the slippery ground of his existence. The temptations of the homosexual which we have described are so great that we must appreciate why it is that Christian theologians often despair in the face of the minimal chances of being able to live ethically with homosexuality and achieve an acceptable partnership. And we ourselves do not venture to credit these chances with anything more than being a possible exception.[10]

Therefore Christian pastoral care will have to be concerned primarily with helping the person to sublimate his homosexual urge. But this cannot be done by exposing the homosexual to defamation of his urge. On the contrary, it is possible only if we are able to help him to see the tasks and the potentialities that are inherent in his abnormal existence. Not infrequently these consist in a pedagogical *eros*, in any case most often in a heightened sense of empathy. Therefore the goal of this sublimation will be found precisely in the actual danger zones, because here is where the charism—the possible charism!—of the homosexual is presented with appropriate tasks. Responsibility toward those who come in contact with persons who are thus constituted requires, of course, that these opportunities be recommended or opened only to those homosexuals who indicate that they are ready for such sublimation and evidence their stability. In most cases even these persons need the continuing ministry of their medical or pastoral counselors.

Toward a Christian Understanding of the Homosexual

H. Kimball Jones

Our discussion would be a lot simpler if there were but one Creation narrative. However, besides the statement "and they shall become one flesh," there is the command, "Be fruitful and multiply." This connection has received strongest emphasis within the Catholic and Anglican traditions. Michael Buckley relates the Catholic position:

> The purpose of coition may be described as conceptional and relational, the former destined for the procreation of children, and the latter for the establishment of the "one flesh union" *(henosis)*. These purposes must never be separated so that one would exclude the other entirely and permanently. The use of the sexual organs, therefore, is permanently limited to an exclusive and lifelong relationship within the married state.[1]

105

Similarly D. S. Bailey relates the Anglican position, stating that the two aspects of coitus—relational and conceptional—cannot be isolated from one another, because the "vocation to parenthood . . . is always implicit in union in one flesh."[2]

The Protestant tradition has not disagreed with these statements, but it has placed the emphasis elsewhere. While Catholics and Anglicans have tended to put more stress on the conceptional aspect of human sexuality, Protestants have given greater emphasis to the relational aspect. This is illustrated in the following statement by Dietrich Bonhoeffer:

> The life of the body is an end in itself. Sex is not only the means of reproduction, but independently of this defined purpose, it brings with it its own joy, in married life, in the love of two human beings for one another. . . . The meaning of bodily life never lies solely in its subordination to its final purpose. The life of the body assumes its full significance only with the fulfillment of its inherent claim to joy.[3]

Despite the different points of emphasis, there is a basic agreement in all three of these views—an agreement based on the Creation narrative in the first chapter in Genesis—that one cannot separate the sexual act from its intended conceptional function. This is both a statement of Christian doctrine and a matter of biological fact. Sylvanus Duvall points out that "from the standpoint of nature, the purpose of sex is to lure people into behavior which will perpetuate the race,"[4] and this fact, with which few would contend, is true of nature before and after the Fall.

Thus, if man is to fulfill his intended nature, he cannot escape the fact this can occur only within a loving relationship with a woman—a relationship which always has beneath it to "be fruitful and multiply." But once we have made this assertion, we must be careful in relating it to the problem of the homosexual. It is very easy at this point simply to say, "Therefore, the homosexual is a sinner whose very way of life is in direct contradiction to the will of God for human sexuality," and to end the matter there. This is what has happened too often within the Church, and it is a mistake we must avoid at all costs.

Sin, Guilt and the Homosexual

We have said that homosexual acts are contrary to the will of God for human sexuality. This would imply that the homosexual is, by his very nature, a sinner and that homosexual acts are therefore sinful *per se*. We must now ask what it means to say that the homosexual is a sinner. Does this mean that it is impossible to envisage an ethical homosexual relationship? Can there be no redemption of the homosexual without change?

Here Thielicke is quite helpful. He points out that we cannot make a distinction between homosexuality as a sinful way of life which is contrary to the will of God and heterosexuality as a good way of life which is in accordance with God's will. Or to put it in another way, we cannot make an automatic distinction between the "sinful homosexual" and the "redeemed heterosexual." The fact is, says Thielicke, that such a distinction is an example of Pharisaism. Whether we like it or not, "we all share . . . in the disordered creation that exists since the Fall," heterosexual as well as homosexual. Therefore, says Thielicke, homosexuality should be seen as "a kind of symptomatic participation in the fate of a fallen world,"[5] and not as an unusually sinful way of life.

While it is true that the homosexual is a sinner, the heterosexual, too, is a sinner. What we have seen to have been the will of God for human sexuality is an ideal state, seldom realized in heterosexual relationships. Certainly it is desirable and possible for a sexual relationship within Christian marriage to be built upon mutual love and devotion, and insofar as it is directed toward the purpose of parenthood, it gains an added dimension of meaning. On the other hand, it is questionable that human beings are capable of consummating perfect marriages in which every act of coitus is a perfect, selfless expression of mutual love coupled with a desire to have children. At most, marriage can only approximate this goal. Due to man's sinful nature, lust and selfishness are never completely absent from coitus, and in most instances they are very much present as inevitable symptoms of man's participation in the fate of the fallen world. Yet the inevitable presence of these factors within the sexual relationship does not make it impossible for a fulfilling, satisfying experience to result. Insofar as love and commitment are present, we expect the relationship to be fulfilling, knowing at the same time that it can never be completely selfless as long as we remain human.

What does this mean for the homosexual? In the first place it means that, given man's sinful nature, the primary problem in sexual relationships is not sex within marriage versus sex outside of marriage, or sex within a heterosexual relationship versus sex within a homosexual relationship. The problem is rather sex as a depersonalizing force versus sex as the fulfillment of human relationship. Thus, the important question would appear to be whether or not it is possible for the homosexual to achieve a responsible, fulfilling relationship.

Such relationships do, in fact, exist. What, then, should be our attitude? Should we condone, or perhaps encourage homosexual relationships which occur in a context of mutual love and devotion, or should we condemn them because they are, by their very nature, contrary to God's purpose for human sexuality?

This is a very difficult question because on one hand it would appear that we should condemn such relationships since they do not offer the same possibility for total fulfillment as heterosexual relationships, even though the latter are not without sin. But this immediately raises several questions. First, what about the heterosexual couple who cannot have children? Or what about the married couple who are not sure whether their marriage is still built up on love? Should we suggest that they immediately refrain from coitus? Or should we not, on the contrary, suggest that this is one means through which their love might become re-ignited, fully aware of the risks involved in such advice? In each of these instances most clergymen would almost certainly recommend a continuation of coitus, knowing that in either case an imperfect relationship might result. The "absolute invert" is, in one sense, in the same position as the man or woman who cannot have children. As we have seen, he is often unable to change his way of life. Normal heterosexual relationships are impossible for him. Does the Church, then, have the right to tell him that he must give up his sexual experiences because they are sinful? Is this really a viable option for him any more than it would be for the childless heterosexual couple? Thielicke states the problem as follows:

> Perhaps the best way to formulate the ethical problem of the constitutional homosexual, who because of his vitality is not able to practice abstinence, is to ask whether within the co-ordinating system of his constitution he is willing to structure the man-man relationship in an *ethically responsible* way. Thus, the ethical question meets him on the basis, which he did not enter intentionally, but which is where he actually finds himself, into which, as Heidegger would say, he has been "thrown."

Thielicke is suggesting here that the absolute invert is not responsible for being what he is, but merely for what he makes himself within his given framework.[7] Thus, a simple condemnation of the homosexual as a sinner, with no further word on the matter, is an irresponsible position for a Christian to take, for it is entirely futile. It places an irrevocable judgment upon those homosexuals who cannot change by saying in effect, "You must change, lest you become unworthy of the love of God." Such judgment will serve only to drive the homosexual to despair or to renounce the Christian faith altogether. It shuts out the possibility of any practicable solution to his problem. If the Church is to be of any help to the homosexual, then it must begin at the point where he finds himself. Thus, the question should not be whether he is *per se* in a state of sin (are not we all!), but rather how he can make the best of a given, and in many cases unchangeable situation. This is the only possible starting point for a practicable Christian ethic concerning homosexuality.

Towards a Practicable Christian Ethic

If ethics constitutes a realm above history, immovable and unconcerned by historical change—how can it influence men, living in history and transformed by history?

Paul Tillich[8]

An ethic will have authority for most of our generation only as it is empirical and starts from the data of actual personal relationships as they now are.

J.A.T. Robinson[9]

Given the complex nature of the problem of homosexuality—the different types of homosexuals, the various causes of homosexuality, and numerous other factors that vary greatly from individual to individual— no single rule can be laid down as to the attitude the Church should take toward the homosexual. It would be nice to be able to lay down a simple dictum—indeed, the Church has done this now for nearly two thousand years—but no one can arrive at a statement that would apply to more than a small percentage of homosexuals. Thus, the answer we are seeking must be contextual and multi-faceted.

As we have seen,   .   .   .   a change is not always possible. How, then, is the clergyman to react to the homosexual who, in all probability, cannot change and does not wish to change? This is the most difficult problem the Church must face in regard to the homosexual. Traditionally, the Church has offered two solutions to this problem, each of which has proven inadequate: 1) We should exhort the homosexual to renounce his evil ways. 2) We should help him sublimate his sexual desires into more creative channels.

Exhortation

For centuries Christians have been telling the homosexual that he must renounce his sinful desires, or at least cease giving overt expression to them. For example, Karl Barth suggests that we must tell the homosexual that "the command of God shows him irrefutably—in clear contradiction to his own theories—that as a man he can only be genuinely human with women."[10]

But does exhortation really serve a purpose? Does Barth honestly believe that if one points out to the invert that his state is unnatural, he will (or, indeed *can*) proceed to renounce it immediately? Along with Thielicke, we must ask whether Barth "has ever accompanied a homosexual pastorally on the 'way' he has to travel."[11] Homosexuality especially for the absolute invert is no slight habit which can be renounced at will. On the contrary, it is a way of life which reaches into the very depths of his soul, and to which he responds with his whole being. In the face of such deep-rooted orientation, moral advice to the homosexual to give up this way of life "is about as effective as advising a normal man to refrain from taking an interest in the opposite sex."[12]

What's more such an exhortation actually serves a negative purpose in many instances. D. J. West has pointed out that, from a psychological point of view, exhorting the homosexual to renounce his way of life, instead of inducing strong-minded self-control . . . leads to great misery and to desperate attempts to deny the very existence of the offending impulses. The repression and mental conflicts so provoked may turn him into a worse social nuisance and misfit than he would have been if he had simply stayed homosexual.[13]

Thus, the simple exhortation to change is a very impractical solution to the problem of homosexuality, reflecting a complete lack of understanding the deep-rooted nature of sexual inversion.

Sublimation

John Harvey[14] and Helmut Thielicke,[15] among others, have suggested that the homosexual who cannot change should be led toward a constructive sublimation of his sexual impulse. It is neither practical nor desirable for the homosexual to sublimate his sexual desires. Both Havelock Ellis and D. J. West have found sublimation to be an ineffective therapeutic goal, and Magnus Hirschfeld found such therapy to be effective with less than 5% of the homosexuals who had attempted it.[16] Gordon Westwood suggests that the reason for this lies in the fact that "sublimation is an unconscious mechanism and therefore not a voluntary process. It can be a useful aid," says Westwood, "but it is rarely a full controlling factor."[17] And the problem is compounded because "forced abstinence from fear and guilt often leads to neurotic disorder."[18] The very professions that are most often suggested as offering opportunities to the homosexual for sublimation are those which are, by and large, inaccessible to him. While he might stand the best chance of sublimating his sexual desires in professions such as scouting, teaching and the Christian ministry—professions which involve what Thielicke calls "a pedagogical eros . . . a heightened sense of empathy"[19]—it is difficult for a professed homosexual to enter such professions. Also, jobs such as these, by offering considerable contact with young people, might provide strong temptations which could be a source of great anxiety to a homosexual who is attempting to abstain from all sexual relations.[20] Thus, sublimation is not a practical answer for the absolute invert. What's more, it is not a desirable one. If we are willing to admit (as Thielicke does) that the homosexual finds himself "thrown" into a particular way of life; and if we assume . . . that the homosexual may be completely "normal" in every sense apart from his sexual anomaly, then we have no right to demand of him that he sublimate his sexual desires simply because the form in which he would express them happens to be disgusting to us.

Surely, such an expression is "unnatural," and as such it can never be a pure expression of human sexuality. But then, given the sinfulness of man, no act of human sexuality can achieve such perfection. Granted, the attitudes of society and the lack of legal and familial ties as well as the absence of a natural mutuality make it difficult for a homosexual relationship to reach the heights of mutual satisfaction and fulfillment that are possible within a heterosexual marriage; however, it is a fact that many homosexual "marriages" have proven relatively fulfilling, reflecting responsible love and devotion.

A Practicable Christian Ethic

Paul Lehmann states that

> the concern of a Christian ethic is to exhibit the intimate relation of sexuality in all its forms to the freedom and the integrity of human wholeness in the most concrete human encounter of belonging.

"Such an ethic," says Lehmann, "can offer no sexual guidance according to a blueprint designed to apply to all sexual behavior in the same way." Thus, he suggests that

> what is called Christian sexual ethics is an approach to sexuality which accents both the fundamental importance of the sexual act for the humanization of man and the setting in which the humanization of man is a concrete and achievable reality. In such a setting the risks of sexual nonconformity must be run.[21]

While Lehmann sees such a setting to exist primarily in an "encounter between male and female under conditions of trust and fulfilment," we would suggest that for the absolute invert such a setting can exist in a similar encounter with another male. While such an encounter can never have the same potential for human fulfillment that is found in a heterosexual relationship, it is, nevertheless, the only sexual setting in which "the humanization of man" can begin to become "a concrete and achievable reality" for the homosexual, however short it may fall of perfect humanity. Thus, we suggest that the Church must be willing to make the difficult, but necessary step of recognizing the validity of mature homosexual relationships, encouraging the absolute invert to maintain a fidelity to one partner when his only other choice would be to lead a promiscuous life filled with guilt and fear. This would by no means be an endorsement of homosexuality by the Church. Rather it would simply be a realistic, and thus responsible solution to an otherwise insoluble problem, for there is no other practicable answer for those homosexuals who cannot change. In the long run such a policy could prove quite beneficial. As Evelyn Hooker points out,

> You must balance the "cost" of accepting homosexuality as a patttern for those who cannot change against the possibility that a very large number of men, who now seek furtive, one-night stands, may have the possibility of establishing more permanent relationships with persons like themselves.[22]

Such an acceptance is not an idealization of the homosexual way of life. Thus, we could not go along with Robert Wood's proposal that the Church perform marriages between homosexuals. It is one thing to say that a homosexual relationship, though necessarily falling short of the will of God, can be an occasion of mutual love and devotion. But it is quite another thing to say that the Church should offer formal sanction of such a relationship. A homosexual relationship can only approximate the marriage relationship as envisioned by the Church. A mature homosexual relationship may be recognized as a valid way of life, a maximum possibility within a given context, but it cannot be recognized as meeting the standards of Christian marriage. However creative and fulfilling it may be (and it may be quite creative and fulfilling), it nevertheless remains an unnatural expression of human sexuality. This immediately raises a question: How can we claim to accept the homosexual and in some instances even go so far as to encourage him to form a lasting homosexual relationship if we see such a relationship as necessarily falling short of the will of God? Does not the latter factor immediately place the homosexual in an inferior position in our eyes? The problem here is one of distinguishing between acceptance and sanction. While we should accept the homosexual as a child of God and recognize his way of life as a potentially creative expression of human sexuality, even encouraging homosexual relationships when necessary, we cannot give the sanction of Christian marriage to these relationships since they, by their very nature, negate the male-female complement and vocation of parenthood, both of which are essential to Christian marriage.

Homosexuality can be a relatively creative and fulfilling way of life for the responsible homosexual, and often it can reach a height of fulfillment equal to that of many heterosexual relationships. However, the homosexual relationship is doomed, by its very nature, to never pass beyond a certain point. Two homosexuals can never complement one another in the same sense that male and female can, and they can never know the joy of having children, a joy that brings a heterosexual relationship into a whole new dimension.

Consequently, we assert that the homosexual who cannot change must be accepted for what he is and encouraged to live responsibly within his own given sexuality; at the same time, we should surely see his position as being unenviable and his way of life as one not to be recommended as being desirable. Where one has the possibility of changing to a heterosexual orientation, he should be strongly urged to do so. But where this is impossible, we would urge him to lead a responsible life within the limits of his situation. He is a sexually-handicapped person, and there is no getting around this; but, by the grace of God, his handicap may become a creative force in his life.

We would suggest that such an attitude on the part of the Church would represent a responsible attempt to come to terms with the problem of homosexuality in the light of the knowledge we have about the problem today. It would be a step of courage and freedom in the light of a Gospel which tells us that we must act with the courage and in the freedom of Christian love if the message of God's love for man is to remain relevant to every age and in every situation.

Such an attitude can only be assumed with fear and trembling. The clergyman who encourages a homosexual to enter into a responsible relationship always runs the risk of being misinterpreted as advocating sexual license. However, this is a risk we must be willing to run if we are truly to open the doors of the Church to the homosexual, offering him concrete and realistic assistance and loving acceptance in the name of Christ.

Sin, Crime, Sickness or Alternative Life Style?: A Jewish Approach to Homosexuality

Hershel Matt

Homosexuality, which in the general community has for some time been a major issue, has begun to be a matter of concern and controversy in the Jewish community as well. This development has come about for several reasons: partly because Jewish homosexuals are, like non-Jews, increasingly "coming out"; partly because some of them are seeking—even demanding—to be accepted as full-fledged members of the Jewish community and of the synagogue; and partly because Jews and non-Jews alike, both heterosexual and homosexual, are turning to rabbis and scholars for a clarification of what Judaism has to say on the subject.

That Judaism must have something to say should be obvious, for the Torah-text-and-tradition, claiming—as it does—to contain the revelation of God's word and will for human life, claims to have something significant—indeed, crucial—to say about every important area of life, surely about such a basic dimension of life as sex. ("He who says Torah is one thing and the affairs of the world are something entirely other is as if he denies God.")[1]

What Judaism has to say about homosexuality would appear to be equally obvious, for all of the relatively few passages in the Torah-text that clearly refer to homosexuality[2] do so in negative terms. The words of the men of Sodom (Genesis 19), who surround Lot's house and say "Where are the men who came to you tonight? bring them out to us, that we may know (or, "be intimate with") them," almost certainly have a homosexual reference. (The usage of the word "sodomy" is, thus, well-founded.) And the horrible story of the "concubine in Gibeah" (Judges 19), probably related to the Genesis passage, similarly involves the threat of homosexual attack. It is sometimes argued that the horror and condemnation expressed in these two stories are directed not against homosexuality as such, but against homosexual rape or against the violation of the sacred obligation of hospitality; it is also argued that the moral abhorrence expressed in the narrative passages does not, in itself, constitute legal prohibition. The two brief passages in the law code of Leviticus (19:22 and 20:13), however, are clear and categorical: "With a male you shall not lie as with a woman; it is an abomination . . . if a male lies with a male as one lies with a woman, the two of them have done an abhorrent thing; they shall be put to death."

References in Talmudic and post-Talmudic sources—likewise relatively few—remain consistent with the biblical prohibition. Whatever the question at issue—whether two men may share the same blanket, or even be together in private; whether two women may sleep in the same room; whether climatic conditions stimulate homosexual temptation; whether Jews are likely to be influenced by the homosexual behavior of non-Jews; whether the age of the homosexual offender should be a factor in determining culpability; what the appropriate punishment is, in theory and in practice; whether the punishment should be the same for male and female offenders; whether rumors concerning a fellow Jew's homosexuality should be given credence; which privileges, communal and synagogal, should be denied to a homosexual—every single decision, pro or con, takes for granted that a homosexual act is a moral perversion, an outrageous and disgusting deed, a serious violation of the Torah's command and, therefore, a grave sin. It would, thus, appear absolutely clear that a Jewish approach to homosexuality must end where and as it starts: with utter condemnation and categorical prohibition.

Yet, such a conclusion, at this point in our discussion, is premature. For if what we seek is a *truly Jewish* approach to a *contemporary* problem, we must not only consult biblical sources and subsequent halakhic decisions but must do two other things as well: a) determine, as far as we are able, the rationale and presuppositions of the traditional stand; and b) inquire whether there are now any changed circumstances or new data in the light of which the Torah's stand today—though based on the same divine and enduring concerns and purposes—might possibly involve changed formulations or different emphases.

Why does the Torah condemn homosexuality so utterly and consider it to be such an abomination? The reason cannot be simply the abhorrence of the unknown, for a law does not forbid the unknown. Besides, the Torah specifically alludes to, and obviously was familiar with, the practice of homosexuality (along with other sexual offenses, often practiced as part of idolatrous cult worship), by both the Egyptians "in whose midst you dwelt" and the Canaanites "into whose land I am bringing you" (Lev. 18:3). Nor can the reason be merely "psychological" and "esthetic"—that homosexuality is inherently disgusting—for that would be begging the question: why was it considered disgusting? Nor can the reason be "statistical"—that the majority of men and women did not and do not practice homosexuality—for Torah-law must surely be based on more than statistics and averages; indeed, the Torah specifically warns *against* following the majority, when the majority is bent on evil.

The reasons for the Torah's condemnation must be related rather to the will of the Creator for the human male and female whom He created: "God created man in His image . . . male and female. He created them (Gen. 1:27) . . . God saw all that He had made and behold it was very good (Ibid. 31) . . . it is not good that man should be alone; I will make a helper for him (as complement and counterpoint to him, his opposite number) (Ibid. 2:18) . . . this one shall be called woman (Ibid. 2:23) . . . let a man leave his father and his mother, and cling to his wife (his woman), and they shall become one flesh (Ibid. 2:24) . . . be fruitful and multiply and fill the earth (Ibid. 1:28) . . . the Lord created the earth to be inhabited (Isaiah 45:18) . . . I will establish My covenant between Me and you (Abraham) and your seed after you, throughout their generations . . . as an everlasting covenant" (Genesis 17:7).

In the light of such Scriptural passages, some of the reasons for the Torah's prohibition of homosexuality become discernible. One reason must be that in the Order of Creation the sexual "nature" and "structure" of the human male and female—including what we refer to as their anatomy, physiology, and psyche—call for mutual complementation, completion, and fulfillment through a heterosexual relationship. Another implied reason is that only through such a relationship, using the organs of generation in a manner conducive to generation, can a new generation appear to populate the earth. A third reason: only with the appearance of a second and third generation can there be a family in the full sense of the word: one that calls for and allows for caring love and reverent responsibility, not only between spouses but also among parents and children and grandchildren. This points to a fourth reason: homosexuality precludes history, not only individual and family history, but history as such—the stage on which both the divine and human roles in the providential drama are to be acted out. In the case of Jewish homosexuality, one further denial is involved: that of the continued survival of the Covenant People Israel, vehicle of God's involvement in the world, "God's stake in history."

It is out of such concerns as these, we must assume, that the Torah-text-and-tradition prohibits homosexuality.

But whenever we speak of the Torah's prohibitions we must be mindful of one of the Torah's key presuppositions: the freedom and capacity of the individual human being to obey. Surely the very creation-in-the-image, which is the basic biblical teaching about human beings, male and female, implies such freedom. How else could the Lord God hold Adam and Eve responsible for the first violation of the first prohibition? And when, in the very next generation, Cain is distressed at God's acceptance of Abel's offering and the rejection of his own, God tells him: "Sin couches at the door: its urge is toward you; yet you can be its master" (Gen. 4:7). Therefore, when Cain proceeds to murder his brother, God "has the right" to confront him with his responsibility for this murder, the first ever committed. In a famous Midrash, human moral freedom and responsibility are made even more explicit. Before conception takes place, "the seminal drop is brought before the Holy One; there and then is it decided, concerning this one, whether it will be strong or weak, wise or foolish, rich or poor—but not whether it will be wicked or righteous." [3] Or, as the famous Talmudic statement puts it, even more succinctly, "All is in the hands of Heaven—except the fear of Heaven." [4] The clear and consistent assumption behind all of the Torah's commands and prohibitions is, thus, that human beings have the freedom to obey or disobey them.[5]

But what if one violates the Torah's command involuntarily, due to circumstances beyond one's control, or with no other options available? Is one still culpable? And is the act still punishable? The Torah-tradition contains numerous examples of such involuntary offenders, who have done what was forbidden or failed to do what was commanded, out of constraint and lack of freedom (me-ones). The cases discussed involve varying degrees and kinds of constraint: threat of torture or death, extreme financial duress; mistaken impression of the facts; forgetfulness; insanity; intoxication; illness; accident; and other factors beyond one's control. Although the halakhic authorities differ as to whether the factor of *ones* should be the governing consideration in any particular case—and whether, therefore, the offender is to be fully exempt, is to be held fully responsible, or partially both—a frequently invoked principle is that "in cases of *ones* the Merciful One exempts." [6] The underlying principle is, apparently, that when forbidden acts are performed in the absence of voluntary choice and free decision, or in the absence of other options, the offenders are judged more leniently than otherwise.

The tradition does not appear ever to have looked upon homosexual behavior in such a light. It appears, rather, to have *assumed* that whenever homosexual acts are performed they are engaged in willingly and willfully, through a free choice from among several options. It is only in our own generation that homosexual behavior has been found to involve not merely a single, overt act, or a series of such acts, but often to reflect a profound inner condition and basic psychic orientation, involving the deepest levels of personality. However deep and numerous are the differences among contempory experts on homosexuality,[7] on one aspect there seems to be *near-unanimity: that for very many homosexuals the prospects of change to heterosexuality are almost nil.*

Now, with regard to one group of homosexuals (and bi-sexuals), those whose sexual behavior represents deliberate rejection of the Torah's standard and a simple indulgence in the hedonistic ethic of "doing whatever gives me pleasure"—and who, if they chose to, *could* live a heterosexual life—it is clear that from any viewpoint that acknowledges the authority of the Torah the traditional prohibition remains in full force. With regard to another group, those for whom the homosexual way has been, psychologically speaking, the "easier" way—but who, with professional help or with strenuous effort, could manage to change—the Torah's standard also remains in effect. With regard to other homosexuals, however, (constituting probably the majority) who are under the constraint of remaining homosexual indefinitely, presumably for life—their only other option being sexual abstinence for life—is there anything less stringent that could, and should, be said by contemporary Torah-interpreters and Torah-observers?

For one thing, a truly Torah approach, taking seriously the injunction of the Torah-tradition not to judge another person until one stands in his place,[8] would acknowledge that no human being is able to know the exact degree of another's freedom; that God alone has that knowledge; that God alone, therefore, has the ability and the right to judge a person's culpability; and that none of us humans, therefore, ought presume to judge a homosexual or automatically regard a homosexual as a sinner—since, as already implied, sin involves not only overt action but also intention, decision, and responsibility.[9]

Furthermore, a Torah approach would look with deep compassion (*rahmanut*) upon the plight of many homosexuals in our society. It would share the anguish of a human being who for years—perhaps since early adolescence—has had to live with a growing sense of being different and "queer"; in constant fear of being discovered; knowing that, if discovered, he might well be looked down upon as perverted, loathsome, dangerous; with the consequent fear of being mistreated, humiliated and ridiculed, perhaps blackmailed, excluded or expelled from many types of employment, and denied acceptance and friendship. ("The Lord seeks the pursued" [10] and we should imitate Him in this regard.)

Not content with withholding judgment and with feeling compassion, a genuinely Jewish approach to homosexuality would require us to *demonstrate* such feelings of compassion by willingly associating with homosexuals and engaging in acts of kindness and friendship—so that the particular individuals whom we meet will not feel grudgingly tolerated but will see that they are included within the circle of our love.

But even more is required, if our Jewish responsibility to homosexuals is to be fulfilled. For it is not enough to attend to our own attitude and behavior; we must be equally concerned with what is felt and done by others, keeping ourselves from falling into the category of those "in whose power it was to protest but did not protest." True, we cannot force a change of heart upon others nor control their actions; we can, however, make a genuine effort to dispel the popular myths and repeal the legal disabilities that have made the life of many homosexuals into a living hell. We now know, for example, that most male homosexuals are not "effeminate" in gait, voice, manner, or dress; that most female homosexuals are not "masculine"; that homosexuality does not mean promiscuity. We should, therefore, avoid such stereotypes in conversation or in attempts at "humor." We now know that the incidence of crimes such as murder, robbery, rape, molestation, and seduction is no higher among homosexuals than among heterosexuals; we should, therefore, work for the immediate repeal of laws, rules, and practices that exclude or discriminate against homosexuals on the contrary assumption. Similarly, in acknowledgement of the relative victimlessness of homosexual relations between consenting adults and in opposition to unneccessary government intrusion upon individual privacy, we should, as Jews, vigorously oppose any legal penalties for such homosexual behavior.[11]

If a homosexual, then, is to be considered neither sinner nor criminal, how *shall* he or she be looked upon? As sick, perhaps?

The label "sick" has some obvious advantages over the other two: if considered sick, the homosexual is saved from being religiously damned, morally condemned, or legally doomed to punishment. But "sick" has serious disadvantages, too. For the sick we prescribe treatment and therapy; upon the sick we often impose restriction, separation, even isolation; toward the sick we feel superiority and show condescension; in the presence of the sick we feel fear. And if these actions and attitudes are true concerning the *physically* ill, how much more so concerning those who are considered mentally, emotionally, psychologically ill. Realizing that the uniqueness of human beings is related to their mind, psyche, conscience and "soul," we tend automatically and recklessly to expand and exaggerate the dimensions of their "emotional illness" and to assume that these "sick people" are maladjusted and malfunctioning in almost all regards and all relationships. We tend, therefore, to shudder in their presence, on the cruel assumption that their illness calls into question their actual humanity. (Do we, perhaps, shudder also from a subconscious fear of becoming like them, or from subconscious horror and guilt at already being at least somewhat like them?)

In the face of these negative connotations of the word "sick" and the negative consequences of applying it to homosexuals, it is quite understandable that hosts of homosexuals bitterly resent and utterly reject such a label, and that even the American Psychiatric Association has, in recent years, removed homosexuality from its list of mental illnesses.

But if the term "sickness" is to be eliminated, what, then, shall be substituted? Some of the terms that have been used—such as defect or perversion—have so many negative connotations and result in so many negative attitudes that they are hardly an improvement over what they replace. Shall we say, then—as urged by many homosexuals, many sexual liberationists and radicals, and some professional experts—that homosexuals should not be singled out at all; that they should receive no special attention, treatment, consideration, description, or label; that their orientation and behavior should be considered equally acceptable with heterosexuality as simply an "alternative life style"?

It is tempting to say "yes," thus avoiding the accusation of indifference and insensitivity to the anguish that so many homosexuals have undergone, and to the discrimination, deprivation, ostracism, and even persecution that have contributed to that anguish.

And yet—once again—a Jew who seeks to be faithful to the Torah and to the divine word which he affirms to be contained therein, though obliged to guard against the temptation of cruelty and lack of compassion, must also guard against the temptation of reckless relativism and simplistic sentimentality. The most truly Jewish stance would be one that takes with equal seriousness both the authority of traditional standards and the significance of modern knowledge. As already indicated, such a stance would maintain the traditional view of heterosexuality as the God-intended norm and yet would incorporate the contemporary recognition of homosexuality as, clinically speaking, a sexual deviance, malfunctioning, or abnormality—usually unavoidable and often irremediable.

Such an approach has a number of advantages. It remains faithful to the Torah-teaching that heterosexuality is, in principle, not merely recommended but commanded, and that homosexuality is not merely discouraged but forbidden. It places upon men and women who become aware of their homosexual tendencies the responsibility for striving, on their own or with the aid of professional counselors, to develop or strengthen their heterosexual tendencies. It removes from those homosexuals who, after making such efforts, find that they cannot change, all burden of blame and guilt[12]—accepting them as they are. It avoids at least some of the negative connotations of "mental illness." It acknowledges that unalterable homosexuality remains theologically unaccountable. And it warns all of us—both homosexuals and heterosexuals—against self-righteousness.

In seeking to do justice to this double claim, the heterosexual majority faces several difficult dilemmas. One is whether homosexuals should *ever* be excluded from any particular roles in society.

Granted, as has been indicated earlier, that such exclusion is, in most cases, unnecessarily cruel and unjustly discriminatory, based on myth or prejudice and, therefore, completely unwarranted and indeed intolerable, are there, nevertheless, a certain few roles—such as teacher, youth leader, or religious guide—which are likely to be so influential upon the lives of young people that when such positions are held by an avowed homosexual those young people whose sexual orientation is not yet set may be influenced toward a homosexual orientation—not through any conscious intention, deliberate effort, or seductive behavior on the part of the homosexual (popular fear of such dangers is based, as we have seen, on myth and prejudice), but simply through functioning as authority figures and role models?

A solution to this dilemma is not easy. Some experts argue that the influence of role models such as teachers or youth leaders is likely to be crucial in a child's life. Others argue that there is little evidence to indicate who are most likely actually to function as role models, and that heroes-at-a-distance, often "present" through the media, can be no less significant as role models than the usual "significant persons" in a child's life. Still others argue that sexual orientation is set at a very early age—according to some, by the age of two!—and is, therefore, very unlikely to be affected by subsequent contact with any other person, however "significant." In the absence of any clear evidence as to harmful effects upon young people, and in the presence of clear evidence of harmful effects upon homosexuals who have been excluded from a host of jobs, we would advocate that the only roles from which homosexuals should be excluded are those of adoptive or foster parent and of religious leader—since these two roles of parent and rabbi are, by definition, meant to serve as models of what a Jewish woman or man should be. And even the role of rabbi should be open to a homosexual *if* he or she honestly holds the conviction—and would conscientiously seek to convey it to others—that, in spite of his or her own homosexuality, the Jewish ideal for man and woman is heterosexuality. (After all, it is accepted that a single or divorced person can legitimately and effectively serve as rabbi provided that he or she holds up marriage as the ideal, and that a childless person may serve as rabbi as long as he or she holds up having children as the ideal.)

For the organized Jewish community a further problem arises, in connection with a request—or demand—which, though formerly unheard of and until recently, indeed, inconceivable, has now been presented by some homosexuals and is likely to be made with increasing frequency and forcefulness: that national synagogue organizations accept congregations of homosexuals as local affiliates. What would be a proper response to this very real dilemma? On the one hand, is not a homosexual synagogue a contradiction in terms? Since Judaism considers heterosexuality to be the norm, how can it accept as legitimate a group which, by name and public identification, represents, celebrates, and makes a principle of its deviation from that norm? And yet, does not any group of Jews have a right to form a congregation and the further right to affiliate, on the same basis as others, with a union of congregations?

Our response to this dilemma would be threefold: a) it would be far preferable for homosexuals to be welcome and feel welcome in existing congregations rather than to feel a need to form their own gay synagogues; b) since the present reality, however, is that such a welcome is not assured and is perhaps even unlikely, the formation of gay congregations is legitimate; and c) a gay congregation, to be eligible for affiliation with a union of congregations, however, must not—by rule, name, practice, or implication—restrict its own membership or leadership to homosexuals.

There remains one further, far more radical, request—again, often couched as a demand—that has been made by some Jewish homosexuals: that rabbis solemnize and all Jews recognize "marriages" between homosexuals, and that congregations admit such couples to "family memberships." Is there any way in which the notion of a homosexual "marriage" could be considered Jewishly valid?

When we speak of "Jewishly valid" with reference to an officially solemnized, publicly recognized pattern of behavior, we must be speaking in terms of traditional Jewish law, the halakhah. Now, though the halakhah has developed and "changed" over the ages, through Rabbinic interpretation of biblical law and Rabbinic enactment for the public welfare, nevertheless, in the three thousand years of recorded halakhic teaching and practice there is apparently not a single instance of halakhic provision for the legitimization of a homosexual relationship. And even if the flexibility and resourcefulness of the halakhah were renewed and increased—as befits the "Torah of Life"—it is hardly conceivable that a homosexual departure from the Torah's heterosexual norm would ever be accepted by halakhically faithful Jews or ever be recognized as *k'dat moshe v'yisrael* (in accordance with the law of Moses and Israel).

How will Jewish homosexuals who cherish both Torah-and-commandments and the Community of the People of Israel, but who must live with the reality of their homosexual condition—how will they be likely to respond to such a categorical halakhic "no"?

Some will probably be so embittered that they may turn their backs on the whole Jewish "establishment" or on Judaism itself. But, perhaps, some may trouble themselves to formulate a response, in the hope of making their position understood, to the "straight" majority of their fellow Jews. And their response might go something like this.

"Granted that marriage in Judaism has always been heterosexual; and granted that one of the major purposes of marriage has been procreation—in order both to populate the world and to pass on the Covenant way of life. But is that the sole purpose and meaning of Jewish marriage? What of the legitimacy of sexual pleasure and release—is that not also Jewish? (Long-term abstinence is no more feasible, bearable, or desirable for homosexuals than for heterosexuals.) And does not marriage have other purposes as well: the fostering of mutual affection, care, trust, sacrifice, and support; the encouragement and sustenance of growth—intellectual, esthetic, moral, and spiritual; the sharing of pain and anxiety; the nurturing of joy and hope; the overcoming of loneliness—all of these on the basis of an enduring commitment of faithfulness? And is not marriage the primary and preferred—and, indeed, the only fully acceptable—context for furthering these purposes? If it is the Torah-teaching that the fullest possible meaning of personhood is to be found in and through marriage, shall we, because we are homosexuals, be denied the right to seek such meaning and to develop such personhood? If God, in whose image we homosexuals, too, are created, has directly or indirectly caused or willed or allowed us to be what we cannot help being—men and women unable to function heterosexually—can we believe, and can you heterosexuals believe, that He wants us to be denied the only possible arrangement whereby we can live as deeply a human life as we are capable of?

"If, as you heterosexuals claim, our condition constitutes a deviance and malfunctioning and abnormality, do we not have the God-given right—indeed, the obligation—to attempt to live with, adjust to, make the best of, and rise above this 'handicap' of ours, just as all of the other handicapped are expected to do?

"If the halakhah can provide marriage only for heterosexuals and cannot speak to our condition, then in this one regard we must live non-halakhically; but we are Jews and we insist on avowing our homosexual condition and our homosexual union, openly and unashamedly, within the Covenant Community of the People of Israel.[13] In our eyes—and, we feel sure, in God's eyes, too—our homosexual bond is worthy, proper, and even holy. We believe that for us, who wish to live as Jews and love as Jews but who, by virtue of our homosexual condition, are not in a position to beget or bear any offspring, God has a word that is no less accepting and no less reassuring than His word to the eunuchs in the Babylonian Exile:

'Let the eunuch not say: behold, I am a withered tree; for thus says the Lord: as regards the eunuchs who keep My Sabbaths, who have chosen what I desire, and hold fast to My covenant, I will give them, in My house and within My walls, a monument and a name better than sons and daughters . . . an everlasting name that shall not perish.' " [14]

IV
Homosexual Acts Are to Be Evaluated in Terms of Relational Significance

Episcopal Diocese of Michigan Report
British Friends' Task Force Report
W. Norman Pittenger

Report of the Commission on Homosexuality of the Episcopal Diocese of Michigan

(1973)

A great virtue of the traditional teaching about sex lies in the fact that it is interpreted as God's creation, and therefore good. It is not characteristic of Christianity to identify bodily life with evil in any way, although specific Christian groups have often acted as if it were. Not only does sexual differentiation provide for the continuation of the human race, it forms the foundation for human community itself. More particularly, the Christian tradition has inherited a unique understanding of the purpose which sexual differentiation enables mankind to fulfill. By conducting their intimate life in such a way as to reflect the reliability and goodness found in God, human beings are given a means of offering a creaturely mirroring of the Divine. This is why the accent in Christian sexual thought is on lifetime personal commitment, a couple's taking of responsibility for one another, mutual love and faithfulness. Sexual differentiation involves interdependence; interdependence opens the possibility for a couple to offer lifelong care to one another. Caring for one another is a reflection of the essence of God's care for mankind.

Thus the whole notion that the bodily, and in particular the sexual life of man is of an inferior, unspiritual order (a notion deriving from a false concept of the dichotomy of body vs. soul) is out of tune with a Christian understanding of sexuality. Such an understanding places sexuality firmly in the context of sacrificial love, which is exemplified in Christ's death for us, a sacrifice that uniquely reveals to us God's goodness. A Christian understanding of sexuality, therefore, requires a responsible, sacrificial use of sexuality as a necessary component of spiritual maturity. Such an understanding is implicit in the traditional Christian ethic; we affirm this ethic and this understanding of it today.

We also discovered, however, that it is impossible to perceive these values in Christianity's traditional sexual teachings and automatically condemn all homosexual persons or relationships. Heterosexual partners by no means possess a monopoly upon sacrificial love and it was far from clear to the Commission that a homosexual relationship is in and of itself incapable of expressing sacrificial love. Social circumstances do indeed make it more difficult for homosexuals than for heterosexuals to aim at sacrificial love in their relationships with each other, but we found no inherent reason for assuming that they could not do so and we know that some homosexuals seriously do. Therefore we contend that it is wrong and presumptuous to deny Christian value to any human relationship which involves attachment to another person in the spirit of sacrificial or self-giving love. Homosexuals seriously seeking to build such relationships with one another are surely as deserving as heterosexuals of encouragement and help from the Church and its ministry. Unfortunately, that encouragement has not often been forthcoming. It is not likely to be forthcoming if the only word of the Church to homosexuals is a word of condemnation and if its ethical counsel to them is to insist upon sexual abstinence. If the Church has prized the potential for love in heterosexual relations, must it not also prize this potential in homosexual relationships as well?

To begin with, the Commission has discovered that it is impossible to study homosexuality in depth without recognizing an element of mystery in the phenomenon that refuses to be wholly dispelled. No scientist has managed convincingly to isolate the "causes" of the homosexual personality. Nor did the theological literature examined by the Commission display any unanimity on how homosexuality was to be assessed. The traditional negativism of the Church on the subject to which we have alluded turned out to be less justified and less convincing than the Commission anticipated. We are persuaded that we are faced less with an aberration than with a mystery: the nature of love itself.

Some Observations About Theological Studies of Homosexuality

Theologians are divided in their interpretations of homosexuality. While most theologians maintain that homosexuality is to be regarded as a manifestation of the fallen state of the race, different theologians draw different conclusions from this fact. But since all men participate in this fallen state and exhibit some manifestation of it, homosexuals can hardly be charged with special guilt.

Catholic thinkers, both Roman Catholic and Anglo-Catholic, tend to utilize the concept of Natural Law in their discussions of homosexuality. Heterosexuality (expressed in matrimony) is thus seen as harmonizing with Natural Law and homosexuality as violating it. To members of this Commission traditional Natural Law seemed less than adequate to handle the question. It has a strong leaning toward "biological fundamentalism" and fails to recognize the extent to which culture rather than reason contributes to any given formulation of Natural Law. Although these tendencies are most apparent in the traditional Natural Law arguments against birth control, they are subtly present as well in Natural Law arguments against homosexuality.

Furthermore, it should be emphasized that Roman Catholic theology is presently engaged in a serious and extensive struggle to deal with the question of Natural Law; though the terminology of the discussion is seldom the one explicitly used in Natural Law argumentation. For example, K. Rahner's writings on the radical unity of love of God and love of neighbor provide a systematic foundation for understanding the law of sacrificial love of neighbor as the very essence of natural law. The recent ethical reflection by Chirico, Robert, Knauer and Schuller deals with principles for translating this fundamental principle of sacrificial love into specific action. While to our knowledge these authors do not deal directly with homosexuality, their basic orientation would seem of necessity to point in the direction we have gone in our discussion above.

Protestant theologians have often approached questions of sexuality by citing passages of Scripture rather than by alluding to Natural Law. Since the Scriptures represent the historical data from which our knowledge of God has been derived they are a potent, legitimate means by which Christians have acquired self-understanding and an interpretation of the world. Nevertheless the practice of citing a given passage of Scripture as the authoritative source for an ethical or theological position creates more problems than it solves.

First of all, the practice very frequently represents the application of a "proof-text" method. Various texts or passages are cited as proof that a given ethical or theological position conforms to Scriptures when in fact the scriptural passages have been pulled out of context in support of some proposition only tangentially related to Scripture. Thus they offer no guarantee at all that the proposition in question actually conforms to the biblical outlook.

Second, when one gathers passages and texts dealing with homosexuality one faces the additional difficulty that many of the passages in Scripture which condemn homosexuality do so because of its association with idolatrous practices such as male temple prostitution. These passages are hardly germane to our contemporary situation for the simple reason that homosexuality does not occur among us in this form. Thus Leviticus 18:22 and 20:13 speak of homosexuality as unclean and provide the death penalty for those practicing it. Yet in context one gathers that the reason for this uncleanness is that homosexuality is associated with the idolatries of Egypt and the worship of Moloch. Similar observations must be made about Deuteronomy 23:17, I Kings 14:24, 15:12, 22:46, and Romans 1:27. The Old Testament passages denounce cult homosexual prostitution and the Romans passage attributes homosexuality to Roman idolatry.

The most famous denunciation of homosexuality in Scripture is undoubtedly the story of Sodom and Gomorrah (Genesis 19:4–11) and deserves close examination. Abraham's kinsman, Lot, has settled as a stranger in Sodom and is visited one evening by two angels. At dusk the men of the town gather at Lot's door, presumably requesting that the guests be brought out and turned over to them so that homosexual intercourse may be performed with them. The upshot of the story is that the angels blind the men of Sodom so that they cannot see Lot's door and the Lord warns Lot to gather his household and flee without looking back at the destruction he intends to visit upon the city. D. S. Bailey first challenged the traditional interpretation of this story by pointing out that Lot had failed to take his guests to visit the elders of the town. As he was a stranger in their midst he owed them this courtesy. Thus Lot's discourtesy is as much the subject of the original story as the sin of Sodom. Further, he indicates that the word for "know" (Yodh) used in this story is used to indicate sexual knowing only ten times in the Bible, out of the 964 times it occurs. ("Bring them out unto us that we may know—yodh—them.") He argues that since this word never indicates homosexual intercourse in any other place, it ought not so be read here. His clinching argument, however, is that the sin of Sodom was not originally thought of as sexual. It received this connotation in the apocryphal Book of Jubilees for the first time, centuries after the original story. Thus Bailey argues that the Church has for centuries used a passage in the denunciation of homosexuality that in fact does not refer to homosexuality.

Whether or not one finds Bailey's arguments persuasive, they do seem to indicate that scriptural opposition to homosexuality was exaggerated by later writers. The question facing the Church today is whether Scripture can legitimately be used to exclude homosexuals from the Church at all. As a Commission we unanimously agree that the time has come to discontinue a use of Scripture that is out of harmony with an understanding of God we have derived precisely from Scripture, a God who has revealed himself in a spirit of love which seeks the lost. Long ago St. Paul argued that Christians were under neither the letter nor the law of Scripture but under its spirit. We believe that our insistence upon the spirit of sacrificial love is fully in harmony with the spirit of Scripture and that we must permit that spirit to guide us more fully in the future than we have in the past.

Secular Studies Reviewed

The Commission found a similar diversity of opinion about homosexuality in the analyses and data it examined from medical and social scientists. We found no agreement as to the causes of homosexuality. Some psychiatric opinions questioned whether the phenomenon could be adequately understood if thought of as "caused" at all. As we have indicated, to these students of the subject, the emergence of homosexuality was regarded as one of life's insoluble mysteries. Depending on the presupposition of the scientist involved, homosexuality can be characterized as an emotional illness, criminal activity, an alternate life style or socially conditioned behavior. Such a disparity of analysis produces an equally disparate variety of responses: therapy, rehabilitation, punishment, acceptance.

The earliest studies of homosexuality were undertaken by medical and psychiatric authorities who drew their conclusion, for the most part, from homosexuals who had come in conflict with the law or were troubled enough to seek therapy. Hence these authorities tended to regard homosexuality as a form of emotional illness or, at the least, of arrested emotional development, and urged the individual to seek help in achieving a more normal—i.e., more heterosexual—development. Unfortunately, not all such authorities agree as to either the causes or the nature of the illness, many contending that it could not be cured in a majority of instances. More recently, psychologists and sociologists have begun studying homophile communities. Some studies seem to draw on homosexuals who have managed to come to grips with their condition and hence found it was quite natural. These scholars are less likely to diagnose homosexuals as ill. They attribute many of the problems of homosexuals to the fact that they are victims of prejudice and repression. For the most part they would agree with homosexuals who feel little reason for changing their sexual orientation to a heterosexual one.

Those who feel that homosexuality presents a grave threat to society or that it would be highly attractive to many people were it not fenced about by heavy sanctions are scarcely supported by the statistics the Commission found. To us such figures indicate society could afford a great deal more tolerance and openness on the subject. For example, in the population Kinsey studied, 4 percent of the men and 2 to 3 percent of the women actually developed patterns of exclusive homosexuality, though 37 percent of the men above the age of puberty and 13 percent of the women admitted to having at least one homosexual experience.

Perhaps the most helpful and realistic device to measure the incidence of homosexuality which the Commission found was a scale developed by Pomeroy reprinted in the volume *The Same Sex* which places the sexual orientation of most persons somewhere on a continuum leading from exclusive homosexual orientation to exclusive heterosexual orientation. (Cf. Weltge, *The Same Sex*, pp. 7–9). None of the studies the Commission examined disclose that homosexuality is concentrated in any particular age group, profession, or class or that there is such a thing as a consistent pattern of homosexual life style. Our studies challenge the popular opinion that there are mannerisms which make it easy to identify the homosexual. They declare that homosexuals have been found in all societies of which we have any knowledge. In accepting societies the phenomenon of homosexuality tends to present few problems.

The Homosexual's Social Lot

Historical studies disclose that persecution and discrimination have been the homosexual's lot in Western society and that the Church bears a heavy share of responsibility for this state of affairs. While the situation seems to be improving in modern society as an increasing number of denominations issue statements renouncing some of their past practices and attitudes which have singled the homosexual out for punitive measures, the most superficial study of the situation of the homosexual today indicates that much remains to be done. Three areas suggest themselves.

First, few homosexuals are entirely free from the danger of losing their employment if their sexual orientation becomes known, especially if that employment is teaching or the ministry. The assumption seems to be that homosexuals are more prone than heterosexuals to act out anti-social sexual impulses and that they are particularly likely to menace the young. Thus, disclosure or discovery of homosexuality is automatic grounds for dismissal, as indicated in a study made by the Executive Council of the Episcopal Church in 1970. To our knowledge such is still the case.

Second, most state governments in this country still attach heavy criminal sanctions to homosexual behavior. Very recently this situation has begun to show a slight change, but in forty-four states the law provides penitentiary terms ranging from twenty years to life imprisonment. Such laws, even when not enforced, are wrong in themselves for they subject homosexuals to police harassment and private blackmail. The Commission on the Reform of Federal Criminal Legislation in its final recommendation to Congress has urged the exclusion of criminal sanctions on any private sexual behavior between consenting adults. Most modern criminal law studies have done likewise. There are proposals currently pending in the Michigan Legislature removing most of the criminal sanctions against homosexual practices. Unfortunately, most of the discrimination in laws and legal practices can be traced directly to the attitudes of the ecclesiastical community.

Third, homophile groups which have developed in recent years to offer homosexuals the acceptance and companionship they have been denied elsewhere and to champion their legal rights have often found difficulty in securing places to meet, especially when they have approached church bodies. In general, members of these groups report that the doors of helping institutions are closed to them unless they admit to being emotionally ill and in need of therapy. Members of the Commission have reached a closer understanding of the deep needs of homosexual persons for love, affection and good will and believe they ought to be given support on the basis of their loneliness as persons rather than their willingness to submit to therapy.

As a Commission we believe the Church is that agency in history called upon to bear witness to the all embracing love of God. We have no evidence that this love does not include homosexuals. The time has come to call upon the Episcopal Church in particular to lay aside its past discriminatory practices and negative attitudes toward persons whose sexual orientation is toward members of their own sex. After long deliberation the Commission offers the following four recommendations as the minimum price of giving substance to that mission to which the Church is committed. For many this will be far from easy. "Love is indeed a harsh and dreadful thing to ask of each of us, but it is the only answer" (Dorothy Day).

1. The Church should take steps to create an atmosphere of openness and understanding about human sexuality and particularly about homosexuality. Programs to assist in this process should be

encouraged at all levels: national, diocesan, convocational, and parochial. Such programs should be at the disposal of institutions of learning and in particular our seminaries and church-related schools.

2. All ministries and professions should be open to otherwise qualified people whatever their sexual orientation. The use that any person makes of sexuality should be open to a reasonable evaluation by individuals competent to judge the relevance of such use to the exercise of the ministry or other profession in question. An oppressive or destructive use of sexuality within personal relationships, whatever the sexual preference or orientation, should give reason to doubt the candidate's fitness for office.

3. All aspects of the Church's life—education, liturgy, pastoral care, fellowship—should be available to all persons, and not contingent upon those persons' guaranteed heterosexuality. Gatherings for homosexuals on church property should be accepted to the extent that they serve the same purpose as other social gatherings—enabling people to meet in an atmosphere of love and acceptance.

4. The Church's concern for individuals and a just social order should lead it to speak publicly for repeal of all laws which make criminal offenses of private, voluntary sex acts between mature persons. The Church ought also to oppose police harassment of homosexuals and investigatory practices which sometimes verge upon entrapment. Likewise the Church should speak publicly on behalf of homosexual persons in the area of civil rights legislation. There should be no discrimination against any person in housing, employment, business services, or public accommodations on the grounds of sexual orientation.

Towards a Christian View of Sex

ed., Alastair Heron
(London, Friends Service Home Committee, 1963)

The task of taking a fresh look at homosexuality is not one which is undertaken with alacrity. That is because homosexuality conjures up more passion and prejudice than possibly any other subject except that of color. The two attitudes have much in common; it is the fear and ignorance behind them that give them their venom.

The word "homosexuality" does not denote a course of conduct, but a state of affairs, the state of affairs of loving one's own, not the opposite sex; it is a state of affairs in nature. One should no more deplore homosexuality than left-handedness. (One can condemn or prohibit acts of course; that is another matter. But one cannot condemn or prohibit homosexuality, as such.)

Secondly, the label of homosexuality is misleading. People are not either homosexual or heterosexual. Most people are predominantly one or the other; most in fact are predominantly heterosexual; many are predominantly homosexual; many are attracted to both sexes fairly equally and may be pushed one way or the other by circumstances, convenience, and social pressure. Before we assume that homosexuality is bad and heterosexuality is good, we should recognize that homosexuals are no more necessarily promiscuous than heterosexuals are necessarily chaste. They may be similar people (or even, it will be realized, the same person) and have similar moral values. But of course, where a heterosexual finds blessing in marriage, a homosexual cannot; and many of the pressures designed to hold lovers of the opposite sex together have the effect of tearing lovers of the same sex apart; it is hardly surprising then that most homosexual affairs (at least among men) are less durable than most heterosexual affairs.

Those who have read so far will recognize how difficult it has been for us to come to definite conclusions as to what people ought or ought not to do. But although we cannot produce a ready-made external morality to replace the conventional code, there are some things about which we can be definite. The first is that there must be a morality of some sort to govern sexual relationships. An experience so profound in its effect upon people and upon the community cannot be left wholly to private judgement. It will never be right to say to each other, "We'll do what we want, and what happens between us is nobody else's business." However private an act, it is never without its impact on society, and we must never behave as though society—which includes our other friends—did not exist. Secondly, the need to preserve marriage and family life has been in the forefront of our minds throughout our work. It is in marriage that sexual impulses have their greatest opportunity for joyful and creative expression, and where two people can enter into each other's lives and hearts most intimately. Here the greatest freedom can be experienced— the freedom conferred by an unreserved commitment to each other, by loving and fearless friendship, and by openness to the world. In marriage, two people thus committed can bring children into the world, provide them with the security of love and home and in this way fulfil their sexual nature. Finally, we accept the definition of sin given by an Anglican broadcaster as covering those actions that involve exploitation of the other person. This is a concept of wrongdoing that applies both to homosexual and heterosexual actions and actions within marriage as well as outside it. It condemns as fundamentally immoral every sexual action that is not, as far as humanly ascertainable, the result of a mutual decision. It condemns seduction and even persuasion, and every instance of coitus which, by reason of disparity of age or intelligence or emotional condition, cannot be a matter of mutual responsibility.

A Christian Attitude

There now comes the difficult matter of a Christian attitude to homosexual problems. On 16th September 1962, in his sermon in Canterbury Cathedral, the Bishop of Woolwich appealed for reform of "our utterly mediaeval treatment of homosexuals" and went on to say "as with capital punishment, one more determined push will see reform of something that is a peculiarly odious piece of English hypocrisy."

It will be clear from all that has gone before that we do not regard the standards of judgement relevant here as being different from those that apply to other sexual problems. Surely it is the nature and quality of a relationship that matters: one must not judge it by its outward appearance but by its inner worth. Homosexual affection can be as selfless as heterosexual affection, and therefore we cannot see that it is in some way morally worse.

Homosexual affection may of course be an emotion which some find aesthetically disgusting, but one cannot base Christian morality on a capacity for such disgust. Neither are we happy with the thought that all homosexual behavior is sinful: motive and circumstances degrade or ennoble any act, and we feel that to list sexual "sins" is to follow the letter rather than the spirit, to kill rather than to give life.

Further we see no reason why the physical nature of a sexual act should be the criterion by which the question whether or not it is moral should be decided. An act which expresses true affection between two individuals and gives pleasure to them both, does not seem to us to be sinful by reason alone of the fact that it is homosexual. The same criteria seems to us to apply whether a relationship is heterosexual or homosexual.

"I seek only to apply to my own life the rules which govern the lives of good men: freedom to choose a partner and, when that partner is found, to live with him discreetly and faithfully." (Peter Wildeblood, *Against the Law*, p. 175.) Is the homosexual to have that freedom, or must he, in Housman's words, "curse the God that made him for the color of his hair?"

It is now necessary to emphasize that we are not saying that all homosexual acts or relationships are to be encouraged. It is difficult shortly to suggest circumstances which may give them a quality of sin. But first of all any element of force or coercion, or abuse of some superior position, must obviously put an act beyond the pale and leave it to be condemned. The authors of this essay have been depressed quite as much by the utter abandon of many homosexuals, especially those who live in homosexual circles as such, as by the absurdity of the condemnation rained down upon the well-behaved. One must disapprove the promiscuity and the selfishness, the utter lack of any real affection, which is the stamp of so many adult relationships, heterosexual as well as homosexual. We see nothing in them often but thinly disguised lust, unredeemed by that real concern which has always been the essential Christian requirement in a human relationship.

But it is also obvious that the really promiscuous and degraded homosexual has not been helped by the total rejection he has had to face. Society has not said, "if you do that, that is all right, but as to the other, we cannot approve of that." It has said, "whatever you do must be wrong: indeed you are wrong."

Only if society is prepared to revise this judgement and to accept even degraded homosexuals as human beings, can they be helped to face the moral implications of their selfish relationships.

The Morality of Homosexual Acts

W. Norman Pittenger

Homosexual acts between persons who intend a genuine union in love are not sinful nor should the church consider them as such. But that short answer is obviously in need of development; and its implications and applications should be spelled out if we hope to deal faithfully and lovingly with homosexuals.

First of all, it is essential that we remember what the word "sin" means. The sinfulness of a sexual act is not primarily a matter of the person with whom it is enjoyed, provided that this person is himself fully and freely consenting to it. There are two things that determine the sinfulness of an act. First there is the inner spirit with which it is performed. The inner spirit means the decision to act in a fashion which will promote the satisfaction of the subjective aim of the person in God's love and with the widest commonality involved in the decision. Second, there is the intentionality which is present in the act and which in some fashion or other is overtly manifest. By this last phrase I am not suggesting a public announcement of intention, although in heterosexual relationships this is the ordinary rule and is the explanation of the marriage service's explicit requirement of such a statement "in the presence of the congregation." It also explains the publication of banns some time before the marriage takes place. I mean by the word "intentionality" that both parties to the act understand the nature of what they are doing, its real meaning, the purpose in all true love of some genuine degree of faithfulness or loyalty, and acceptance of its implications for both of them.

139

Since these two criteria are the determinants of the goodness of a sexual act or of its sinfulness, it is important to see how what we have said about the characteristics of human love applies in the case. The two persons must be committed one to the other, in such a fashion that neither is "using" the other. They must give and receive in tenderness, so that there is no element of coercion, undue pressure or imposed constraint which denies the freedom of either partner. They must intend some loyalty to each other, accepting what we might style a mutual belonging. They must purpose to entertain in respect to each other an expectation of fresh and new manifestations of personality, which they will not only "put up with" but which they will welcome and appreciate. Their relationship must involve a genuine union of lives in which each will preserve its own identity and its own freedom, but in which each will also contribute (through the mutuality which is theirs) to the creation and the strengthening of a bond that can keep them together. The consequence will be the fulfilment of each in relation to the other, bringing to more complete realization the subjective aim which is proper to each and to both.

We have admitted frankly that by such a set of tests every human being is a "sinner," since no human being—save, in Christian faith, Jesus Christ himself—has realized all that it means to be a man; and when I say "realized" I am speaking not of some mental apprehension but of a genuine making real through the whole effort of a life lived under the mastery of supreme love. Yet I have also insisted that what is most important at this point is not the achievement of status nor some specious appeal to the facts at the present moment in its imperfection and frustration as well in its failures and deficiencies because of human weakness and wrong decision. The important thing is that the person shall be on the way, moving towards the goal and open to possibilities which conspire to promote such actualization. He is not yet fulfilled; he is being fulfilled. Man, like the rest of the creation, is "in process" towards the greatest good; he has not yet arrived there.

Hence the question we must ask does not concern specific acts considered in isolation from their context. It concerns specific acts in relation to the total context, above all in the movement or direction of the human life involved. The agent is much more important than his particular and supposedly "discrete" (or separate and separable) acts. No acts are entirely discrete in this sense; no acts are ever separable nor separated; for human life is what it is precisely in its bringing of the past to bear on the present, in its contemporary relationships, and in its aim or purpose. Thus I should phrase the real question in this way: does this or that act, whatever it is, contribute in its own proper way to the movement of this person to the attainment of the subjective aim which establishes him as the man he is meant to be—always remembering, and I repeat this once again lest what I have just said be criticized as individualistic, that no person is "discrete" either. He is always and inevitably, precisely because he is a man, a participant in the human race and in its movement towards its intended goal of a society of love and in love. We may borrow a word from biology, and say that every human person and every act of every person is symbiotic in relation to every other human person and to every act of every other person. There is always the give-and-take, the sharing or participation which is characteristic of man's processive nature, just as that sociality is characteristic of the world-process as a whole in and under the divine Love that is God.

How do homosexual acts fit into that total pattern?

In so far as they contribute to the movement of the persons towards mutual fulfilment and fulfilment in mutuality, with all the accompanying characteristics of love, they are good acts. In so far as they do not contribute towards mutual fulfilment in love, they are bad acts. But that statement is too brief to be exact. For in every act, however "bad" it may be in the circumstances, there is some element of good. This is the point which St. Thomas Aquinas emphasized in his splendid Christian insistence that nothing, literally nothing, is *malum in se*—evil in and of itself. One of the grand strains in the Thomist moral theology, whatever else may be rigid and static about it, is its recognition of what I call contextuality; things are good or bad in the context in which they do or do not contribute to an end which in itself is judged to be good.

Mention of St. Thomas brings to our mind the concept of "natural moral law," which he did so much to develop. This "law of nature" is often supposed to rule out altogether the possibility of homosexual acts of a physical nature. But to speak in that way is to assume that we have knowledge of "normality," or "natural" behavior, revealed to us in the very fact of our being human. We have no such knowledge, beyond the normality and naturalness of becoming genuinely fulfilled men and women. As it stands, and in the light of our present knowledge about sexuality, a heterosexually-oriented person acts "naturally" when he acts heterosexually, while a homosexually-oriented person acts equally "naturally" when he acts in accordance with his basic, inbuilt homosexual desire and drive.

Any notion of divine law as somehow revealed to men in spite of their humanity, as if such a law cut across all human insight and experience, is a most tragic misunderstanding of the way God works in his world. And the later idea that there is some moral "law of nature" which in its specificity is known to men is equally an impossibility, however hallowed this idea may be in certain strains of historic Christian thought. As it happens, I am myself very sympathetic to the notion of "natural law" and can see its profound value. It *can* be the statement that man is "to avoid the evil and do the good," which is exactly how Aquinas defined its ultimate meaning. But then we must ask what is evil and what is good? When "natural" is brought down to details and is used to rule out mechanical or chemical contraception, to give a very relevant example, it has become nothing short of demonic. For in that case the "natural law" comes to mean a series of precise commandments which turn morality into a new variety of ancient legalism of the worst sort.

But if we speak, as Aquinas also does, of "love in our hearts," or of the Holy Spirit at work in men's minds as they think seriously, carefully and in a prayerful mood about moral questions, then we are on the way to a thoroughly Christian understanding of the matter. This kind of approach gives us freedom in our own day and for our own problems; but it also relates us to the deepest insight of past ages and to the accumulated wisdom of great Christian thinkers. That wisdom and insight is never to be treated as if it were the utterance of God from on high. Yet it will help us in our thinking provided we take it not literally but with utmost seriousness. We must listen to our fathers, but we need also to see that even the wisest of them was not infallible. We have our own decisions to make, in the light of the gospel of God as Love in action in the world; and it may be that we shall have to disagree with those ancient worthies in this or that, perhaps in many of their views.

One of the places where I think we must disagree is exactly in the matter of homosexuality. They did not know what we now know; nor can we blame them for not knowing, since they were men of their own time. Furthermore, the dependence which they felt upon Jewish ideas, as well as other aspects of inherited thought, prevented them from seeing some of the implications of the gospel to which they were committed. They cannot be blamed for that, either. Nor am I claiming that we in this day have come to know all the truth. We like them are the creatures of our times and of our circumstances. Yet some things we do know; and it would be false humility to pretend that we do not. One of the things we know is more of what homosexuality is about. Obviously the subject is by no means a matter of complete and precise knowledge; it is in many ways mysterious in respect to its genesis, its developmental aspects and its physiological-psychological context. But so also is heterosexuality. On the other hand, we know that the homosexual is like other men. His drives and desires are like theirs, although the sex of the person he can love is different. We know that if the homosexual is to fulfil himself in a sexual way through genital activity it can be only with a member of his own sex. He may try intercourse with a person of the other sex but the result is usually tragedy for both parties. The male homosexual is able to give himself, whole and entire, only to another man; the female homosexual, to another woman.

So much is generally conceded today. But now we come back once again to the question of homosexual acts, in distinction from the homosexual state or condition.

What are we to say? I have already indicated my own answer to this question. I cannot see that when two men or two women are committed to each other, wish to be loyal to each other, are hopeful about each other, in such mutuality that each gives and receives, acting with tenderness and with no force or pressure of one on the other, seeking a union which will bring their lives together as fully and completely as possible: I cannot see, if all this is true, why two such persons should be condemned for committing sin when they desire, as almost inevitably they will desire, to act on their love—and that means, of course, to engage in physical acts which for them will both express their love and deepen it.

Nothing that I have seen, in the dozen of books that I have read asserting the sinfulness of homosexual acts, has convinced me that they contain much more than special pleading, inherited or personal prejudice, outworn patterns of thought and inadequate or even erroneous factual data. They say that such sexual contacts are sinful, but their views seem to be nothing more than rationalizations of a sense of disgust or horror which many heterosexuals feel at the very thought of such physical acts. I know perfectly well that at this point some might try to hoist me by my own petard. If such discussions are only rationalizations, what then about my own discussion? I confess frankly that I do not feel the distaste or disgust or horror which others feel when they read or think about what these physical acts involve. But surely the point is, not whether any of this is just rationalization, but how good a rationalization it is. Dr Leonard Hodgson once said in a lecture that the question is whether our rationalizations, granted they exist, can stand up to the test of sound reasoning, common sense, knowledge of the relevant facts and vigorous critical attack. For my part, none of the books to which I refer nor the countless articles I have read seems able to face that kind of test.

Whether my own discussion can stand up to it I am not able to say. But at least I can claim that I have tried very hard to think my way through this whole question and that the conclusions which I have reached were not purchased save by "blood and sweat" and sometimes, I confess, "tears." I began with a quite different attitude; I have found myself driven to the attitude which this paper has tried to present.

There are one or two other matters about which something should be said. If promiscuity seems to be a denial of that love which is the point of all sexual union, including homosexual union, what about those relationships which are not in fact permanent but yet continue for some considerable time? Here I suggest that the question has to do with the "inner spirit" and intention to which I have called attention . . . (What) about the meaning of "fidelity" and "permanence" in homosexual relationships? Here I content myself only by pointing out that nobody can predict with absolute certainty whether any given couple will remain permanently in love; but if the decision in freedom is there, with some intention of permanence, it seems to me that the situation is not very much unlike that which is found in heterosexual marriage. If and when all Christian communions become realistic about marriage and approach the question of divorce with something other than sheer obtuseness, they may be able to see that heterosexual marriages can "die," as our Eastern Orthodox brethren say. When a marriage has died, despite every effort that has been made to keep it going, it is a shocking violation of human personality to pretend that it still exists. George Tyrrell once said, I believe, that "two cats tied together by the tail do not constitute Christian marriage." May it not be similar in a homosexual relationship? It has aimed at permanence; but the couple find themselves unable to achieve it. One of the jobs of a counsellor or priest ought to be to do everything in his power to keep the relationship going, in the hope that it will become permanent in fact as well as in intention. The homosexual pair are at a terrible disadvantage here. Society seems to be against them; they have many problems which the ordinary heterosexual couple never face; they cannot have children to bring them once again to a renewed awareness of the "togetherness" which will give those children a happy and secure home. But instead of using these obvious facts to destroy the relationship, I believe that those who are able should do all they can to assist in promoting its maintenance. If then, after all possible effort on the part of the two persons and of those who would help them, the attempt fails to be effective, they must separate. For if they do not separate, two lives will very likely be ruined. The same is true also, in my judgment, in respect to heterosexual unions, whatever ecclesiastical authority may say.

If what we have been saying about the basic meaning of human sexuality is well-grounded, it will follow that every human being must of necessity "employ" (if that is the right word for my meaning, which is "express himself through, use as an instrumental medium, and find enhancement of personality by means of his sexual nature") his sexuality in the fulfillment of his subjective aim or integrating purpose. This will be done in various ways, of course. There will be a very few who by what they may call "vocation" are able to refuse all overt physical expression of their sexual nature. The majority of human beings find the mode for sexual life in union with a member of the other sex. For the homosexual the only possible way for sexual activity is with a person of his own sex; for him the alternative is either complete celibacy or a distorting of his own experience and nature by attempting union with a person of the other sex—and in that case, as I have said, the likelihood is that both partners will be unhappy and the "end of the affair" will be tragedy for each of them.

Furthermore, even those who claim that they do not in any fashion "employ" their sexual nature are fooling themselves. If such persons do not healthily and openly acknowledge their sexuality and seek to express it in ways such as we have indicated, such as dedication to some cause or task or perhaps another human being to whose service they give themselves, they become warped and twisted in their inner lives. We all know the type known as "the spinster"—who can be of either sex, let it be remembered—people who by refusal to acknowledge sexuality and use it in externalizing activity have become embittered, hostile, perhaps even neurotic personalities. Suppressed sexuality is still sexuality; but it is hateful and terrible in its consequences.

Those who urge that all homosexuals should thus suppress their sexuality are asking that they should become incipient or actual neurotics. One has known instances where this has been most dreadfully true, in which a man who could love only another man has killed in himself, as he thought, all that drive of his affection. As a matter of fact he has not killed his sexual desire, however he may seem to live asexually; what he has done is to push it deep down inside him, where it festers and twists back on itself. This tragic victim of social pressures then becomes sour and warped in his human relationships, seeing evil sex in everything around him and losing the capacity to "live in love and charity with his neighbours." In such a case, I make bold to say, even promiscuity would have been better; although (as I have made clear) I am not for a moment commending easy and consistent promiscuity, among homosexuals or for anybody else. But I recall a woman whom once I knew, so nasty in her attitudes and so hostile in her responses that a friend of mine said of her, 'What *she* needs is sex!' He had a point.

The title of a famous story by Tolstoy is "Where Love is, there God is." Love can show itself in strange and unexpected places. I am ready to say that in homosexual love of the kind I have been discussing, God is present. He is present in the loving relationship and present also in the acts which express and cement that love. I know quite well that the very idea that this is the case will appear shocking to many of my friends and to the majority of clergymen. But I am convinved that what I have said is true because I have seen it to be true. Such human love where God is hiddenly present always needs for its best realization the further "infusion" of the divine love which we who are Christians believe that Christian fellowship, sacramental worship and the reception of the sacramental elements can provide. The fellowship and the sacraments are not ours, but the Lord's. Who are we, to "fence" that table from any needy and hungry child of God? How can we, who are ready to confess ourselves ignorant and prejudiced and misguided men, refuse that gracious gift of Love to any man or woman who honestly comes asking for it?

V

Homosexual Acts are Natural and Good

Michael F. Valente
Neale Secor
Robert Wood

A New Direction

Michael F. Valente

In the present situation, one has a choice. If one can abstract from the ideological fight in progress and escape embroilment in the theological controversy over orthodoxy and authority and institutionalism, then the choice is to heed the pope and the traditionalist interpretation of sexual ethics, or to opt for the revisionist tack on contraception and with it arrive at the destruction of the natural law doctrine and the recognition of the need to rethink the whole of sexual ethics.

The currently prevailing sense of option in sexual matters is based principally upon man's psychic achievement of a new world view within the context of which theologians have moved towards an acceptance of nonprocreative intercourse as ethical. This has been the work of the revisionists.

The question is one of ethics: In terms of man's fulfilment of his destiny, is human sexuality separable from procreation? If so, does the separation imply separation in marriage, from heterosexuality, or from deep interpersonal relationship? Or are human sexuality and procreation indissolubly linked? Is procreation not merely a good but an absolute good? Is the meaning and purpose of human life simply to exist? Is human existence under any circumstances preferable to never having existed at all? Does the biological differentiation between the respective procreative functions of male and female dictate an inviolable norm for nonprocreative sexual relationships? Must every sexual relationship have a profound interpersonal dimension to it in order to be ethical?

The issue of contraception is the logical starting point because it is against the sinfulness of contraception—as opposed to other acts such as fornication, masturbation, homosexuality, or bestiality—that the contemporary protest against the Church's sexual ethic was initiated.

The 1951 acceptance by Pius XII of the rhythm method of birth control implied that intercourse and procreation were not indissolubly bound together. Science had discovered that nature did not always so link them; man by his inventive ingenuity could capitalize on the discovery. Implicit in the pope's statement was a rejection of the traditional idea that mankind's procreation was an absolute duty of those who enjoyed marital intercourse, and that any violation of that duty by means of intervention in the biological was a direct offense against God because it contravened the very order of nature. On the contrary, nature can be made subject to reason. Reason therefore liberates man from a so-called "natural law," when that law is unreasonable.

Such a revisionist reinterpretation of the significance of the Church's teaching is not fanciful. It represents an effort of reason, taking its impetus from the pope's own lead, to reflect on what man believes. The power of such a reinterpretation lies precisely in the very notion of revision or reformation which it suggests. Removed from the frozen state of divinely absolutized "natural law" biology, the subject is always open to new revision by means of reasoned human decision.

The separation of human sexuality in itself from human sexuality as procreative leaves open the possibility that where it is nonprocreative—whether in circumstances that are marital or nonmarital, heterosexual or nonheterosexual, inseminative or not—it does not have to be surrounded by the kinds of restrictions hitherto placed on it. To put it in a different way, if sexual activity can be guaranteed nonprocreative, it is no longer hemmed in by the rules and guidelines previously established out of reverence for the life of the potential child.

The guidelines for nonprocreative sexual activity are . . . very definite, and they are concerned with the preservation of the integrity of the human personality. To engage in sexual activity that would be destructive of one's own or another's personality is ethically wrong and dangerous. It may be worth noting at this point, that the more seriously dangerous it is, the more it is usually associated with and stems from psychological illness. But the mentally ill are hardly models for responsibility in terms of sin.

One must abandon the traditional prohibition of nonprocreative forms of sexual indulgence, at least insofar as that prohibition is based upon the idea that sexual acts must be ordered to procreation. If nonprocreative activity is accepted as licit in marriage, then one is necessarily left with the obligation to reconsider all such forms, both inside and outside of marriage.

It may be necessary for one individual, on account of his personal circumstances—either extrinsic or intrinsic—to adjust to a sexual mode of existence quite different from that of others. Shepherds have customarily sought sexual release with their sheep. Prisoners have traditionally resorted to homosexuality for the same reasons. These circumstances are extrinsic to be sure, but there might be intrinsic circumstances of an inseparable kind which might demand similar adjustment.

In the arena of fundamental sexual orientation, individuals most often choose as a sexual object that which their sexual impulse seeks. Yet the biological and psychological makeup of some persons is such that homosexuality is their mode of sexual relationship and response. The prohibition against homosexuality stemmed from the traditional belief that sex was necessarily and intrinsically procreation-oriented. Persons suffering from this socially unaccepted difficulty should be made to realize that their relationships can be good, especially if love is present. They should be encouraged to seek relationships that are meaningful and constructive, and that can contribute to the development of their personality as loving.

It must not be forgotten that the homosexual is at a distinct disadvantage in a society which condemns and persecutes him. He is deprived of certain social and sexual freedoms granted to his heterosexual equals and is burdened with fears and guilt which his heterosexual peers are not forced to share. It is perhaps because of these fears and guilt feelings that homosexuals allow themselves to be so deprived of their human rights—for example, the right to show affection in public.

One of the cruelest aspects of a majority's attempts to lord it over any minority is not merely the inequity involved in the situation, but the way in which the majority evokes the penalty of ostracism. An individual gets his psychic vitality, his desire to be, from his identification with his group, the community of man. Hence to relegate him to minority is, in effect, to exclude him from the group. No punishment on earth is crueler that this, for to ostracize him is to doom him to ultimate psychic disintegration. To ostracize him because he is black, because he is a homosexual, because he is a Jew, because he is anything else—especially when what he is cannot be remedied—is to chart that person's doom.

Society has tended to encourage the repression of homosexuality (although there seems to be some ambivalence in the way it treats the male homosexual as opposed to the female homosexual). This is unfortunate. Suppression (a conscious act as distinguished from repression which is at least partly subconscious) makes much more sense, since it allows the individual to be a fully human person, one who can savor, appreciate, and enjoy tender feelings for another person of the same sex.

Repression is also a consequence and reinforcement of the notion of the intrinsic evil of homosexuality. It tends to close off a part of the personality and thereby to damage it. It is an effect of closed-mindedness, another example of society's enforcement of conformity at the terrible price of maimed and maladjusted personalities, rendered so by the stifling of individuality and free expression. It is an effect following upon feelings of guilt engendered by fear of authority. The role-playing which religion and society require of the homosexual is no different from the role-playing they require of all who would be truly free. The individual is compelled to repress his true individual identity and to behave according to socially and religiously sanctioned patterns fashioned by consensus. Thus conformity causes him to rip himself apart in order to lead two lives, as it were.

For those who prefer to see homosexuality as a psychological illness, the rate of recovery is so slight as to call seriously into question the legitimacy of referring at all to an apparent cure. This seems particularly true if "cure" is taken to mean the adoption or attainment of a psychological attitude unaffected and uninfluenced by the individual's prior homosexual actions. To speak of achieving a state of growth and development in which the individual attains a state of psychological integration untouched by his previous experience is to describe the unreal.

What is really of significant interest is whether or not an adult who has been an overt homosexual can, through any means, attain to a greater or lesser degree a successful adjustment to the predominantly heterosexual society in which he lives and even, in some cases at least, to a heterosexual life-style of his own. What is at issue, then, is individual comfort in life. Such comfort is often precluded however, by the guilt, stemming from their sexual needs, which oppresses individuals. That guilt may be religious, or it may be neurotic. Many are victims of a societal neurosis which has as its symptom guilt brought on by fear of social rejection.

Yet the inadequate description of individuals as heterosexual, homosexual, or bisexual in their orientation provides us with a more important insight. Some persons are not consciously aware of the extent of their sexual adaptability; but they know it subconsciously and fear anything that threatens to burst their sociosexual balloon because they are afraid of possibilities of their own subconsciously imagined behavior. If society were truly tolerant, there would be no pressure of this sort, and the effect might be a realization that the division of persons into heterosexuals, homosexuals, and bisexuals is artificial and arbitrary. The division, in fact, is the result of a former world view that saw the preferences of the apparent majority as the norm for what it means to be human. It saw human beings as being limited to what they were "given," as it were. It could thus see deviations as illnesses, perversions, and evils. A new world view, however, makes it clear that each individual is uniquely capable of turning every interpersonal encounter into something new, something creative. We are not forced to limit our encounters to recapitulation either of our own past encounters or of the patterns of the majority. We can instead vivify each encounter with creativity. And that creativity can extend to the use we make of our sexual potential as well. For we are not bound to be classified as creatures limited to a given set of sexual habits hemming us in and assigning us to one sexual category or another, some "acceptable" and some "deviant."

Now is the appropriate time for the adoption of new attitudes toward acts prohibited in the past, such as contraception, fornication, masturbation, homosexuality, and bestiality. A genuine innovation in sexual ethics is possible. But such an innovation implies a new creation. And the creation of a new sexual ethic can only follow upon the existence of a new attitude. That new attitude does exist. It is part of a new world view, itself the effect of man's achievement of a new consciousness. And because that new consciousness transcends the old, and that new world view transcends the old, so too that new creation of a sexual ethic transcends the old.

What is new, therefore, is an attitude which of necessity rejects the past approach to sexual ethics, with its blanket prohibition of acts as intrinsically evil and always gravely serious if they do not conform to a specific concept of "nature."

It may be objected that besides tradition there is a scriptural basis for prohibiting acts such as fornication, homosexuality, masturbation, bestiality, contraceptive intercourse, and the like. Yet all would agree that Christian morality is almost entirely the morality of the Old Testament, especially as it concerns Christian attitudes toward sexuality. And advances in scriptural scholarship make it clear that moral pronouncements found in Scripture are simply the expressions of the author's convictions as to how everyday problems of living must be resolved in accordance with the thrust of the Judaic-Christian ethical message. They cannot be assigned in themselves—as isolated pronouncements—the absolute value of inerrancy. This value is attributable only to the total scriptural narration of the crucial necessity of faith as man's response to God's revelation, on the basis of which he is alone saved from all that threatens him with loss of meaning and intelligibility. In short, values being protected at a particular period may lose their validity in another time and place.

The attempt to codify an intrinsic objective morality of sexual acts is another example of the self-righteousness which stands as the very antithesis of true Christian morality. Christ's standard of ethical righteousness and love teaches what men—especially when they are in the majority—find most difficult: tolerance. Indeed, where sexuality is concerned—as in so many areas of human life—tolerance and vision are perhaps at once the most uniquely Christian, the most self-fulfilling, and the most important aids to authentic spiritual discovery.

A Brief for a New Homosexual Ethic

Neale Secor

This paper is a critique of the liberal Protestant ethic which concludes that Christians should "accept" the homosexual as another sinner. It is an argument against too easily agreeing with that view. In the following pages "homosexuality" is considered to be that historical, cultural phenomenon of human beings' proclivity toward and desire for union with the same sex.

The modern Christian of liberal persuasion no longer considers homosexuality an unspeakable taboo. He is speaking out. He condemns irrational societal prejudice. He worries about unfair employment practices. He wrestles with intolerably hostile military and civil service regulations. He fights for statute reform. He establishes counseling centers. He attends conferences on homosexuality. He even periodically enters into face-to-face dialogue with persons of admitted homosexual proclivity.

The modern moralist has been liberated from the suffocating overlay of what Wainwright Churchill calls our "erotophobic" and "homeophobic" culture. The liberated moralist can now look more realistically into socially deviate sexual behavior patterns that according to Marcuse symbolize an "instinctual freedom in a world of repression." What

Christian interested in the future of situational-relational ethics can help but breathe a sigh of ecclesiastical relief—at last, liberation from twenty-five long centuries of a Levitical world view!

The chapters in the present volume give vigorous and thoughtful evidence of the waning influence of the long era of the old moralistic school which, although different in many ways, saw in homosexuality nothing but a demonic, carnal threat to the very existence of man under the will of God. Supposedly we are no longer irrevocably bound to biblical literalism. D. S. Bailey has lead us out of Sodom by discrediting the alleged homosexual implications of that myth. Other interpreters have revealed the priestly codes in their culture-bound irrelevance for today's world and have reinvestigated Paul's sexual attitudes. The poison of biblical homosexual death penalties has been diluted.

Free at last. Free at last!

Free, however, to what? For what?

Free to join the venerable Helmut Thielicke (*The Ethics of Sex*) and the thoughtful Kimball Jones (*A Christian Understanding of the Homosexual*) so exemplary of the new ethical spirit, in accepting the homosexual into the Christian community for what they claim he is: not an idolater, nor a criminal, nor a leperous outcast; but a genuine product of the "fall," the result of original sin. Free to recognize and accept the awful "burden" of the "constitutional" homosexual's "irreversible situation." Free to help carry this "unnatural expression of human sexuality." Free to help the "absolute invert" realize his "optimal ethical possibilities." Free to understand this "pathology," which like all such pathologies "falls on the same level with abnormal personality structure." Free to help the homosexual man who, after all, is "not responsible for being what he is." Free to feel sorry for, accept, and help this "unnatural" phenomenon of human personality.

It is probably a principle of progress that liberation movements must have their pitfalls and newfound freedoms their limitations. So the ethical response that moves from thoughtless repression toward enlightened tolerance is no exception. The pitfalls and limitations reflect no discredit on the new freedom or its liberators. But they warrant caution to those who too quickly would buy in the marketplace of ethical freedom only to find that they have purchased but half a loaf. The pitfall of the recent ethical liberation as it regards homosexuality is revealed in the failure to fully come to terms with the implications of relying primarily upon the Genesis creation myths to define the essential fundamentals of what it means to be "human" in God's image. The limitation upon the ethicist's newfound freedom is his too easy reliance upon questionable psychological data in order to support his definition of sexual humanity.

The modern moralist's thesis of accepting the homosexual appears to be premised upon two basic, if sometimes unelucidated, assumptions. The first is the theological assumption that the homosexual condition is only expressive of the *post-lapsum* deviations from God's essential will. In this instance, it is postulated as a deviation from the God-willed, natural human state of pure maleness or pure femaleness as expressed in Genesis and so is not the subject of particular condemnation. Surely the homosexual is "queer," runs this assumption—but are we not all in some sense deviates from God's pure will and do not all of us therefore participate in the queerness of sin after the fall? The second assumption is the psychological one that the homosexual is mentally ill or "sick"—irreversibly sick like one physically riddled with terminal cancer—and should therefore be encouraged to come to grips with both the liabilities and potentialties of his pathology, but not be ostracized.

Fair enough—certainly better than past ecclesiastical judgments! But what if the assumptions are faulty? Where does that leave the new ethical desire for tolerant acceptance of the homosexual?

I contend that these assumptions are indeed faulty; that the ethical thesis for acceptance of the homosexual as a "sick sinner like the rest of us sick sinners" is, accordingly, questionable; and that we therefore either have to revert to the past—and in some ways more historically honest—posture of moral condemnation, or somehow find new bases for future acceptance.

The elements of the theological problem are clear, if their delineation elusive. The key is some determinator of the divine will. A requirement of Christian ethics (the "science of human conduct as it is determined by divine conduct"—Brunner) is that human moral decisions should reflect God's will. Catholic moralism—both Roman and Anglican—historically has relied most heavily upon the authoritative tradition of the church as it attempted to define and ascertain the will of God. A rather intricate scheme of values has been developed in the creation of a moral theology. Protestantism, in its search for a Christian ethic, has more often placed reliance upon the biblical word and upon personal faith experience; it has no such worked-out system of moral values for easy reference.

The words of the Bible and the numerical "normalcy" of heterosexuality in the history of human experience provided classical Protestantism with a conception of sexual polarity to be deemed essential to the definition of "human" personality. (By a somewhat different route Catholic moral theology reaches a similar conclusion—e.g., Bailey.) Although teachers of Protestant ethics may disagree regarding the treatment of the homosexual, there is no disagreement about his theological nature as a human being. Both the renowned Karl Barth, who had little tolerance for homosexuality, and the able Helmut Thielicke, who has counseled acceptance of the homosexual condition, have a common understanding of God's will of creation as found in the book of Genesis.

So basic is this common understanding of creation in discovering an ethic for human sexuality that I am persuaded it must be dealt with as a condition precedent for reaching an ethic of homosexuality. The temptation of recent moral investigation has been to move on to interpretations of Levitical statutes and of Pauline statements on sexual relations (especially 1 Corinthians 5 and Romans 1), and to overlook the basic assumption upon which such later interpretations rest. It does not suffice to demythologize and liberalize later biblical words without first coming to terms with the biblical assumptions upon which the later words depend—thus, the crucial importance of the Genesis myths of creation.

"Male" he created them. "Female" he created them. And in his own image! Male *and* (a separate) female. Traditional Christian ethics has tended to interpret the conjunctive "and" as a disjunctive "or," so that sexual differentiation has become part of the essential definition of man.

So strong has been this conviction of polarity that it has not only been deemed theologically normative for human relationship (a thou to a thou), but it has also assumed metaphysical significance in the very constitution of "man." To be human becomes, by hypothesis, to be purely male or purely female. Only in monogamous marriage desirous of reproduction is this essential duality preserved in proper balance.

In contrast to this understanding, however, one might recall that also in biblical mythology Adam ("man") was created by God prior to Eve's separation from Adam; one might therefore postulate that the "essential" quality of the God-desired image is a mixture, or combination, of both sexes rather than a strict sexual duality. One might urge that, although the Genesis stories point to an *existential* biological separation of sexual relational *function*, the *essential* mythological separation was of the androgynous "male-female" Adam from God, and not Eve from Adam.

One might continue this corrective process by delving into the rather late times when the Genesis traditions were formed for a greater appreciation of the then cultural needs of the monogamous agrarian family unit, the real fear of Canaanite and other apostate idolatrous sexual-religious practices, the primitive reverence for the semen, and the biological misunderstandings regarding the conception and birth processes. Such investigation might reveal a perspective into which to place the Genesis traditions.

One might even suggest to the liberal ethical interpreter that to equate functional sex differences with essential being is to resort to a literalist biblical anthropology which not only is inappropriate and perhaps completely meaningless in modern discussion, but also is embarrassingly inapposite to his otherwise nonliteralistic ethical methodology.

These suggested possibilities of biblical interpretation must be left to those more interested and skilled in pure hermeneutics.

It well may be revealed by further work by those scholars that Genesis does indeed presume an essential, God-willed strict polarity between male and female, and not just a God-willed functional, relational differentiation. It even may be that a literal interpretation of the Genesis myth will be considered primary for a firm foundation for ethics. It must suffice to say that these are issues of biblical interpretation not fully considered by otherwise thoughtful explorers into the ethical content of homosexuality, even though they are very much considered by the very same explorers when they treat the ethics of heterosexuality! At this point, conclusions simply have been drawn too hastily from predetermined biblical assumptions.

Should an understanding of the Genesis myth requiring an essential male "or" female polarity be agreed upon, ethical students in the days of study ahead must still face the next ethical issue; whether the failure of persons to rejoin as man and woman in monogamous marriage (henosis) for the presumed purpose of propagation is a sin which is susceptible to easy Christian "acceptance."

The resolution of this issue is of concern to more persons than just those with homosexual preferences. It is of concern to the bachelor, the unmarried woman, the divorced person, the separated couple, the widow, the widower, and to those young people who in increasing numbers are "living together" or who after a sanctified marriage purposely decide to remain childless. The resolution of this issue likewise has consequences for the behavior patterns of masturbation, sexual abstinence, premarital relationships, extramarital relationships, and nonmarital relationships. Are all of these relationships and all of these sexual practices—along with a gender identification and behavior which prefers the same sex—results of the fall? Are only monogamous child-filled relationships expressive of God's essential divine will for man in relationship? And what might be the status of a thesis like Norman Pittenger's that to be human *means* to be a "lover" and not merely a heterosexual acting-out identifiable object?

Having considered the first leg of Protestant authority, the biblical word, what must we say of the second, the authority of human faith experiences? This authority of personal, cultural experience, as it informs an understanding of homosexual relationships and practices, is instructive in understanding the other nonhenotic practices and relationships as well.

Other writers in this book have set forth in some detail historical, cultural, biological, and anthropological data regarding homosexuality. Within the detail two parallel themes of experiential expression are relevant for our discussion here: (1) Throughout history, the Western church (and in consequence the legal and social codes derived therefrom) has said a loud "No" to homosexuality. (2) Throughout primitive and recorded history, animal life (including human) and certain entire cultures have said either a loud "Yes" or at least an audible "Maybe" to homosexuality.

That many leaders of history, Christian and non-Christian, past and present, have been, or are, homosexually inclined and active hardly validates homosexuality as an ethical possibility. But neither do ecclesiastical injunctions or moral laws eliminate actual homosexual proclivity and behavior. The facts of the historical matter are that homosexuality is a human social phenomenon, has always been so, and has always received cultural recognition, whether pejoratively or positively. The Western church has condemned, and the Western state has outlawed; but the cultural phenomenon itself has continued into the present quite unabated.

One is struck not so much with the efforts to eradicate this human propensity as with its dogged capacity to persist and even flourish in the face of such efforts. This awareness is not at all dissimilar to the repeated confessions of modern-day churchmen about how surprised they are at the "normalcy" of the homosexually inclined persons they have come to know as persons rather than as clinical entities or pastoral charges.

I am not at all sure how much weight should be given this experiential, historical evidence as over against (if that finally be the conclusion) a contrary biblical imperative of sexual polarity in the Genesis myth. I am convinced, however, that it must be accorded some weight as ethical authority in attempting to elicit and comprehend what it means to be human in the divine image and what God's will is for modern man. We simply cannot ignore what the social scientists, cultural historians, anthropologists, and modern-day investigators have been attempting to tell us about homosexuality. At least we cannot ignore this data unless we conclude, a priori, that such human experience and investigation are outside the realm of the divine will. And this I am hesitant to do.

In the realm of "social" or "community" ethics, such data rather than being ignored usually is accorded a high priority as expressive of God's continuing action in history. Within the realm of "personal" ethics, however, there appears to have been a much greater difficulty in giving credence to any authority outside of biblical interpretation, or (as will be discussed below) psychiatric studies.

At this point in the ethical investigation of homosexuality, one cannot state with any assurance whether or not the authority of human historical experience will affront the authority of biblical interpretation. More work, much more work and thinking, needs to be done.

Until it is done, however, the moralist who would accept the homosexual on the theological assumption that he is just another *post-lapsum* sinner might best pull up his ethical reigns a bit. It might well be that the homosexual, as traditionally has been held in Protestant ethics, is not just "another" sinner, but rather an idolater of the first order who is thwarting the very divine purpose of essential humanity as pure male or pure female joined together in monogamous reproductivity. On the other hand, that might not be the essential quality of "man" as God's likeness at all; or even if it is, it might be understood differently in the light of God-given historical experiences of homosexual patterns and practices.

The one area of human experience to which the "acceptance" ethicist has given close attention is psychology, or at least psychiatry. In fact a strong assumption underlying the plea that Christians "accept" the homosexual is that he is mentally ill. One suspects that in his efforts to come to terms with nonheterosexually oriented persons, the moralist of liberal persuasion has become a bit enamored with psychiatry and has perhaps given that modern field of human understanding an undeservedly high-priestly place in his conclusions.

This chapter is not the place for a full discussion of the various emotional theories regarding homosexuality or of the value systems of the professional psychiatrists which undergird those theories. This can be left to the reader's evaluation of such as Thomas Szasz. It is the place, however, to remind ourselves, as Rollo May has repeatedly urged, that psychiatrists and therapists do have values, that they are socially "conservative" values, and that such values previously are informed and molded by traditional cultural and ethical values. Psychiatric diagnoses and prognoses of homosexually oriented patients are not devoid of a priori ethical values. To the contrary, those values define the very meaning of mental "health" or mental "disease," and usually do so in a highly protected, isolated doctor-patient relationship.

The conclusions of a Dr. Bieber (or Hadden, or Ellis, or Erikson, or Berg, or Allen, or the many others) that the homosexual is mentally "ill" must be put into the perspective of Bieber's own admission that "all psychoanalytic theories assume that adult homosexuality is pathological," even though the various theories differ because they "assign differing weights to constitutional and experiential determinants." Freud, of course, made similar assumptions although his psychic phenomenology allowed him to call homosexuality a "symptom" of neurosis rather than the neurosis itself. Irrespective of such nice distinctions, the homosexual remained for Freud pathologically "arrested" or "fixated" at some oral period a long way off from healthy maturation.

Certainly the psychiatric diagnoses of homosexuality must be, by hypothesis, pathologically determined. The question for the psychiatrist is not whether a person of homosexual proclivity is mentally sick. He assumes that. His question, rather, is What kind of mental disease is it, and can it be cured?

For the Christian ethicist to rely, therefore, upon the psychiatrist's "findings" that a homosexual is mentally ill or in a "constitutional," "irreversible" pathological state, and therefore to conclude that the homosexual should be "accepted" as such is questionable. What the ethicist is doing in such reliance is basing his assumptions upon the psychiatrist's assumptions, when the psychiatrist originally received his assumptions (values) from the very ecclesiastical ethical predecessors from whom the ethicist feels he is liberally departing. This not only is tautologist reasoning and circuitous investigation; it also participates in a kind of understanding which simply is not helpful to ethical inquiry.

A particular psychiatric theory of homosexual pathology or a particular therapist's etiological findings regarding a particular disturbed person of homosexual orientation hopefully will continue to be helpful to the pastoral counselor. This, however, is not the issue of ethical theory and formulation. The moral issue is with the nature of homosexuality, so that the ethical promulgator might better determine whether or not such nature and the personal decisions made therefrom accord with or deviate from what he perceives to be God's will for men in relationships.

In helping to identify the ethical nature of personhood in general, or the nature of homosexual personhood in particular, psychiatric theory continues basically to be enculturated ethical theory in different dress using different labels. Alleged theoretical differences that have little or no logical distinction when placed under the microscope of cultural data investigation are not limited to ethics and psychiatry. Regarding homosexuality, the same process has occurred between Christian ethics and the law. One is hard put to find real distinction between the "sin" of homosexual behavior and the "crime" of homosexual behavior. The labels are different and the sanctions are different, but the nature of both the ethical sin and legal crime of homosexuality are as similar as its alleged mental "illness." Labels do not make fundamental distinctions in value hypotheses and assumptions.

No profession or field of human investigation is of course without its values and prior unconscious assumptions. Sociology, cultural anthropology, and psychology must be included with law and psychiatry. There is a difference, however. The difference is that psychiatry like religion and the law does not—or at least should not—hold itself out as attempting to be "scientifically objective." The political and healing professions of a society require active values and beliefs to bring to the political and healing processes. The behavioral social sciences of sociology—including cultural anthropology—and psychology, however, do attempt to fulfill the task of ascertaining objective data for the sake of intellectual and scientific purity, much the same way that physics and biochemistry do in the physical sciences. Application of the data of scientific conclusions to specific problems is someone else's job. It is within these two behavioral fields, therefore, that one concerned with ethical foundations receives clues as to the nature of the issue with which he is concerned.

Within this perspective Evelyn Hooker's findings based on clinically objective testings, that there are no observable psychological differences between homosexually and heterosexually oriented men except their gender-object preferences, and that therefore as a "clinical entity" homosexuality is "neutral" and not pathological are of unusual ethical pertinence. Of similar relevance and pertinence are the related social-psychology findings of Pomeroy and Simon and Gagnon.

These and related anthropological studies lend support to the behaviorist belief that society itself and not the homosexual basically is the "sick" patient which in its illness "causes" persons to "become" homosexually oriented—so, in varying degrees and emphases, with the studies of Lindner, Marcuse, Churchill, Mead, Malinowski, Beach, Benedict, Weinberg, Kardiner, Van den Haag, Ruitenbeek, et al. England's famous "Wolfenden Report" follows Hooker and others in the conclusion that there is no medically scientific basis for homosexuality as a separate clinical entity.

Whichever tack one prefers to take, a thesis that holds out the homosexual as irrevocably mentally ill and therefore ethically concludes that he should be accepted as such, ignores to its peril much scientifically informed data.

As with the theological assumptions discussed above, the present failure of psychiatry to provide an unassailable standard of psychic health does not mean that, upon further investigation, homosexuality may not be found to be a historical, cultural (and psychological) aberration of a pathological (diseased) nature. And I certainly am not implying that there are not many emotionally disturbed persons who are otherwise homosexually inclined. What I am arguing is that at this point of initial inquiry into the human experience of homosexuality there simply are too few data cards on the table of honest investigation, and that the cards which are revealed point in diverse and often conflicting directions. The only fact that appears with some certainty is that homosexual identification and practice are learned in the human growth process, much the same way as are all personality identifications and practices. Definite conclusions, ethical or otherwise, simply cannot be made upon the available data.

Let us suppose for a moment, however, that a future consensus should be reached in the position that homosexual propensity is an uncontrollable disorder of the basic psychic nature of man, and not merely a deviation from the social sexual patterning of the majority of persons. The Protestant moralist remains faced with at least three more fairly basic questions prior to making definitive conclusions: What place should ethics give to such a psychiatric consensus within the experiential authority referents for deciding God's will for man's sexual being and behavior? If the consensus is given a priority place, then will Christian ethics "accept" *all* homosexually inclined persons, or only those constitutional *in*verts who have no choice in the matter but not the willful *per*verts? If only the *in*verts are accepted, then is Protestant ethics participating in a moral theology of a gradation of sins (material-venial vs. formal-mortal) more acceptable in Catholic than Protestant tradition?

Understanding and appreciation should be accorded honest Christian motivations behind the desire to forgive and accept downtrodden minorities. It is an admirable desire. Caution likewise should be accorded lest these motivations partake in questionable hypotheses and thus stand open to Camus' reflection that the "welfare of the people . . . has always been an alibi of tyrants, and it provides the further advantage of giving the servants of tyranny a good conscience."

As indicated at the outset these pages have been argumentative and exploratory rather than definitive; they have raised more questions than they have provided answers; they have offered more criticisms than they have constructive suggestions. I have deliberately assumed this argumentative, critical, question-raising role in the firm belief that this is the appropriate ethical stance at this stage of inquiry regarding the ethics of homosexuality. I am impressed by a Christian history of near obsession with sexual issues and therefore am requesting that, regarding the specific issue of homosexuality, we draw a halt on making hasty theological-ethical conclusions, particularly when they appear founded on untested assumptions and incomplete data.

It probably is the case that, in this particular arena of human conduct, the Christian church has been thrown from its accustomed role of teacher and into that of learner. The learning posture understandably is awkward and at times abrasive, perhaps especially so for those accustomed to promulgating ethical theory and positions. It is a necessary posture, however, if the Christian community is to overcome the oppression and repression of the homosexual minority for which it has primary historical responsibility, deal with the collective guilt resulting from that responsibility, and then move on to an ethical stance which is both intelligible to and workable for the homosexual and churchman alike.

In the learning process we are not left bereft of starting points and working hypotheses. The starting points of honest biblical reinterpretation and open investigation into the human historical experience of homosexuality as recorded by the social sciences are obvious ones if Protestantism is to take seriously its traditional ethical authority referents. A third starting point would be for today's Christian to test his present faith understanding of man against the reality referent of the homosexual himself; this might be accomplished by many more personal meetings and confrontations between the Christian and the homosexual in dialogue settings or within the homosexual subcultures.

I would further suggest that, until proved inadequate or incorrect, the following tentative working hypotheses provide an ethical framework during the learning process:

1. All human sexual identifications and behavior patterns, irrespective of desired gender object, are morally neutral; i.e., avoid making prior ethical judgments regarding sexual behavior on the basis of the object of sexual drives alone.

2. No matter what the particular sexual behavior (hetero, homo, mono), the test for sin is whether or not that behavior meets presently understood and approved Christian standards (what God wills for man) for all human relational behavior; i.e., avoid making prior ethical judgments regarding sin on the basis of sexual behavior alone.

3. Christian ethical concern for the homosexual exists not because he has a certain sexual proclivity but because he is a person; i.e., avoid making prior ethical judgments regarding concern for people on the basis of socially aberrant behavior alone.

I am aware that these suggested working hypotheses can be stereotyped—positively or negatively—as mere tenets of the so-called new morality. They are suggested, however, not as truths or tenets of anything. Rather, they are working hypotheses; and if certain aspects of the new morality provide an open-ended framework for further ethical inquiry into the nature of homosexuality and homosexual behavior, so be it. It is exactly that open-endedness for which I have been arguing.

Christ and the Homosexual

Robert Wood

These . . . are the three conditions wherein I find homosexuality and the expression of it by a homosexual capable of being moral:

(1) for its adverse effect on the birth rate;
(2) as another avenue for sacramental love;
(3) and as a vehicle for self-expression.

Homosexuality and the homosexual, either together or apart, must not always and automatically be labelled with the stigma of "immoral"! Moral acknowledgment removes the onus of such behavior, reduces the opportunities for blackmail, and eliminates the dead weight of constant public censure.

If God does have a purpose in permitting homosexuality, what is that purpose? I believe there are three conditions which make homosexual expression by the homosexual moral, and which demand that society, the courts and the Church cease blindly labelling homosexuality always and in all cases "immoral."

The first condition whereby homosexuality has a moral basis is that HOMOSEXUALITY IS A GOD-CREATED WAY OF PROTECTING THE HUMAN RACE ON THIS PLANET FROM THE SUICIDE OF OVERPOPULATION.

Indeed, since homosexuality appears to have existed among mankind as long as heterosexuality, can we not conclude that this form of sexuality is a built-in safety valve of human behavior devised by the all-knowing deity to permit sexual expression without a corresponding increase in population, followed by the necessity of eliminating people already born? As we become alarmed by the spiralling birth rate, and wonder how all the mouths are going to be fed and all the children educated and all the hands employed, we can pause to give thanks for the presence of homosexuality and its adverse affect on the birth rate. Plato and his fellow Greeks seem to have recognized this factor in their permissive attitude toward homosexuality.

The second condition whereby homosexuality has a moral basis is, MAKING AVAILABLE OPPORTUNITIES FOR LOVE FOR SOME WHO ARE UNABLE TO FIND THEM IN HETEROSEXUAL RELATIONS, A LOVE WHICH CAN TRULY BE SACRAMENTAL. Anyone who has ever been in love and remembers its esctasy certainly welcomes such an experience for all mankind. Fortunate, indeed, are those who can find such love through the socially-acceptable channel of monogamous heterosexual marriage. But, alas, many of God's children cannot find love this way. The all-knowing deity, the God and Father of Jesus Christ, has in His infinite mercy provided not one but two avenues of expressing physical human love: heterosexual *and* homosexual. Through homosexuality, a great many more people can have a love experience, and this is good, it is moral, it is a positive help to both individual and society.

Homosexuality provides both integrity and freedom for the lover who cannot love within heterosexuality: he may retain his personal integrity by loving a fellow human, and he also attains freedom from the either/or of heterosexual or animal love. It is quite possible for homosexual love to become sacramental and thus moral.

The third condition under which homosexuality has a moral basis is that it PROVIDES AN OUTLET FOR THE EXPRESSION OF THE HUMAN PERSONALITY FOR THOSE WHO CANNOT EXPRESS IT FULLY WITHIN HETEROSEXUALITY.

The human personality is a divine mark of distinction for each individual. The Church seeks a resurrection experience for each person, but there can be none without the free expression of one's own sacred personality. If the freedom is lacking, then the moral quality is absent; and if there is no self-expression, there can be no chance of a resurrection.

There never has been and never can be an absolute *external* standard for right, for this immediately removes the freedom of choice upon which all morality rests. Rather, the moral standard must come from within, and this constitutes the source of one's motivation in a particular instance.

Since it is the motive which determines the moral quality of an act, let us investigate the motive of a homosexual acting to express his personality through homosexual channels. I suppose there are as many individual motives as there are homosexuals; but the primary motive is self-expression. This does not mean hedonistic indulgence, egocentric aggrandizement, or narcissistic pleasure. The primary motive for a homosexual's seeking to express himself through homosexuality, rather than what for him is stupefying heterosexuality, is his sincere attempt to find self-expression. We applaud this effort on the part of heterosexuals; so why is it any less moral on the part of homosexuals? I maintain that it is not; that this motive can be as worthy, as beneficial, and as free from selfishness for the homosexual as for the heterosexual, and thus the condition becomes moral. But when choice is offered permitting self-expression beyond an area where none could be experienced hitherto the factor which opens this gate and makes the offer becomes a moral condition. Whether or not the response is moral is another question.

The opportunity for freedom for homosexuals who can find no moral satisfaction within heterosexual confines is what the phenomenon of homosexuality offers. In enabling the homosexual to attain fuller expression of his personality (why his personality needs such expression is not the question here), the condition of homosexuality exerts a moral influence on both the individual and society.

VI
Critiques

Charles Curran
James B. Nelson
Theodore Jennings
Lisa Cahill

Homosexuality and Moral Theology: Methodological and Substantive Considerations

Charles E. Curran

The Morality of Homosexuality

Within the pale of Christian ethics there appear to be three generic answers to the question. The more traditional approach sees homosexual acts as immoral. A very few Christian ethicists argue that homosexual acts are in themselves neutral. A more sizeable minority has proposed a mediating position which, while not commending such acts, does not always condemn them.

Homosexual Acts Are Wrong

Different methodological approaches have been employed to arrive at the conclusion that homosexual acts are wrong. Roman Catholic theology in its treatment of theology in general and homosexuality in particular follows the approach and the conclusions of Thomas Aquinas. Right reason is the ultimate moral norm, but right reason builds on the order of nature. In sexual matters, Thomas accepted Ulpian's understanding of the natural as that which is common to man and all the animals. The order of nature which man shares with animal life calls for the depositing of male seed in the vas of the female so that procreation will occur and the species will continue in existence. Thomas and the manuals of moral theology divide the sins against chastity into two categories: the sins against nature *(peccata contra naturam)* and the sins according to nature *(peccata secundum naturam)*. The sins against nature are those acts which do not follow the order of nature and thus prevent procreation—pollution, imperfect sodomy, sodomy, and bestiality. Sins according to nature, but against the ordering of reason, include simple fornication, incest, adultery, rape.[1]

Thomas's condemnation of homosexual acts follows from his systematic understanding of human sexuality and its purposes in human life.[2] Since Thomas refers to homosexuality as a sin against nature, one might imagine that he attributes a special heinousness to such acts, but the expression "sin against nature" is a technical term incorporating the understanding of Ulpian. The term "sin against nature" includes sexual acts other than homosexual acts and does not argue for a special heinousness in relation to all other sins, although such sins are more grave than other sins against chastity.[3]

Until recently Catholic theologians have generally repeated and developed the Thomistic consideration of homosexuality. John F. Harvey, who has written more extensively on this subject than any other Catholic theologian, well exemplifies the best of the older Catholic approach. Harvey in his overall consideration of the morality of homosexuality sorts out three aspects of the question: the responsibility of the homosexual for his condition, the objective morality of homosexual acts, and the subjective responsibility of homosexuals for their actions.[4]

Harvey maintains that the homosexual is not responsible for his condition. In an individual case compulsion may diminish the subjective responsibility of the homosexual for his overt homosexual acts, but

Harvey believes that the homosexual can and should develop proper self-control. Harvey's discussion of objective morality begins with the natural law presupposition that the homosexual act, since by its essence it excludes the transmission of life, cannot fulfill the procreative purpose of the sexual faculty and thus constitutes a grave transgression of the divine will. No explicit mention is made of the love union aspect of sexuality, although a brief sentence describes the homosexual act as a deviation of the normal attraction of man for woman.[5]

Recently many criticisms have arisen concerning such an understanding of sexuality in general and homosexuality in particular. The older Catholic approach inordinately places great emphasis on the biological and physical aspect of the sexual act; the procreative aspect becomes the primary and sometimes the only purpose of sexuality. Poor medical and biological knowledge merely heightened the inadequacies of such an approach. Likewise, an older approach with its stress on the individual acts did not pay sufficient attention to the condition of homosexuality. Harvey improved on this by indicating that the homosexual is not usually responsible for his particular condition, although he is ordinarily responsible for his wrong homosexual acts. The fact that such an approach based on the natural law either ignored the scriptural teaching on a particular point or else merely tacked on a few proof texts has already been mentioned.

Other approaches have arrived at the same conclusion as the natural law approach followed in Roman Catholic theology; in fact, the vast majority of Christian ethicists have come to this condemnation of homosexual acts.

Karl Barth insists that theological and ethical judgments about sexuality, i.e., the command of God in this matter, must constitute a form of knowledge which rests on secure foundations. But these foundations obviously cannot be the empirical sciences.[6] "That man and woman—in the relationship conditioned by this irreversible order—are the human creatures of God and as such the image of God and likeness of the covenant of grace—this is the secure theological knowledge with which we ourselves work and with which we must be content." [7] The command of God thus does not involve any consideration of the data of the empirical sciences.

On the basis of his "secure theological knowledge" without any reference to concrete experience or the data of science, Barth characterizes homosexuality as "the physical, psychological and social sickness, the phenomenon of perversion, decadence and decay, which can emerge when man refuses to admit the validity of the divine command. . . ."[8] "From the refusal to recognize God, there follows the failure to appreciate man and thus humanity without the fellow-man.

And since humanity as fellow-humanity is to be understood in its root as the togetherness of man and woman, as the root of this inhumanity, there follows the ideal of a masculinity free from woman and a femininity free from man." [9]

Barth's position represents a confident and straightforward theological position based on the divine command, although he does remind one counseling homosexuals to be aware of God's command and also his forgiving grace.

John Giles Milhaven has approached the question of homosexuality with a methodology quite different from that of Barth, although they both reach the same ethical conclusion that homosexual acts are wrong.[10] Milhaven explicitly claims to be following the methodology of the new morality. The primary and ultimately the only ethical criterion is love which includes "free determination, commitment, of a man or woman to further the good of a certain person" and can be identified with the promotion of human good.[11] "To understand what is good for a person, he, a man of the twentieth century, relies exclusively on experience." [12] Milhaven's man of the new morality turns to the experience of the community. In this cast those who have the critical experience are "preeminently the psychologists, psychiatrists and analysts." [13] Although there is no unanimity among experts, the most commonly held opinion is that all homosexuals are mentally ill or neurotic. "Thus a Christian moving in the spirit of the new morality condemns homosexual behavior more severely than one using traditional arguments." [14]

The dramatic opposition between the approaches of Barth and Milhaven to the question of homosexuality illustrates the methodological question of the place of the empirical sciences in moral theology. The theological approach of Barth in general does not give enough importance or place to human knowledge in general, let alone the specific empirical sciences of psychology and psychiatry. The Christological monism of Barth prevents any way into the ethical problem from the viewpoint of philosophy and human wisdom, although at times Barth's antiphilosophical rhetoric seems stronger than his actual practice. I would reject any methodological approach which would be so narrowly Christological that it would exclude all human wisdom as helpful for the Christian ethicist.

Milhaven's method of relying exclusively on experience, which in this case is preeminently the findings of psychology and psychiatry, also appears too one-sided. Milhaven himself seems to contradict his exclusive reliance on such experience near the end of his article, for he alludes to "a second and older way a Christian can answer the ethical question of homosexual behavior."[15] This involves the real but limited role of the pastors and teachers of Christ's body. "For many Christians, heeding the words of their pastors and teachers is a wiser, and therefore more loving response to the question of homosexual behavior than reading the evidence of the psychiatrists and psychologists of the secular city." [16] Thus the concluding sentence of the essay appears to stand in contradiction with the approach of one who relies exclusively on experience. Perhaps Milhaven could avoid some of the apparent contradiction by showing that the teaching of the pastors relies on experience, but in the article he does not take this tack. Coming at the end of his article and proposed as a second and older way, this approach seems to stand in opposition to an approach which relies exclusively on experience.

From the viewpoint of theological ethics there are problems with a methodology which relies exclusively on such experience. The Christian realizes that existing man is beset with the limitations of creatureliness and sinfulness. Likewise, resurrection destiny and Christian eschatology introduce a transcendent aspect by which man is always called upon to go beyond the present. What is presently existing can never become totally normative for Christian ethics with its horizon which includes creatureliness and sinfulness as well as the eschatological pull of the future. Elsewhere I have illustrated from history the dangers of accepting the present experience as normative.

Perhaps one could counter the above theological criticism by showing that human experience, properly understood, does include all these aspects. I personally would accept an understanding of human experience which can include man's saving relationship to God and all that such a relationship includes. Such experience, however, would have to be related to the full reality of the world around us and could never be reduced to the data of psychiatry, psychology, and analysis. In fairness to Milhaven, the formulation of his method does not call for exclusive reliance on the behavioral sciences themselves but upon human experience. However, in his method in the question of homosexuality, his reliance on these sciences is total to the exclusion of any other considerations of human experience or of historical or scriptural data.

Homosexual Acts Are Neutral

There exists today a comparatively small but significant number of ethicians, including some few Christian ethicists, who would not judge homosexual acts to be wrong. A succinct statement of this position is found in the statement made by the English Quakers:

> One should no more deplore homosexuality than left handedness. . . . Surely it is the nature and quality of a relationship which matters. One must not judge it by its outward appearance, but by its inner worth. Homosexual affections can

be as selfless as heterosexual affection, and therefore we cannot see that it is in some way morally worse.[17]

Robert W. Wood in his book *Christ and the Homosexual* was one of the first writers in the area of Christian ethics to adopt such a generic opinion about homosexuality and homosexual acts.[18] *Christ and the Homosexual,* however, is more of a propagandistic polemic against the way Christians have treated the homosexual in the past and consequently betrays many theological shortcomings and inconsistencies, e.g., a constant confusion between the morality of homosexual acts and the proper Christian attitude towards the homosexual person, a literalistic interpretation of the words of Jesus not to judge another which would really destroy any attempt at Christian ethics.

Wood proposes as his thesis that homosexual acts are not always and everywhere wrong, but three reasons indicate that homosexual acts for the homosexual are moral. These three reasons are: (1) Homosexuality is a God-created way of protecting the human race on this planet from the suicide of overpopulation; (2) homosexuality makes available opportunities for love for some who are unable to find them in heterosexual relations, a love which truly can be sacramental; (3) homosexuality provides an outlet for the expression of the human personality for those who cannot express themselves fully within heterosexuality.[19]

Neale A. Secor presents a more adequate theological reasoning as outlined in three hypotheses which he proposes in the context of an open-ended approach.[20] (1) All human sexual identifications and behavior patterns, irrespective of desired gender object, are morally neutral; i.e., avoid making prior ethical judgments regarding sexual behavior on the basis of the object of the sexual behavior alone. (2) No matter what the particular sexual behavior (hetero-homo-mono), the test of sin is whether or not the behavior meets presently understood and approved Christian standards (what God wills for man) for all human relational behavior; i.e., avoid making prior ethical judgments regarding sin on the basis of sexual behavior alone. (3) Christian ethical concern for the homosexual exists not because he has a certain sexual proclivity but because he is a person; i.e., avoid making prior ethical judgments regarding concern for people on the basis of sexual behavior alone.[21]

In a sense, Secor's three points readily are reduced to the fact that sexuality in itself is neutral, and ethical judgments cannot be made on the basis of the object of the sexual behavior alone. Interestingly, Secor implicitly even goes one step further than those who would maintain that the ultimately determining norm is the quality of the relationship. Secor maintains that monosexuality could be moral and thus not against "presently understood and approved Christian standards for all human relational behavior." Can the relationship to self in monosexuality really be expressive of a proper Christian relation? It would be difficult to argue that monosexuality is an expression of Christian love which should require some type of giving to another. Perhaps Secor is guilty of a contradiction by asserting that monosexuality can be in accord with "standards for all human relational behavior."

The difference between the two opinions on homosexuality centers on the meaning of human sexuality; i.e., does human sexuality have a meaning in terms of a relationship of male and female in a procreative union of love? Generally speaking, I accept many of the arguments proposed by those who maintain that human sexuality in the Christian perspective has meaning in terms of the relationship between male and female. The scriptural data undoubtedly points in this direction, even to the possible extent that the likeness to God is precisely in terms of the sexuality by which man and woman are able to enter into a covenant of love with one another.

The Christian tradition has constantly accepted the view that homosexuality goes against the Christian understanding of human sexuality and its meaning. I would agree that historical circumstances could have influenced the condemnation of a particular form of behavior. Likewise, it is possible that the Christian tradition could have been wrong at a particular point. However, there seems to be no sufficient evidence for such a judgment in the case of homosexuality. Despite all the methodological shortcomings and one-sidedness of the natural law approach proposed by Aquinas, it still seems to correspond to a certain human connaturality condemning homosexuality as wrong. Also, the majority of all the data from the human sciences seems to point to the fact that human sexuality has its proper meaning in terms of the love union of male and female.

Interestingly, those who argue that sexuality is neutral and all sexuality should be judged in terms of the quality of the relationship fail to come to grips with the accepted fact that most homosexual liaisons are of a "one night stand" variety. Thus there is not a sexual union as expressive of a loving commitment of one to another. One might argue that the prejudices of society make such sexual behavior almost necessary for the homosexual, since he cannot easily live in a permanent relationship with a person of the same sex. However, at least those who are arguing in favor of such an understanding of homosexual acts should come to grips with what appears to be a generally accepted fact about the nature of homosexual relationships in our society. No one can deny there are many somewhat stable relationships, but these do not clearly constitute the majority of the cases.[22]

There remains another important ethical consideration which also appears in connection with other problems which are posed today in the area of genetics and the new biology. Does sexuality or the sexual union have any relationship to procreation? The position of the hierarchical magisterium in the Roman Catholic Church would argue that every single act of sexual intercourse must be open to procreation. Obviously such an approach gives one a strong rule and criterion to use in condemning homosexual acts or other seemingly errant forms of sexual behavior. However, even many who would accept the moral use of contraception would not deny all connection between human sexuality and procreation. Paul Ramsey, for example, argues that man cannot put asunder what God has put together in terms of the procreative and love union aspect of human sexuality. Ramsey is well aware that there are marital unions in which the couple either do not intend to have children, or are not physically able to bear children, but these are still accepted as true marital unions. Ramsey argues that these couples still realize that love union and the procreative aspects of marital sexuality belong together, for they admit that, if either had a child, it would be only from their one-flesh unity with each other and not apart from this.[23]

Modern developments in genetics raise the possibility that bearing children can and should be separated from the one-flesh union of man and wife. In general, I believe that the joining together of the love union and procreative aspects does appear to be the meaning of human sexuality and marriage, but it is evident that neither Scripture nor Christian tradition could respond to the questions raised by the new biology. There does seem to be a strong presumption in favor of such an understanding which cannot be overturned without grave reasons. All too often biologists think that whatever is biologically possible is also humanly possible and desirable. But there are many other important questions from the viewpoint of psychology, sociology, and anthropology which have to be thoroughly investigated before I would be willing to overcome the presumption in favor of the union of the procreative and love union aspects of sexuality.

The fact that human sexuality might be neutral and not structured in accord with the union of male and female seems to be compatible with some new trends in Christian ethics and moral theology. Note how often those who favor the morality of homosexual acts will base their theological arguments on premises proposed in other contexts by such authors as Lehmann and Fletcher. However, there seem to be some unacceptable presuppositions in a theological methodology which would presume that man and human sexuality have no meaning in themselves and in their relationships but are completely neutral. Again, this does not mean that one would be forced to adopt the view that the biological and physical structures of human existence understood in an exclusive sense become morally normative for man—a mistake that Roman Catholic theology has made in the past. But one can, and in my opinion should, maintain that there is a certain structuring or meaning to human existence which contributes to an ethical criterion so that humanity does not appear as something which is morally neutral and capable of doing or becoming anything under certain conditions.

Christian ethics in general and Roman Catholic moral theology in particular have recently emphasized the creative aspect of human existence. Likewise, contemporary theology emphasizes the importance of the self-transcending subject and the meaning which he gives to reality. Too often an older theology merely viewed the subject as one who passively conformed to an already existing order. In the light of these new emphases the model of responsibility seems to be the best model for understanding the moral life of the Christian and overcomes dangers involved in the older teleological and deontological models. Contemporary man realizes that he does have the power and the responsibility to shape his future existence in the world and he cannot merely sit back and wait for things to happen.[24] In this contemporary context Rahner's description of man as a self-creator is pertinent.[25]

The crucial moral question concerns the limits placed on man as self-creator. In this particular essay perhaps Rahner over-emphasizes this aspect of self-creator and does not spell out the limitations of man which he does frequently mention in a generic sense throughout the article. Man cannot be considered as self-creator in the sense that he can make himself into whatever he wants to be. There are definite limitations in human existence which narrow down the possibilities open to man. In our personal existence we realize the built-in limitations in our own personalities and how difficult it remains to change our character and personality. Such changes do not take place overnight but proceed rather very slowly, if at all. There is no doubt that the optimistic exuberance of the 1960's led theology to an overly optimistic and utopian view of the possibilities of human existence. In general, Christian theology constantly reminds us of two very important human limitations: creatureliness and sinfulness.[26] Sober reflection on the last few years reminds us that, especially in the area of social ethics and reform of institutions, there are many built-in limitations and obstacles. Those who were naively optimistic in the early 60's have often become embittered and alienated precisely because their creative desires for radical change have not come into existence.

Intimately connected with an over-exaggerated understanding of man as self-creator stands an anthropology which defines man primarily in terms of freedom. Freedom is a necessary characteristic of human existence, but man cannot be understood solely in terms of freedom. Pope

John XXIII insisted on a fourfold basis for a just social order—truth, justice, charity and freedom.[27] I would urge the inclusion of power as another important consideration in social justice.

In the understanding of the state, Catholic theology well illustrates its basic understanding that there is a moral meaning or structure to man. The state is a natural society precisely because man is by nature a social and political animal. Living together with others in the social order does not constitute a limitation or restriction of man's freedom, for man's nature is such that he is called to live in society with his fellows.[28] Thus Catholic theology viewed the state as a natural society which was not an intrusion on the freedom of man. Orthodox Protestant theology in general viewed the state as resulting from the sinfulness of man precisely because the state with its power is necessary to keep sinful men from devouring one another in society.[29] The limitations of the state in Catholic theology do not constitute an infringement of the freedom of the human person because man is by nature a social person destined to live in society with others.

In general, an argument from within the historical context of Roman Catholic theology (I do not mean to imply that one ceases to be a loyal Roman Catholic if he theologizes in a different manner) places greater emphasis on the structure of love.[30] The structure, corporeality, or visibility of love underscores the Roman Catholic approach to the Incarnation, ecclesiology, and sacramentology. No one can deny that at times Catholic theology has overemphasized the place of structure both in ecclesiology and ethics, but it does not follow that there is no structure whatsoever to love in the Catholic theological tradition today. Thus Catholic theology is quite compatible with an understanding of human sexuality which sees love structured in terms of the bond of love between male and female.

The very fact that Roman Catholic tradition favors the visible and structured aspect of love in many areas does not necessarily make this the correct view. Likewise, one could hold to a concept of visible or structured love and still perhaps argue in favor of the morality of homosexual acts. The argument proposed here is one of "fittingness" rather than proof. The Catholic theological tradition is logically more compatible with an understanding of sexuality structured in terms of the love union of male and female. However, the precise argument for the male-female structure of human sexual love rests on the reasons already advanced.

An unnuanced acceptance of the concept of man as self-creator and a unilateral emphasis on freedom cohere with a totally extrinsic approach to morality. In the past, Catholic morality in the name of an intrinsic morality has tended to canonize physical and biological structures. In the above paragraphs I have refrained from using the word "structure" without any qualification precisely because of the errors of an older Catholic theology. Too often an historically conditioned reality was acknowledged as an essential structure of human existence. However, there is still a meaning to man and his relationships which cannot be described as totally neutral. The danger will always exist of absolutizing this meaning when it must be seen in terms of all the elements entering into the human act. However, we do admit there are certain inalienable rights of man which cannot be taken away from him. Certain human relationships, such as slave-master, student-teacher, employee-employer, citizen-government, have a definite moral meaning or structure, so that freedom is not the only aspect involved. Man, human existence, and human relationships can never be merely neutral.

A Third Position

A third or mediating position on the morality of homosexual acts has emerged somewhat frequently within Protestant ethics in the last few years and is now also appearing in Catholic ethics. I have briefly proposed such a solution based on a theory of compromise theology, but a consideration and critique of other mediating positions will clarify the theoretical and practical ramifications of this theology of compromise.[31] In general, a mediating approach recognizes that homosexual acts are wrong but also acknowledges that homosexual behavior for some people might not fall under the total condemnation proposed in the first opinion.

The mediating position implied by Helmut Thielicke applies his total ethical vision to the question of homosexuality. Homosexuality in every case is not in accord with the order of creation. Man's homosexual condition, however, deserves no stronger condemnation than the status of existence which we all share as human beings living in a disordered world which is the result of the Fall. The homosexual must try to change his condition, but Thielicke realizes that such a change is often not possible. Is homosexual behavior for such a person acceptable? Thielicke appears to set the theoretical framework for the acceptance of such behavior in these circumstances, but at the last minute (and somewhat illogically) he hesitates to grant such acceptance and counsels the need of sublimation.[32]

H. Kimball Jones has articulated a mediating position which develops the theoretical framework proposed by Thielicke and explicitly acknowledges that homosexual behavior in certain circumstances can be morally acceptable, since there is nothing else the person can do.[33] Jones's approach, however, remains open to the charge of inconsistency—a danger which constantly lurks for any mediating position. One cannot fault any Christian ethicist for appreciating the pathos of the concrete dilemmas of human existence—in this case the agonizing problems confronting the homosexual—but such pastoral sympathy and understanding must find solid and rigorous theological support.

Jones concludes his investigation of Scripture, the theological tradition, and the contemporary psychological data by asserting "that man is by nature heterosexual in a very fundamental sense and that his sexual nature can be fulfilled as intended by God, only within a relationship of love between a man and a woman. This becomes more apparent when we consider the connection between human sexuality and procreation."[34]

But Jones then accepts and develops Thielicke's understanding of man existing after the Fall and the consequences of the disorder wrought by sin. One cannot make a clear distinction between the sinful homosexual and the redeemed heterosexual, for even in marriage the relationship does not escape the disorder of sin. Thus one cannot formulate the problem in terms of sex within a heterosexual relationship versus sex within a homosexual relationship. "The problem is rather sex as a depersonalizing force versus sex as a fulfillment of human relationship."[35]

This argument implies an understanding of sin which I cannot accept and also involves a logical inconsistency with what the same author proposed earlier. Catholic natural law theology has definitely erred by failing to consider the reality of sin in the present world. Nature was considered as existing in itself unaffected by the disordering reality of sin and likewise unaffected intrinsically by the transcendent aspect of the supernatural or grace. In Thielicke and Jones, however, the effect of sin appears to be too total and unnuanced. In the Catholic tradition theology has been more willing to accept degrees of sinfulness and the relative gravity of sins as exemplified in the distinction between mortal and venial sin. Likewise, in the Catholic tradition sin does not totally destroy or totally disfigure the order of creation, to use the phrase more traditionally employed in Protestant theology. The force of sin cannot be such as to entirely change the question so that it is no longer the difference between "sex within a heterosexual relationship versus sex within a homosexual relationship" but rather sex (either hetero or homo—or for Secor even mono) as a depersonalizing force or as the fulfillment of a human relationship.

Jones earlier asserted quite categorically that sex is naturally heterosexual. In my understanding, sin does affect creation, but it does not necessarily abolish the already existing structure of human existence and human sexuality. To use a phrase frequently employed by Thielicke himself, in the darkness of night not all cats are gray.[36] In other words, sin does not totally destroy the order of creation so that the distinctions between right and wrong based on creation are now totally broken down and these structures no longer point out what is morally good. All must admit that heterosexual relationships can be wrong and sinful. No one doubts that even in marriage sexual relations can be immoral, if one partner merely uses the other partner for a variety of reasons. However, there is a basic meaning of human sexuality in terms of maleness and femaleness which sin neither eradicates, neutralizes nor reduces to the same ethical significance as homosexual relations.

Jones not only accepts a concept of sin which destroys the ethical difference which he admits creation establishes between hetero- and homosexuality, but he also appears to accept a theological methodology in developing his argument which contradicts the methodology employed in his earlier affirmation of the heterosexual nature of human sexuality. In developing "his practical Christian ethics," he rightly rejects the absolute validity of either exhortation or sublimation as the answer to the homosexual's dilemma. Jones accepts, after citing Paul Lehmann, the criterion of a relationship that contributes to the humanization of man. If the homosexual relationship contributes to the humanization of man, then such a relationship, even though it is not the ideal, can be accepted and even encouraged by the Church:

> Thus, we suggest that the Church must be willing to make the difficult, but necessary, step of recognizing the validity of mature homosexual relationships, encouraging the absolute invert to maintain a fidelity to one partner when his only other choice would be to lead a promiscuous life filled with guilt and fear. This would by no means be an endorsement of homosexuality by the Church.[37]

I can agree almost totally with the conclusion proposed by Jones, but he has unfortunately employed a way of argumentation which seems inconsistent with some of his earlier assertions. Granted the existence of the disorder of sin, Jones apparently accepts the quality of the relationship argument which in principle he derives from Paul Lehmann. This type of argumentation is at odds with the earlier reasoning which established the heterosexual nature of human sexuality. Likewise, in words he accepts the pervasive disorder of sin to such an extent that the question can no longer be raised in terms of heterosexual versus homosexual relationships; but he never fully accepts his own statement, for he emphasizes that homosexual behavior will always fall short of the will of God and is doomed to never pass beyond a certain point.

Two other somewhat related mediating positions have also been proposed within the context of Roman Catholic theology. The one solution has been adopted in practice by a team of Dutch Catholics dealing with the practical counseling of homosexuals. In this book first published in 1961 the authors attempt to adopt a "more lenient pastoral approach" which could be explained in terms of the classical distinction between formal and material sin which in certain circumstances can be tolerated as a lesser of two evils.[38]

In a final chapter written for the second edition five years after the original publication H. Ruygers mentions the older classical approach of moral theology to homosexuality but also suggests a new anthropological approach which would not have a biological or physiological concept of nature but rather attempt to develop a more human understanding of man. Ruygers recognizes the danger in such an approach and explicitly affirms that an anthropology which is not based on the biological nature as such but uniquely on the possibility of attributing a free and fully human meaning to that which concerns man does not leave itself without resources for objecting to those who would see no difference between heterosexual and homosexual intimacy. But such a theory is not developed by the author. In general, the theological discussion in this book remains quite sketchy, since the team is more concerned with pastoral counseling.[39] On the level of pastoral counseling they conclude that one cannot a priori exclude the fact that two homosexuals should and could live together.[40]

John J. McNeill, S.J., has recently summarized much of the literature in the field and has tentatively concluded that the suggestion "that a homosexual can in his situation be morally justified in seeking out ethically responsible expressions of his sexuality" could possibly be understood as falling, in traditional terminology, within the principle of choosing the lesser of two evils.[41] McNeill maintains that celibacy does not offer a viable alternative for all; consequently, a relatively ethical and responsible relationship tending to be permanent between two homosexuals would be a lesser evil than promiscuity.[42]

While in general agreement with the practical conclusions proposed by McNeill, I cannot totally agree with his reasoning about the principle of choosing the lesser of two evils. I also believe that one can and should go beyond this principle to propose a somewhat more adequate theoretical solution to the dilemma frequently facing the homosexual and his counselor.

McNeill maintains that Catholic theologians in the past have not applied the principle of the lesser of two evils in the case of homosexuality because they considered "any use of sex outside of marriage, or in such a way that renders procreation impossible is always objectively seriously sinful. Where both courses of action represent mortal sin from a theological viewpoint, there can be no 'lesser of two evils' to be chosen among them; the only moral and 'ethically responsible' course of action would be total abstinence."[43]

McNeill then develops several new emphases in moral theology which call into question this judgment about objectively serious sin. The first emphasis is the equal importance given to the love-union aspect of sexuality even in the documents of Vatican II. The second emphasis is the rejection of an act-centered moral theology in favor of a responsible orientation toward growth and reconciliation. From these two emphases he wants to prove that the principle of the lesser of two evils applies in this case, because a more permanent and stable homosexual union would not be always objectively seriously sinful.[44]

McNeill's reasoning appears to be somewhat hazy in this section, for he never explicitly says that he is trying to prove that such actions would not be objectively seriously sinful. I am not too sure that his brief treatment of the question really does furnish conclusive proof. However, a more serious objection questions his understanding of the principle of counseling the lesser of two evils. Catholic theologians have admitted as a probable opinion that, even in the case of two objectively mortal sins, one can counsel the lesser of two evils.[45] The famous example given by Alphonsus and others refers to counseling a man only to steal from another rather than to kill him.[46] Catholic theology, as alluded to earlier, willingly admits not only a distinction between mortal and venial sins but also a distinction in the gravity of various mortal sins. Thus, even if homosexual behavior were always an objectively grave wrong, one could still apply here the principle of counseling the lesser of two evils.

The principle of counseling the lesser of two evils, like the distinction between formal and material sinfulness which in its more positive formulation today respects the need for moral growth so that one might have to be satisfied at times with what is materially wrong,[47] offers one way of solving the practical dilemma of the homosexual. Such an approach remains within the traditional principles of Catholic thought, but I do not believe it goes quite far enough. In this opinion the act is still objectively wrong, although, for McNeill explicitly, it might not be grave, objective sin.

Gayness and Homosexuality: Issues for the Church[1]

James B. Nelson

The Gay Caucuses now active in virtually every major American denomination no longer will let any of us forget that the church must face this issue more openly, honestly, and sensitively than it has yet done.[2] Beyond the legitimate pressure which the caucuses are exerting, there are numerous compelling reasons for the church to reexamine its theology and practice. Among them are these:

• Gay Christians are sisters and brothers of every other Christian, and a great many are earnestly seeking the church's full acceptance of them—without prejudgment on the basis of sexual orientation.

• While antihomosexual bias has long existed in Western culture generally, the church must take responsibility for its significant share in shaping, supporting, and transmitting negative (and often hostile) attitudes toward gay people.

• The Christian mandate to seek social justice will not let us forget that discrimination continues against millions of gay people in employment, housing, public accommodations, education, basic civil liberties—and in church structures.[3]

• The church must do its ongoing theological and ethical work with a

186

high sense of responsibility. Fresh insights from gay Christians, from feminist theologians, and from those secular scholars who frequently manifest God's "common grace" in the world remind us of the numerous ways our particular sexual conditionings have colored our perceptions of God's nature and presence among us. If the Protestant Principle warns us against absolutizing historically relative theological and ethical judgments, so also an openness to continuing revelation should convince us (as it did some of our ancestors-in-faith) that "the Lord has yet more light and truth to break forth."

• Finally, the heterosexually-oriented majority in the church has an immense amount to gain from a deeper grappling with this issue and a deeper encounter with gay Christians: an enriched capacity to love other human beings more fully and less fearfully, and a more faithful response to God's will for social justice.

The Bible and Homosexuality

It is a curious but unmistakable phenomenon that a great many Christians treat so literally the references to homosexual practice in the Bible, while at the same time they interpret biblical texts on almost every other topic with considerable flexibility and nonliteralness. Why this may be so is an important question, and we shall return to it later. But at this point the major texts which mention the subject engage our attention.

A brief survey of these passages needs to be prefaced with a word about interpretive principles.[4] Let me suggest four. First and most fundamental, Jesus Christ is the bearer of God's invitation to human wholeness and communion. Jesus Christ is the focal point of God's humanizing action, and hence he is the central norm through which and by which everything else in Scripture should be judged. Second, the interpreter must take seriously both the historical context of the biblical writers and our present cultural situation. Third, we should study and interpret the Bible with awareness of the cultural relativity in which we ourselves are immersed, and through which we perceive and experience what Christian faith means. Finally, our scriptural interpretation should be informed by the revelations of God's truth in other disciplines of human inquiry.

Nowhere does the Bible say anything about homosexuality as a *sexual orientation*. Its references to the subject are—without exception—statements about certain kinds of homosexual *acts*. Our understanding of homosexuality as a psychosexual orientation is a relatively recent development. It is crucial to remember this, for in all probability the biblical writers in each instance were speaking of homosexual acts undertaken by persons whom the authors presumed to be heterosexually constituted.[5]

Even though it does not deal with homosexual activity, it is well to begin with the Onan story (Genesis 38:1–11), for it has significantly influenced attitudes toward this subject. Onan's refusal to impregnate his widowed sister-in-law—a refusal expressed through his deliberate withdrawal before ejaculation (*coitus interruptus*)—was seen by the writer as so serious a violation of divine decree that Onan was killed by Yahweh.

Three interpretive observations are particularly relevant to the subject of homosexuality. First, the Onan story clearly points up the strong emphasis upon procreation which is characteristic of the Hebrew interpretation of sexuality. The historical context is one in which a small tribe was struggling for its very survival, and thus the reproduction of children was of exceptional importance. Any sexual activity that "wasted the seed" was a threat to the tribe. Our own situation on an overcrowded planet is markedly different.

The second observation is linked to this, and I repeat this point made in earlier chapters. The Onan story illustrates a biological misunderstanding which is present throughout the Bible. The prescientific mind (particularly the prescientific *male* mind) assumed that the man's semen contained the whole of nascent life. With no knowledge of eggs and ovulation, it was assumed that the woman provided only the incubating space. Hence, the deliberate and nonprocreative spilling of semen was equivalent to the deliberate destruction of human life. Whether it occurred in *coitus interruptus* (as with Onan), or in male homosexual acts, or for that matter in male masturbation, the deserved judgment was as severe as that for abortion or even murder.

The third observation follows: male homosexual and masturbatory acts have been condemned far more vigorously than have similar female acts throughout the whole sweep of the Judeo-Christian tradition. The sexism endemic to a patriarchal society ironically bore with its logic a heavier burden upon the "deviants" of the "superior" gender. But the central irony of the Onan story interpretation through the centuries is this: its major point does not concern sexual sin as such but rather has to do with human greed (over property inheritance) and with the disobedience of God's commands.

However, it is another Genesis account which has emerged as the chief text in Christian history for the summary condemnation of homosexuality: Sodom and Gomorrah (Genesis 19:1–29). Traditional explanation has held that the destruction of the two cities is the positive sign of God's utter disapproval of homosexuality. Yet, there are compelling reasons to doubt the accuracy of this interpretation. Current Old Testament scholarship generally holds that the story's major themes are the affront to God's will in the breach of ancient Hebrew hospitality norms and persistent violations of rudimentary social justice.[6]

There are multiple reasons for preferring the latter interpretation. For one, some scholars doubt that the verb "to know" (*yādáh*) in this story refers to sexual intercourse. More probably it means the crowd's rude insistence upon *knowing who* these two strangers were. Lot, in their eyes, was not properly qualified to offer hospitality to strangers inasmuch as he himself was an outsider, a resident alien in Sodom.

That inhospitality and injustice coming from the mob and generally characterizing the community were "the sin of Sodom" is plausible when one examines parallel scriptural accounts (e.g., the crime of Gibeah, Judges 19:1–21:25). Even weightier evidence comes from subsequent Old Testament references to Sodom, none of which identifies homosexuality with that city. Ezekiel is typical: "Behold, this was the sin of your sister Sodom: she and her daughters lived in pride, plenty, and thoughtless ease; they supported not the poor and needy; they grew haughty, and committed abomination before me; so I swept them away; as you have seen" (Ezekiel 16:49–50). The other Old Testament references to Sodom's sin are similar (ef. Isaiah 13:19; Jeremiah 49:18, 50:40), and the identification of Sodom with inhospitality is made by Jesus as well (Luke 10:10–13). It was not until several centuries after it was written that the Sodom story was given a dominantly sexual interpretation—in the intertestamental Book of Jubilees and then in two late New Testament texts (2 Peter 2:4–10 and Jude 6–7). But if Sodom had consistently been understood as the major symbol of divine judgment on homosexual acts, we would expect that the other biblical references to such acts would also mention Sodom and its fate. None does.

Though there is considerable agreement among scholars that the basic ethical theme of the Sodom account is that of justice and its basic theological theme is God's righteousness in the face of social guilt, we can still acknowledge the possibility that homosexual acts did play some role in the story.[7] If the verb "to know" does signify homosexual intercourse, it is also patently clear that what is being threatened here is homosexual *rape*. Moreover, the men of Sodom have threatened to rape the two visiting *angels*, and since the angels represent Yahweh's presence there is a direct sin against God here portrayed. In all fairness to the text, it is extremely difficult to construe this account as a judgment against *all* homosexual activity.

Fr. John McNeill writes a fitting conclusion to our brief look at the Sodom story. Observing that its dominant use in Christianity may well be one of the supreme ironies of history, he says: "For thousands of years in the Christian West the homosexual has been the victim of inhospitable treatment. Condemned by the Church, he has been the victim of persecution, torture, and even death. In the name of a mistaken understanding of Sodom and Gomorrah, the true crime of Sodom and Gomorrah has been and continues to be repeated every day."[8]

If the dominant homosexual interpretation traditionally given to the

Sodom account fails to stand up to critical examination, there are, nevertheless, several other Old Testament passages which unmistakably condemn homosexual acts. It is crucial to see in these, however, that the pervasive theme is that of cultic defilement and idolatry. There is no general condemnation of same-sex *orientation* (a notion foreign to the writers), nor is there any reference to genital *love* between gay persons who are committed to each other. What is clear is that sacral male prostitution is anathematized, for it involves the cultic worship of foreign gods and denies Yahweh's exclusive claim (see Deuteronomy 23:17; I Kings 14:24, 15:12, 22:46).

Cultic defilement is also the context for the Holiness Code in Leviticus (see 18:22 and 20:13).[9] Canaanite fertility worship involved sacral prostitution and sexual orgies, and this constituted a direct threat to Yahweh's exclusive claim. For Yahweh was the One who worked through the freedom of human history and not, primarily, through the cycles of biological life. If so, sexuality was not to be seen as a mysterious sacred power, but rather as part of human life to be used responsibly in gratitude to the Creator—a basic perspective of continuing relevance.

For those who do not accept this as the more appropriate interpretation of the Leviticus references, some exceedingly difficult issues of biblical interpretation emerge.[10] What is the principle of selection by which cultic injunctions against homosexual acts are held valid today but at the same time most other parts of the Holiness Code are deemed irrelevant? Should the death penalty be used against male homosexuals as the law stipulates? Why are female same-sex acts unmentioned? What is the link between female subordination and the fear of male homosexuality, both evident in these laws? And how shall a church which grounds its life in the grace of Jesus Christ deal with the law codes of ancient Israel?

Part of the Old Testament context for this issue, worthy of note, was a common Middle East practice in that day: the submission of captured male foes to anal rape. It was an expression of domination and contempt, a powerful symbol of scorn in societies where the dignity of the male was held in such high esteem. Here a man was using another *man* as he might use a woman. As long as homosexual activity of any sort had this connection, it is not difficult to understand some of these texts.

Nevertheless, at a number of points in the Old Testament there are beautiful affirmations of same-sex *love*. Two notable examples come to mind. David's love for Jonathan was said to exceed his love for women. And the relationship of Ruth and Naomi can only be described as a bond of deep love. There is no indication that there was genital expression in either of these. The point is simply that in these instances, deeply and emotionally expressed love between two persons of the same sex is affirmed. Indeed, the accounts suggest that it is something of a cause for celebration.

In the New Testament we have no record of any words of Jesus about homosexuality either as an orientation or as a genital expression. The major New Testament references are found in two Pauline letters and in 1 Timothy.

Paul's statement in Romans 1:18–32 traditionally has been taken as the strongest New Testament rejection of homosexuality, yet this passage deserves more careful examination than is often accorded to it. The writer is clearly concerned about the influence of paganism on the Roman Christians, and he had good reason to be. The moral climate of Hellenistic Rome was marred by various forms of sexual commerce and exploitation. Yet, in this passage while Paul sees homosexual acts as a *result* of idolatry, he does not claim that they are the *cause* of divine wrath. Idolatry clearly is the major issue at stake. Further, when Paul uses the word "nature" he "apparently refers only to homosexual acts indulged in by those he considered to be otherwise heterosexually inclined; acts which represent a voluntary choice to act contrary to their ordinary sexual appetite."[11] Thus, he speaks of homosexual acts as those in which people are "leaving," "giving up," or "exchanging" their regular sexual orientations. It is difficult to read into Paul's words at this point the modern psychosexual understanding of the gay person as one whose orientation is fixed very early in life and for whom "natural" (heterosexual) relations would be felt as basically contrary to his or her own sexual constitution, and might well be impossible at that. In addition, in this passage we are given a description of homosexual *lust* ("consumed with passion for one another"), but hardly an account of interpersonal same-sex love—about which Paul does not speak.

Thus, it is difficult to construe Paul's statement as applicable to acts of committed love engaged in by persons for whom same-sex attraction is part of the giveness of *their* "nature." In point of fact, Paul uses the word "nature" in his writings as a flexible concept, expressing varying concerns in different contexts. An ethical position which condemns homosexuality as a violation of natural law will have to turn to non-bibilical philosophical materials for its justification—the Pauline material will not sustain it.[12]

Finally it is worth noting that in this entire section of the letter to the Romans the author's concern is to demonstrate that all persons are under the power of sin. They cannot extricate themselves from it through meritorious works of the law. In spite of his own moral judgments, Paul reveals this basic point in Romans 2:1. There he declares that those who pass judgment on others (for the various acts which he has earlier mentioned) are no better off. They condemn themselves beause they stand under the same power of sin. And in Romans 3:21–25 comes the central premise of these first chapters of the letter: all have sinned and fallen short of God's glory, and all who open themselves in faith are justified by God's grace in Jesus Christ.

The point of all this is not that Paul sees homosexual acts as neutral or, much less, that he looks upon any such acts with favor. Clearly, he does not. He understands homosexual practices to be the result of idolatry. But, as David L. Bartlett has observed, Paul's argument here is not "purely" theological. It is partly based on his interpretation of Old Testament concepts of idolatry, partly based on the common wisdom of his day, and partly based on his own empirical understanding of homosexuality's nature and consequences. In regard to the latter, he looked at the Gentile world and saw idolatry but also saw homosexual practices and the prevalence of venereal disease—and he linked them firmly together. As Bartlett comments, to be genuinely "Pauline" in our understanding of homosexual practices today, we would have to demonstrate that there does indeed exist a clear connection between idolatry and homosexual acts—and then one would wonder, given the widespread idolatry of our times, why more people had not been so "punished." In addition, a Pauline methodology would have us discuss homosexuality today with our best biblical interpretation, our best common wisdom of the contemporary day, and the best empirical understandings we can find. "If our understanding of homosexuality and our empirical perception of its nature and consequences have changed, then we will not be able to understand the issue precisely as Paul did, even if we share Paul's reverence for the Old Testament, his abhorrence of idolatry, and his conviction that we are all sinners saved by grace through faith."[13]

Paul's other reference to homosexual acts (1 Corinthians 6:9–10) is similar to that of the writer of 1 Timothy (1:8–11). Both passages contain lists of practices which will exclude people from the kingdom. They are acts which dishonor God and harm the neighbor, including such things as thievery, drunkenness, kidnapping, and lying. Homosexual acts are not singled out for special censure, but they are unmistakably part of the list. What then should we make of Paul's moral judgment in this case? Perhaps we should just accept him for what he was: a faithful apostle and a profound interpreter of the central message of the gospel, yet one who was also a fallible and historically-conditioned human being. Paul's central message is clear: we do not earn righteousness by anything we do nor are we justified by anything we are—we are justified by the grace of God in Jesus Christ, and the gifts of the Spirit are equally available to all persons. If the norm of the new humanity in Jesus Christ together with our best current moral wisdom and empirical knowledge would cause us to question some of Paul's moral convictions about the status of women and about the institution of human slavery, surely his moral judgments about homosexual acts ought not be exempt.

The central biblical message regarding sexuality seems clear enough. Like every other good gift, it can be misused. The idolatrous dishonoring of God inevitably results in the dishonoring of persons, and faithfulness to God will result in sexual expression which honors the personhood of the other. Our sexuality is not a mysterious and alien force of nature but part of what it means to be human. It is a power to be integrated fully into one's selfhood and to be used in the service of love. That message, I am convinced, applies regardless of one's affectional orientation.

The Range of Contemporary Theological Opinion

Four theological stances toward homosexuality represent the range of current conviction.[14] The first can be called a *rejecting-punitive* orientation. The person who holds this unconditionally rejects homosexuality as Christianly legitimate and, at the same time, bears a punitive attitude toward gay persons.

The rejecting-punitive motif, tragically enough, is a strong one in Christian history. If we have been ignorant of the persecutions, it is not without reason. Unlike the recognized histories of other minority groups, there has been no "gay history." Heterosexual historians usually have considered the subject unmentionable, and gay historians have been constrained by the fear of ceasing to be invisible. A conspiracy of silence has resulted. Yet, the facts are there. For many centuries stoning, burning, sexual mutilation, and the death penalty were fairly common treatments for discovered homosexuals. While the church frequently gave its blessings to the civil persecutions, official ecclesiastical practice tended to be less physically violent. Nevertheless, spiritually it was even more severe, for it usually meant refusal of the sacraments and ostracism from the common life.[15]

Today no major contemporary theologian holds the rejecting-punitive position and most church bodies in their formal statements have moved away from it. Yet in practice it may still be by far the most common orientation throughout the length and breadth of the church in our society. Its theology rests on a selective biblical literalism—selective, again, because other moral issues are not treated with the same kind of literalism at all. Its punitive attitudes might be expressed less violently than was typical in the past, but they are still highly punitive and ostracizing.[16] The attitudes are rooted in familiar stereotypes: all lesbians are tough and all male gays effeminate; homosexuals are compulsive and sex-hungry; they are by nature promiscuous; male gays have an inherent tendency toward child molestation. Each of these stereotypes has been thoroughly discounted by reliable research, and yet they persist in the minds of countless Christians. And the key criticism of this whole orientation—beyond its untenable biblical interpretations—must be the incongruity of a vindictive stance with the gospel.

The *rejecting-nonpunitive* position must be considered more fully. No less a theologian than Karl Barth represents this view. Since humanity is always "fellow-humanity," Barth argues, men and women come into its fullness only in relation to persons of the opposite sex. To seek one's humanity in a person of the same sex is to seek "a substitute for the despised partner," and this is "physical, psychological and social sickness, the phenomenon of perversion, decadence and decay."[17] Moreover, this is idolatry. One who seeks same-sex union is simply seeking oneself in a quest for self-satisfaction and self-sufficiency. Hence, homosexuality is unnatural and violates the command of the Creator. But, Barth hastens to add, the central theme of the gospel is God's overwhelming grace in Jesus Christ. *Homosexuality* must be condemned, but in light of grace the homosexual *person* must not.

If Barth's arguments emphasize that there is something inherently wrong with the homosexual condition as such (it is idolatrous, a sickness and a perversion), the rejecting-nonpunitive position can also be argued on more consequentialist grounds. William Muehl does this.[18] Muehl clearly recognizes the cruelty, injustice, and hypocrisy all present in the persecution and prosecution of gay persons. He fully supports the church's obligation toward their civil liberties. Theirs, he believes, is not the only form of sexual irresponsibility, but it *is* irresponsibility which cannot be approved by Christian conscience. Human dignity is threatened by gay relationships. Homosexuality is an illness comparable to alcoholism, and sheer acceptance of it would have "implications for our view of marriage, the limitations appropriate to sexual activity, the raising of children, and the structure of the family." Since we are relatively ignorant concerning such potentially grave social results, Muehl argues, we should respect the historic position of the church, which rejects homosexuality.

The rejecting-nonpunitive stance appears to rest upon two major arguments and upon two major unspoken assumptions, each of which is open to serious question. The first argument is that of natural law and idolatry. At this point we return to Barth. Barth seems to forget our human historicity, apparently assuming that human nature is an unchangeable, once-and-for-all essence given by the Creator. Actually, our human nature is shaped in some significant part by the interaction of people in specific periods of time with specific cultural symbols and historic environments. In fact, the notion of a fixed human nature is highly questionable from a biblical point of view. "Where we read 'created' in our Bibles, the tense in the Hebrew is often in fact the continuous present, i.e. God is 'creating.' And from this understanding comes a statement that may be held to give us our vocation as '*being* created in the image of God.' . . ."[19]

Committed to human historicity, Gregory Baum fittingly declares, "In other words, human nature as it is at present is not normative for theologians. . . . What is normative for normal life is the human nature to which we are divinely summoned, which is defined in terms of mutuality. This, at least, is the promise of biblical religion." After examining the evidence of mutual fulfillment in committed gay couples, Fr. Baum concludes, "Homosexual love, then, is not contrary to human nature, defined in terms of mutuality toward which mankind is summoned."[20]

In addition, Barth's claim that homosexuality is idolatrous rests on questionable assumptions which I have earlier touched upon—the norm of procreative sex and the notion of essential gender complementarity. Regarding the first, Barth (like Paul Ramsey) affirms responsible family planning, but contends that even if every sex act is not procreative, all sexual relations must be oriented to that possibility. On one level it can be countered that while responsible *love* and sexual expression ought not to be sundered, procreation (even the procreative possibility) and sex ought not to be irrevocably joined. "Be fruitful and multiply" has now overfilled the earth. On another level it can also be argued that the possibility of procreation has not consistently been insisted upon by Christian orthodoxy, as witness the validity of the marriage between a man and a woman, one of whom is known to be irreversibly sterile.

What of the notion of essential gender complementarity? Barth claims that there is no "fellow humanity" apart from the covenanted relationship with one of the opposite sex. But it is more theologically defensible to affirm that there is no genuine humanity apart from *relationship* and *community*. To insist that the relationship which constitutes the image of God must be heterosexual assumes that the psychic natures of women and men are somehow biologically-given and ontologically unchangeable. Rosemary Ruether speaks vigorously to this point: "Such a concept of complementarity depends on a sadomasochistic concept of male and female relations. It covertly demands the continued dependency and underdevelopment of woman in order to validate the thesis that two kinds of personalities exist by nature in males and females and which are each partial expressions of some larger whole. Such a view can allow neither men nor women to be whole persons who can develop both their active and their affective sides."[21]

Still another contention of Barth's position is that homosexuality means a "despising" of the other sex. But this lacks both logical and factual foundations. It equates an aversion to intercourse with an aversion to persons. Actually, many gay people exhibit the ability to establish particularly meaningful and loving relationships with members of the opposite sex precisely because sexual "conquest" in whatever form is excluded from the situation. Moreover, current research indicates the widespread amount of antipathy between persons of the *opposite* sex because of the dominance-submission patterns ingrained in our sex-role stereotyping.[22] Indeed, the logic of Barth's argument would seem to be that *heterosexuals* by *their* very nature should despise members of their own sex—an unsupportable assumption.

And finally, Barth maintains that homosexuality is idolatrous because it is basically self-worship and narcissism: the gay person is just loving in the other the reflection of the self. But this claim does grave injustice to both the uniqueness of persons and the capacities which gay people amply demonstrate for self-giving love. When a person in a committed relationship deeply loves another of the same sex, it is difficult to understand how this can be construed as self-love—except if one adopts an untenable "biologism" about human relatedness and ignores the unity of the body-self.

We return to Muehl to examine the second major argument of the rejecting-nonpunitive position: that undesirable social consequences most likely would result from homosexuality's acceptance. Underneath Muehl's fears for the future of the family seems to lie the unspoken conviction that the church's approval of same-sex orientation would bring in its wake a significant increase in numbers of those choosing to be gay. But this is highly unlikely. Research shows no demonstrable increase in homosexual behavior in the quarter century since Kinsey's study in spite of some lessening of punitive attitudes in recent years.[23] Indeed, if one's dominant sexual orientation is, for the great majority, not a matter of conscious choice, this is quite understandable. It may be the case that some heterosexual people, perhaps quite unconsciously, assume that there is something so attractive in the gay experience that if it were not stringently forbidden many others would choose this orientation.

The great majority of gay persons do not appear to have any more choice about their affectional orientation than do the great majority of heterosexuals. There is no general agreement about the causes of homosexuality. Major theories cluster around two different approaches, the psychogenic and the genetic, but both remain in dispute.[24] Some researchers are now admitting that when we know more about the causes of heterosexuality (about which we know precious little at present) then we shall also know more about the causes of homosexuality. At least one thing is increasingly clear, however: sexual orientation is relatively fixed by early childhood through processes about which the individual makes no conscious choice.

If sexual orientation for the great majority of heterosexuals and gay persons is not freely chosen, neither is it easily reversed. Positive therapeutic results in that minority of gay people who have sought treatment to reverse their orientation have been minimal. One study contends that there are actually no validated instances of successful sexual preference reorientation through therapy.[25] Behavioral modification programs using "aversive therapy" have been able to condition some gays against attraction to their own sex but have been notably unable to replace that with similar attraction to the opposite sex. In 1975 the therapist who had developed and popularized the orgasmic reorientation technique disavowed his own treatment and called upon other behavioral therapists to cease, because such attempts were proving harmful to the subjects' whole personality structures—a particularly dehumanizing result.[26]

The adverse social consequences argument also hinges upon the assumption that gay people are inherently less capable of interpersonal and social functioning than are heterosexuals. It is significant, however, that in 1974 the American Psychiatric Association removed homosexuality from its list of mental disorders, saying "homosexuality *per se* implies no impairment in judgment, stability, reliability, or general social or vocational capabilities." Those clinicians who have attributed personality problems to gays *because* of their sexual orientation usually have drawn their observations from their own patients without recognizing or admitting that their heterosexual patients *also* have personality problems—and that is why they have come for therapy. The best comparative study to date remains that of Evelyn Hooker who found that when batteries of personality tests were administered to samples of male heterosexuals and male gays, neither group of which was in therapy, the clinical psychologists evaluating the test results could neither distinguish sexual orientation nor find "demonstrable pathology" among those later identified as homosexually-oriented.[27] "Neurotic" traits typically ascribed to gay persons are essentially the same for members of any oppressed minority group, and in cultures where homosexual behavior has been fully accepted such traits do not discernibly appear.[28]

Harmful consequences for the institution of family life is another fear expressed in this position. Even if gay persons were no less prone to emotional instability because of their sexual orientation, if society endorses same-sex coupling what will happen to the concept of the Christian family? Thus, Muehl asks, "Can the battered institution of Christian marriage stand the sight of gay unions being solemnized at the altar?"[29]

It is likely, however, that gay acceptance would actually bring constructive family consequences. There are several reasons for this. At present a fair number of marital difficulties and divorces stem from the fact that one of the spouses is primarily homosexual in orientation and has been pushed into marriage by social expectations and by the desire to escape detection. One priest who serves as a canon lawyer in a Catholic marriage tribunal contends that in over a third of the divorces with which he has dealt, one of the partners was homosexually inclined, a fact of major disruption for the marriage.[30] It seems highly probable in this regard that marital stability would be well served if heterosexual union were not viewed as the only avenue to respectability.

Other beneficial results for family life can be foreseen as well. Greater acceptance of homosexuality is likely to ease the current pressures toward the heterosexual's living up to rigid sex-role stereotypes. The acting out of such stereotypes when they are not authentic to one's unique personality is predictably a major factor in marital difficulties. Moreover, emotional intimacy between heterosexual family members of the same gender is likely to be enhanced. Such intimacy—between father and son, for example—too often is still inhibited by unrecognized homosexual fears. And, of no minor importance, the syndromes of alienation and rejection within families when a child is discovered to be gay would be ameliorated. Speaking to this point, Peggy Way writes out of an extensive counseling experience with gay people and their families: "I feel terrible sadness and pathos over the beautiful 'children' many parents are missing because sexuality gets in the way. All the rich humanness, spirituality, commitment, kindness I get to enjoy and share is lost to parents who cannot deal with the homosexuality of their own children, regardless of their other fine qualities."[31] In short, the picture of invidious consequences to family life from gay acceptance is highly overdrawn. In fact, the greater likelihood is quite the other way around: there are positive benefits to be foreseen.

Positive benefits more than negative consequences can also be foreseen for society as a whole. Societal health is always integrally related to social justice, and justice is served when discrimination against minority groups on the basis of unfair stereotypes is mitigated. Justice is also served when violence and the more destructive forms of competition are mitigated, and our attempt to understand the exaggerated aggressiveness of many male heterosexuals must take seriously the presence of conscious and unconscious fears of homosexuality. In a difficult-to-measure but predictable way, society would also benefit from the creative energies released in countless gay people, were they to be fully accepted. At present, closeted gays time and again report the daily energy drain inevitable for one forced to live a double life. If of a different sort, the drain on the personal resources of publicly-avowed gays is surely no less. Society presses them to make their homosexual orientation central to their identities, coerces them into spending time and energy defending their acceptability, and then through its various door-closing discriminations deprives itself of their best talents. Once again, not only is the case for harmful social consequences difficult to demonstrate, but the more persuasive arguments lie on the side of social benefit.

There is a basic flaw which underlies the entire rejecting-nonpunitive position: the assumption that it is possible to reject the homosexual orientation as such and still be nonpunitive toward gays as persons. Further comment on this is warranted, but I shall do so in the context of the next position.

Qualified acceptance might be the term for a third theological option regarding homosexuality. Helmut Thielicke is its best example, and his argument follows several steps. Similar to Barth, Thielicke first argues, "The fundamental order of creation and the created determination of the two sexes make it appear justifiable to speak of homosexuality as a 'perversion' . . . [which] is in every case *not* in accord with the order of creation."[32] But Thielicke is more open to contemporary psychological and medical research on the subject. Hence, he takes a second step: "But now experience shows that constitutional homosexuality at any rate is largely unsusceptible to medical or psychotherapeutic treatment, at least so far as achieving the desired goal of a fundamental conversion to normality is concerned."[33] Further, he says, homosexuality as a *predisposition* ought not to be depreciated any more than the varied distortions of the created order in which all fallen people share.

But what about genital expression? If a gay person can change in sexual orientation, such change should actively be sought. Admittedly, however, most cannot. Then, Thielicke contends, such persons should seek to sublimate their homosexual desires and not act on them. But some constitutional homosexuals "because of their vitality" are not able to practice abstinence. If that is the case, they should structure their sexual relationships "in an ethically responsible way" (in adult, fully-committed relationships). They should make the best of their painful situations without idealizing them or pretending that they are normal.

Thielicke's argument is important. For one thing, it is more empirically informed than the rejecting-nonpunitive position. Further, this argument now represents the position of a number of church leaders and several recent denominational statements on the issue. But the argument still is unacceptable, in my judgment. This position, like Barth's, is grounded in an essentially nonhistoricist, rigid version of natural law. And, in spite of its greater humanness, the position becomes self-contradictory. In effect, the gay person is told, "We heterosexual Christians sympathize with your plight, and if you *must* give genital expression to your orientation you must do it in a morally responsible way—but do not forget that you are a sinner *because of your sexual orientation* and do not deny that you are a sexual pervert."

An ethics of the gospel ought never forget that the capacity for moral responsibility is intrinsically related to self-acceptance which, in turn, depends on one's acceptance by others and, ultimately, by God. Gay persons frequently have been told by their families that they do not belong to them, by the church that they are desperate sinners because of their affectional orientation, by medical doctors that they are sick, and by the law that they are criminals. In the face of this onslaught, it is amazing that so many are emotionally stable and sexually responsible. If loneliness, self-doubt, depression, and promiscuity do have a higher incidence among gays, it is fully understandable. Then we should cut through the vicious circle of self-fulfilling prophecy and strike at the root of the problem—social oppression. Thielicke fails to do this. More liberal though his position might be, by continuing to label same-sex orientation as a perversion of God's natural law, he encourages the continuation of punitive attitudes toward gays. If it be argued that we can reject the sin without rejecting the sinner, the question must be asked, but what if the so-called "sin" is as much a part of the person as the color of the skin? The upshot of it all is that Thielicke's position effectively undermines its own hopes for responsible and faithful sexual relationships.

The fourth major theological possibility is *full acceptance*. Those who affirm this position most often make the assumption that the homosexual orientation is more of a given than a free choice. More fundamentally, however, this position rests on the conviction that same-sex relationships can richly express and be the vehicle of God's humanizing intentions.

Though still in a minority, the advocates of full acceptance are increasing in number. In 1963 the English Friends stated in their widely-read *Towards a Quaker View of Sex,* "One should no more deplore 'homosexuality' than left-handedness. . . . Homosexual affection can be as selfless as heterosexual affection, and therefore we cannot see that it is in some way morally worse."[34] From the Catholic side, in 1976 Fr. John McNeill published his impressive case for gay acceptance, *The Church and the Homosexual.* Among other issues, emphasizing the positive contributions which homosexual acceptance can make to church and society, he contends, "The objective acceptance of the homosexual community will potentially leave both communities (homosexual and heterosexual) free from the need to conform to narrow stereotypes, and positively free to develop all the qualities that belong to the fullness of the human personality."[35]

Among theologians it has been Norman Pittenger, however, who has articulated the full acceptance position most persistently over the years.[36] God, he affirms, is the "Cosmic Lover," ceaselessly and unfailingly in action as love, and manifested supremely in Jesus Christ. God's abiding purpose for humankind is that in response to divine action we should realize our intended humanity as human lovers—in the richest, broadest, and most responsible sense of the term. Our embodied sexuality is the physiological and psychological base for our capacity to love.

For all of its continuity with animal sexuality, human sexuality is different, continues Pittenger. As persons our sexuality means the possibility of expressing and sharing a total personal relationship in love, a relationship which contributes immeasurably toward our intended destiny. Hence, abnormality or deviance should not be defined statistically, but rather in reference to the norm of humanity in Jesus Christ. Gay persons desire and need deep and lasting relationships just as do heterosexuals, and appropriate genital expression should be denied to neither.

Thus, the ethical question which Pittenger poses is this: what sexual behavior will serve and enhance, rather than inhibit, damage, or destroy the fuller realization of our divinely-intended humanity? The answer is sexual behavior in accord with an ethics of love. This means commitment and trust, tenderness, respect for the other, and the desire for ongoing and responsible communion with the other. On the negative side, an ethics of love mandates against selfish sexual expression, cruelty, impersonal sex, obsession with sex, and against actions done without willingness to take responsibility for the consequences. Such an ethics always asks about the meanings of acts in their total context—in the relationship itself, in society, and in regard to God's intended direction for human life. Such an ethics of sexual love is equally appropriate to heterosexual and gay Christians. There is no double standard.

Further Reflections

Reinhold Neibuhr argued that Christians must learn to live with the tension of "having and not having the truth."[37] "Tolerance" in its truest sense, he maintained, comes when we can have vital convictions which lead to committed actions and, at the same time, recognize that our own "truth" is always incomplete and subject to distortion. Living with convictions we also then live within the reality of divine forgiveness and with respect for the convictions of those who sincerely differ from us. That spirit is always essential, I believe, but when we confront issues like homosexuality on which feelings are particularly deep and divided, it is especially crucial.

At various times I have felt the force of each of the first three stances which I have described, beginning as a teenager with the full complement of anti-gay stereotypes and prejudices. Having moved somewhat later into the rejecting-nonpunitive and then the qualified acceptance positions, several personal friendships with remarkable gay Christian people jarred me into further reflection. I came to believe that nothing less than full Christian acceptance of homosexuality and of its responsible genital expression adequately represented the direction of both gospel and contemporary research. While full acceptance means a rather sharp turning from the majority opinion in the Christian *moral* tradition about homosexuality, I am convinced that it does not mean an *ethical* change from the central thrust of the gospel. Rather, it means its fuller implementation.

There are times when we must challenge specific moral traditions of our heritage in the light of new empirical knowledge, new experience, and God's on-going revelation. Our ancestors-in-faith did not know what we now know about homosexuality as a psychosexual orientation, nor can we blame them for being persons of their own historical time. And the dependence of early Christians on certain cultural traditions prevented them (on this issue as on some other moral matters) from seeing some of the implications of that gospel to which they were sincerely committed. We ought neither blame them nor pretend that we have the full truth. Our judgments—whatever they may be—are conditioned and imperfect. But we do have some insights about homosexuality now that they did not have access to, and it would be unfaithful not to use the best lights that we have.[38]

We have little definitive knowledge about the causes of homosexuality, however—or of heterosexuality, for that matter.[39] We do know that homosexuality is extraordinarily difficult to define as a coherent phenomenon, simply because gay people like heterosexuals are diverse and unique. They differ in behavior and feelings, in levels of sexual interest, in roles and ways of lovemaking, in the amount of genital activity, in attitudes about their own and others' homosexuality, in the extent to which they are open or covert about their orientation. This conclusion from the Institute for Sex Research at Indiana University bears emphasis: "Our data appear to indicate that homosexuality involves a large numer of widely divergent experiences—developmental, sexual, social, and psychological—and that even after a person has been labeled 'homosexual' on the basis of his or her preferred sexual object choice, there is little that can be predicted about the person on the basis of that label."[40] One thing, I would add, can be predicted, however, precisely because it is common to all human beings: gay persons desire and seek meaning and wholeness in and through their sexuality, and their sexuality is for them (as for anyone else) of intrinsic importance to their capacity for any kind of human love.

This chapter's emphasis thus far has been upon one of the two directions appropriate to sexual theology: the movement from Christian faith to sexuality. But we need also to make inquiry in the other direction as well, asking how our own experience as sexual persons tends to give shape to our perceptions of the faith and its moral values. In doing so we can understand more fully something of the persisting power of anti-gay stereotypes as well as the intensity of feeling about this whole issue.

Some of the anti-homosexual emotion might stem from the repugnance some people feel about the physical acts of gay sexual expression. It is well to recall just what they are. The chief expressions are hand-holding, kissing, mutual caressing, and mutual masturbation (for both sexes), cunnilingus (for women); and fellatio and anal intercourse (for men). The point is that all of these physical techniques are the property of heterosexuals as well, some statistically more common than others but all widely used. It is unlikely that the foreignness of the physical act to heterosexual experience explains very much.

It may be that heterosexuals feel less personally defined by their sexual orientation and that the apparent centrality of homosexuality to the gay's personal identity is disturbing. But, to the extent that this is true, it is more effect than cause of discrimination—just as racial minority people are typically more conscious of their own skin color, through countless daily reminders from the majority. It seems, on the whole, more accurate to say that heterosexuals simply tend to be preoccupied with the narrowly sexual aspect of the gay person's life, in spite of the fact that gays "vary profoundly in the degree to which their homosexual commitment and its facilitation become the organizing principle of their lives."[41]

For this reason language becomes highly significant. The term "homosexual" is clinically correct if it refers simply to the fact that an individual's primary affectional and genital orientation is toward the same sex. Thus, to speak of "homosexuality" meaning a psychosexual orientation or to speak of "homosexual acts" where the reference is specifically to genital and other physical expression is quite accurate. But unfortunately the word carries other associations for many—especially that of clinical pathology and a focus on sexual acts *per se* rather than on human beings. Thus, gays are entirely appropriate in their insistence that *persons* who have this alternative form of sexual orientation be called gay. It is a way of saying more comprehensively and more accurately that one's identity as a sexual human being is far broader than what one does in bed. It is a way of resisting the corrosive effect of having to deal with one's own self-image so constantly in genital terms, in spite of the majority's desire to keep the focus there.[42]

To press the causes of anti-gay feeling more fully, we need to reflect once more on the two alienating sexual dualisms. Consider spiritualistic dualism. By the strange twist of heterosexual emotional-logic, it would appear that gays are resented because they seem to have succumbed less to the spirit-body dualism which afflicts us all in various ways. Feeling the internally divisive affects of spiritualism, we yearn (unconsciously as well as consciously) to be whole, to reclaim the essential unity of the body-self. But since majority stereotype insists that gays are more sexually defined and simply *more sexual* than the rest, they may well become the targets of subconscious envy precisely for that reason. Thus, the stereotype bears its curious and unintended harvest, but one which roots it even more firmly in the feelings of many who hold it.

The problem of patriarchal or sexist dualism may be even more basic to anti-gay feeling. This might be experienced in several related ways. One is the heterosexual's possible anxiety about homosexual feelings within the self. While for the sake of economy I have been using "gay" and "heterosexual" in ways that might suggest two sharply distinct and mutually-exclusive groups, current research indicates that people commonly tend toward some degree of bisexuality. Most, for reasons not yet fully understood, develop a *dominant* orientation toward one side or the other. Kinsey's early hypothesis, however, has been repeatedly confirmed by subsequent research: on the scale of zero to six, relatively few persons fall near the zero end (exclusively heterosexual in *both* feelings and behavior) and relatively few near the six mark (exclusively homosexual). Most are somewhere in between, though with a clearly felt and expressed bias toward one orientation rather than the other.

A recent study draws this conclusion: "Although we *suspect* that approximately four or five percent of American males—and half of that percentage of females—are exclusively homosexual in their behaviors throughout their lives, much larger numbers are exclusively homosexual in their behaviors at any given time, and even larger numbers engage in both homosexual and heterosexual acts from time to time. For a given individual, ratings on this homosexual-heterosexual continuum may go up or down depending upon the person's age, life circumstances, and the culture in which he or she lives."[43] Further, there is not necessarily a perfect fit between one's feelings and one's behaviors regarding sexual orientation.

Even for those whose genital expression beyond puberty has been exclusively heterosexual, there may be homosexual feelings present even if relegated to the unconscious level. Freud's notion of reaction formation becomes pertinent at this point: one way of coping with unwanted impulses felt in the self is by attacking it in others.[44]

Because of patriarchalism and exaggerated images of masculinity, such anxiety is frequently felt more strongly by men—an additional reason why male gays have consistently been more the objects of negative majority feeling than have lesbians. It seems highly probable that the much more severe condemnation of male homosexual acts in the Old Testament expresses this patriarchal phenomenon: "If a man lies with a male *as with a woman,* both of them have committed an abomination; they shall be put to death, their blood is upon them" (Leviticus 20:13; italics added). If male dignity was a primary consideration, then "sodomy" could not be tolerated, because when a man acted sexually like a woman he was committing a *degradation*—literally, a loss of grade or status—not only in regard to himself but also, by implication, for every other male. But this is not true of the early Hebrews alone. Anthropologists have noted the strong tendency of patriarchal cultures, wherever they may be, to view (especially male) homosexuality as "the unspeakable sin," while matriarchal cultures have been strikingly different on this issue.[45]

A male is supposed to feel masculine in any patriarchy. A psychiatrist comments, "I believe that homosexuality is also abhorred by men because it is felt by them to represent confused, poorly defined and poorly delineated boundaries of what constitutes so-called normal male feelings. Homosexuality, the word and the symbol, threatens masculine gender identity, and identity generally, because it is felt as potential eradication of safe limits and borders within whose confines we can rest easy and sure of what and who we are supposed to be and what we are supposed to feel."[46] Pollution rituals as studied by anthropologists provide added insight. Those rituals and punishments, in both ancient tribes and modern societies, tend to focus upon the marginal person who does not clearly represent society's patterns and symbols of order. Such persons may be doing nothing morally wrong, yet their status is indefinable. But this places them very basically "in the wrong" for they have "developed some wrong condition or simply crossed some line which should not have been crossed and this displacement unleashes danger for someone."[47]

In spite of the lack of any demonstrable connection between male homosexual orientation and "effeminate" behavior patterns, the gay male seems particularly threatening to many other men. He seems to belie the importance of super-masculinity, and his very presence seems to call into question so much that many other men have sacrificed to be "manly." But many heterosexual women likewise have difficulty coping with the lesbian. The lesbian is independent from male control in ways that other women are not, and when a heterosexual woman has deeply internalized sexist dualism such independence becomes a considerable threat. Furthermore, both men and women of heterosexual orientation can feel diminished by the presence of a gay person of the opposite sex. Consciously or unconsciously there is awareness that the gay person has no specifically sexual interest in them. To the extent that sexual attractiveness is vital to one's sense of basic self-worth, this, too, is threatening.

There are additional ways in which gay people raise the anxieties of many heterosexuals. Because of their sexual orientation, gay folk appear to disvalue commonly-held values concerning marriage, family, and children. And because we so frequently judge others using our own standards as the ultimate and unquestionable norm, those who so obviously deviate from our experience seem to be seriously deviant indeed. Curiously enough, gay people can also awaken in others a dimly-recognized fear of death. Sometimes the hope of vicarious immortality through children and grandchildren is, in fact, stronger than the resurrection faith for many Christians. If so, the presence of the gay person who (usually) does not have children can awaken the fear of death, even though consciousness of that might be only a nameless anxiety.[48]

At its root, the issue goes beyond the insights of the psychologists, anthropologists, and sociologists, valuable though those insights be. It is finally a theological matter, an issue of faith. If we must find an important part of our personal security in a status which depends upon the negative definition of those who differ from us—and if we must find the security of our social order through rigid demarcations of behaviors regardless of their causation, their motivations, their moral intent, or their actual consequences—then we are living by something other than the grace of God.

On the other hand, through that very grace we might know something of the healing possibilities for the sexual dualisms that beset us. To that extent we will not need to project our own alienation onto others but can join with them in our common liberation. It will be liberation from a hierarchical and intensely power-conscious attitude toward life. It will be liberation from the need to organize the proper membership of both church and society around a principle of sex orientation. It will be liberation from the need to blame a minority group for the erosion of all of "our" values. But more, it can be a liberation into greater equality, more sensitive abilities to care about persons, augmented justice, in short, a freedom to love more fully—others and also ourselves.[49]

Implications for the Church

The church's unequivocal support of civil rights for gay people ought not depend upon Christian agreement about the theological and moral appropriateness of homosexuality. The matter of civil rights is a matter of basic Christian commitment to social justice for all persons.[50]

The present legal situation is highly uneven. A few states and municipalities have legislated civil protection for gays, prohibiting discrimination in employment, public accommodations, housing, and licensing on the basis of "affectional or sexual preference." But the majority have not, nor has the federal government. And the passage of such legislation is no guarantee that it will not be rescinded.[51]

Most states still have punitive legislation concerning gay people on their books, though in actual practice enforcement is varied and unpredictable.[52] In any event, laws labeling "sodomy" or "unnatural sexual intercourse" as punishable offenses have a number of inherent problems.

They violate the rights of privacy. They are ineffective and virtually unenforceable except through objectionable police methods such as entrapment and enticement. Yet, whether they are enforced or not, sodomy laws stigmatize as criminal the person whose only "crime" is preference for the same sex, and inevitably such laws will take their toll in the gay person's sense of self-worth. Moreover, an important principle of church-state separation may be involved. What some Christians on fairly narrow doctrinal grounds consider a *sin* ought not to be made a *crime* unless that moral judgment can be defended on broader grounds of public welfare and unless the behavior in question constitutes a provable threat to public decency and personal well-being.

What about the internal life of the churches?[53] If and when the churches were to affirm homosexuality and its responsible expression as Christianly appropriate, the implications for church life would be many. Full acceptance of gay Christians into the ongoing life of Christian congregations is basic. Because it is still so largely absent, gay movement toward congregations organized by themselves and principally for gays will undoubtedly continue. It is completely understandable, and in the present day it may be necessary. It is also regrettable, for the majority's exclusionism then continues to fragment the body of Christ. It is an irony, indeed, for while the human sciences and contemporary culture at large have been urging the church to take sexuality more seriously, the church in regard to gays and women has made sexuality primary: it has been used as the organizing principle by which these people have been excluded from full participation.[54]

Congregational affirmation of gays would involve significant attitudinal changes on the part of many other members of the church. Full acceptance of gays as persons, for example, means that all of those gestures and behaviors which are appropriate for heterosexuals are also appropriate for gay people.

Effective pastoral counseling and support for gay persons is crucial. By training, profession, and calling the clergy should be those to whom gay people might turn in complete confidence. At present it often is not so. Lack of sufficent information, lack of insight into the problems which gays confront in a hostile environment, and lack of some deep understanding and acceptance concerning their own sexuality remain formidable problems with many clergy. And this constitutes an important agenda item for theological education.

The church's ministry is to the gay community as well as to gay individuals. While full integration into the richly diverse body of Christ is the ideal, there is also need for supportive gay Christian groups now and in the foreseeable future. A study of male gays in the United States and two European countries points this out: "Perhaps our most salient finding pertains to the benficial effects (in terms of psychological adjustment) of a supportive environment—social relations with other homosexuals, their own institutions and publications."[55] From gay coffee houses in local churches to denominationally-supported gay caucuses, these things are needed. That gay bars and baths are still virtually the only institutionalized meeting places in many urban areas should make a claim upon the church's conscience.

The ordination question continues to be difficult. Not only division over theological and ethical issues but also differing patterns of ministerial placement and job security cause reservations for otherwise sympathetic church leaders. While there are undoubtedly ordained homosexually-oriented ministers right now in every denomination, the vast majority of them quite understandably continue their secrecy. It was not until 1972 that a major American denomination, the United Church of Christ, ordained a publicly avowed gay candidate, and the second instance took another four years, this time an Episcopalian event. There will be others, but the process is painful and painfully slow. The recommendation made by the United Church's Executive Council to its ordaining bodies is worthy of consideration by other denominations: "that in the instance of considering a stated homosexual candidacy for ordination, the issue should not be his/her homosexuality as such, but rather the candidate's total view of human sexuality and his/her understanding of the morality of its use."[56] Though presently this may be difficult to implement in some denominational situations, it is the logic of full acceptance. Church assemblies may continue to claim "prudential grounds" as their main reason for barring gay ordinations for some time to come, but one day perhaps that form of prudence will sound as thin as when it was used to bar women and racial minorities from ministry.

Most difficult of all for the church at present is the idea of "homosexual marriage." Heterosexuals of the "rejecting-punitive" and "rejecting-nonpunitive" persuasions, of course, are adamantly opposed to any such thing. But in the "qualified acceptance" position there is a curious ambivalence. One the one hand, there is an insistence that the non-celibate gay person have a genitally-exclusive permanent relationship; homosexual relationships are tolerated only insofar as they approximate heterosexual monogamy. (This insistence, I believe, often does not represent a genuine attempt to understand the range of meanings in homosexual relationships, nor does it do justice to the different social circumstances under which gay women and men must live.)[57] But when gay persons *do* want to relate their genital expression to life commitment, as many do, "the church in its concern for morality turns away from these moral hungers and concerns."[58]

It is true that the issue of marriage is complicated by the nature of symbolic traditions. As an ordinance or as a sacrament, marriage has a long theological and ecclesiastical history, and that history has been an exclusively heterosexual one. Deeply-rooted symbols are organic. They grow and develop, and sudden changes are seldom successfully legislated. But when existing symbols do not meet legitimate needs, new symbols and rites may be developed. A "Blessing of Union" rite (by whatever name), for example, might function for gays in ways fully parallel to the marriage rites. Such an ordinance would convey the Christian community's recognition, affirmation, pledge of support, and prayer for divine blessing to the gay couple whose intention is lasting fidelity.

Predictably, acceptance of this is a long time off. Heterosexual Christians who want to affirm individual gays but reject all homosexual genital love will argue that since genital expression belongs only in heterosexual marriage, gay Christians have only one legitimate and responsible choice—celibacy. "Just as we expect the heterosexual to be continent outside of marriage, so, too, the homosexual."[59] But this demonstrates lack of sensitivity to the gay person's socially-imposed dilemma. The heterosexual's abstinence is either freely chosen for a lifetime or it is temporary until marriage. But the celibacy some Christians would impose upon the gay person would be involuntary and unending.[60]

Those others who urge the non-celibate gay to seek a permanent relationship, and yet would withhold any liturgical blessing, are saying something different but also insensitive. By withholding full recognition of such sexual covenants the church only, if unintentionally, promotes promiscuity, for it says in effect, "*Whatever* your relationship is, it is not fit for public Christian affirmation, support, and celebration." To urge a course of action, fully-committed relationships, and then to deny communal and ritual support to those very relationships is to engage in a humanly destructive contradiction.

When and if the church moves toward liturgical support of gay unions, it should also press toward civil recognition. Such legal matters as tax laws, property rights, and inheritance rights are of legitimate concern to a gay couple and, I believe, are a matter of the equity to which love's justice presses us. Moreover, the symbolic affirmation given by the civil community through legal recognition ought not to be minimized.

On the difficult question of whether previously-married gay persons should be allowed to retain custody of their children when they enter into a gay union, the courts have taken a variety of positions. Yet the main difficulty of the question is not principally the matter of whether the children themselves would be shaped into a homosexual orientation. Dr. John Money speaks to the point: "Society's apprehensions notwithstanding, it is not inevitably psychically dangerous for children, boys or girls, to live with a divorced parent who sets up a new household with a partner of the same sex. . . . It is not the sameness or difference of the sex of the adults that counts, but the quality of the relationship between them, and the quality of the relationship they establish with the child." [61] The real difficulty lies in the fragmenting pressures which the social environment can put upon a same-sex couple, to the detriment of children. For this the church itself must acknowledge its share of responsibility—but it can also respond to the opportunity with its still considerable capacity to influence public opinion on such moral issues.

The ecclesiastical implications of full gay acceptance are doubtless complex, at least in their effective implementation. Understandably, however, many gay Christians are tired of waiting for all of the complexities to be resolved to the full satisfaction of the majority group. These minority Christians have waited—and have hurt—long enough.[62] Pushed away from the Lord's Table by subtle or blatant pressures, they have been pushed to find community in the gay bars, baths, and ghettos. One gay Christian puts it in these haunting words: "Usually, for most gay women and men, coming out *in* the church has meant coming out *of* the church. . . . Coming out of the closet, a process the church should be enabling and ennobling, is a process which must be experienced more often in the secular world rather than the Christian community. . . . And for most of those numerous gay persons who choose not to come out in the church because they want to *stay* in the church—in Christian communi-ty—the church has meant more than just a closet . . . the church has become for them a giant tomb, smelling of death rather than life." [63]

Surely there is much research on homosexuality (and on heterosexuali-ty as well) that still needs to be done. But this much is clear: our sexuality is vitally important to the dignity of each of us. The basic issue is really not about "them," but about all of us. How can we live less fearfully and more securely in the grace of God? What is the nature of that loving humanity toward which the Spirit presses us? And what does it mean to be a woman or a man in Jesus Christ?

Homosexuality and Christian Faith: A Theological Reflection

Theodore W. Jennings

The question of the appropriate relation of the church to homosexuals and homosexuality has emerged as one of major importance in the deliberations of denominational bodies. The ensuing debate too often takes the form of a contest between defenders of traditional morality on the one hand and apologists for homosexual life style on the other. What is too often lacking in this conservative-liberal confrontation is attention to pertinent theological reflection. In what follows my aim is not so much to provide as to provoke that kind of reflection.

From the outset I should indicate how I became interested in this subject and what my biases are. I have over the past several years had a number of friends and associates who were quite self-consciously homosexual. Many of these have been related in significant ways to the church. Some are committed laymen and laywomen, some are active

211

clergy, some are seminary students. Some of these friends are extraordinarily talented and powerful people. Others are haunted by self-doubt and self-loathing. All of them share a concern to understand themselves in the light of Christian faith. As pastor and as friend I want these folk to know that the Christian faith is ultimately a word not of judgment but of grace. I know how difficult this is when the church, through its official pronouncements and its unofficial atmosphere, reinforces in them the impression that they are neither understood nor wanted, neither loved nor even to be "tolerated." One of my biases is to want to defend these folk against the church. But I also have another bias: namely, that heterosexuality is a fundamentally superior form of sexuality to homosexuality.

As a theologian I have tried to ask whether either of these biases is appropriate or pertinent. I have had to discipline both my knee-jerk sympathy and my knee-jerk heterosexual certainty.

In the meantime the issue of homosexuals in the church has come to the fore in unexpected ways. I believe that the debate has both raised and obscured important issues, but it has seemed important to me that theologians address themselves to these issues in such a way as to help clarify them and to serve the church as it struggles to determine the appropriate stance.

What I will *not* do is propose a theology of homosexuality. That is, I do not intend to discover special principles which apply to this complex of issues in an ad hoc way. Rather I propose to ask how the fundamental principles of Christian theology illuminate this question or complex of issues.

God's Grace and God's Judgment

The basic principle of all theology, but one most forcefully brought to expression in this century by Karl Barth, is this: that in Christian faith we have to do with the gracious God whose one and supreme intention is to justify, save and redeem humanity not on the basis of a discrimination between better and worse persons but solely on the basis of God's own gracious election. Followed through with consistency, this principle maintains that no human act or condition can of itself constitute an insuperable obstacle to God's grace.[1]

The violation of this theological principle places in human hands the capacity to effect our own salvation. But this is justification by works, and therefore a counsel of human pride whose end result can only be despair or self-righteousness. Thus whatever is said in "Christian ethics" must always stand under this first principle and cannot be allowed to rescind God's gracious decree, election and activity in Christ in justifying the ungodly. With respect to the understanding of homosexuality, therefore, neither homosexual condition nor homosexual inclination nor specifically homosexual acts may be interpreted as excluding one from the domain of God's gracious intention.

A second principle, closely and indeed inseparably connected to the first, has to do with the universality of God's judgment in relation to which our fundamental human condition is disclosed as unrighteous whether as observers or as violators of "the Law." Thus the negative import of the gospel of God's grace is the radical undermining of all our attempts to establish ourselves in the pursuit of either "righteousness" or "unrighteousness."

What this means is that no "natural" human condition or life style is intrinsically justified or righteous—neither heterosexuality nor homosexuality, closed nor open marriage, celibacy nor profligacy. This negative assertion therefore stands against all attempts to argue for the autonomous or intrinsic legitimacy of any "life style" and against those who condemn homosexuality from the standpoint of an assumed righteousness of heterosexual marital fidelity or those who, condemning the obvious hypocrisies and oppressions ingredient to the institution of marriage, claim the autonomous validity of a homosexual life style.

These two principles in their interconnection (in which priority belongs to the first) make clear that no absolute or ultimate distinction can be made between homosexuality and heterosexuality. In both we have clearly exhibited the sinful condition of human beings—which human beings in this condition are encountered in a shattering and redeeming way by God's gracious will.

The use of the notion of "sin" in this connection frequently betrays a large-scale misunderstanding. As both Jesus and Paul make almost excessively clear, they address themselves only to "sinners" and the "lost." One should therefore view with alarm discussions of this question which, discovering that homosexuals are sinners, conclude that they are unfit for the ministry and, almost, for Christian community. Are we then necessarily to conclude that since homosexuals are sinners—and healthy heterosexuals are less so—that Christ died for homosexuals but not for us? Out of our own self-righteousness we therefore have condemned ourselves.

The Otherness of the Other

Now if the matter were left here in the ultimate context of God's judgment and grace, we would not have a Christian ethic. What we want but also what the Christian tradition provides is guidance in matters penultimate as well as ultimate.

I will begin here with another principle forcefully illuminated by Karl Barth. It is that our created, fallen and redeemed humanity is to be understood as co-humanity. This assertion derives from the clue of Genesis 1:26 that the image of God in us is expressed in that we are created male and female. I believe Barth is correct to take co-humanity, as evidenced in the two-gender character of our existence, to be the crucial determinant of our humanity.

This principle is applied by Barth and others in such a way as to place homosexuality in the wrong when contrasted with heterosexuality. Barth does not do this in a way that violates the first set of principles, but other theologians (e.g., Otto Piper) do. In either case we must ask whether this application is justified.

I believe the answer must be negative. That our humanity is co-humanity cannot be interpreted only in a sexual or genital way. If this is done, nothing remains of the symbolic and thus ethical significance of co-humanity. We then would have literalized the metaphor so as to deprive it of its general ethical significance. That significance is this—that human beings differ from one another; that this difference is that which we constantly seek to abrogate, so as to make the other conform to our desire (on the sexual level this is lust, on the political level it is oppression). But the otherness of the other is God's gift to us, by which gift we are summoned out of our isolation and into the co-humanity of love (Bonhoeffer).

Thus with respect to any relation the principle of co-humanity leads us to inquire: To what extent is this relationship predicated upon the reduction of the other to our own desire, and to what extent does it, however brokenly, embody the mutuality of co-humanity? Thus the principle of co-humanity does enable us to distinguish between better and worse relationships, but it cannot serve to dismiss homosexual relations as worse a priori.

Procreation and Family-Centeredness

A further principle often adduced in the discussion of homosexuality is that of natural law. As it applies to this context the argument goes: sexuality belongs to the law of nature, but it is ordered toward a particular purpose; namely, the procreation of children. Sexuality which does not have this end in view violates that order. Homosexuality is thus a perversion of the natural order and therefore of the law of God. This position, of major importance in Catholic moral theology, is also used in some Protestant discussions.

Obviously, all forms of human sexuality which do not have procreation as their goal fall equally under this principle: masturbation, contraception, nongenital sexuality between husband and wife, homosexuality. It is simply inconsistent to apply this principle to only one member of this set. Protestant sexual ethics in general have a more celebrative and less goal-oriented understanding of sexuality, and it is on this basis that contraception is not proscribed by Protestant theology. On what basis, then, can we revive this understanding of natural law to condemn homosexuality?

In the American situation the ghost of this natural-law principle lives on in the "sanctity of the home and family." Christianity in American Protestantism has been linked closely with the preservation of the life of the family, and on this basis homosexuality is understood as a clear violation of the ideal of family life.

Now as a theologian I am inclined to ask whether the "family-centeredness" of American Christianity can be justified theologically, and here (against many of my own instincts) I must answer No. We have only to remind ourselves of how suspicious of family ties both Jesus and Paul were to see what an anomaly the identification of Christian life with family life is. But if this identification is an anomaly, then we certainly cannot argue that because homosexuality (as a permanent and exclusive sexual pattern) precludes marriage and family, it must be ruled out a priori as unchristian.

The Biblical Proscriptions

Let us turn to the scriptural passages which are frequently adduced to buttress the proscription of homosexuality. Of course a responsible application of Scripture cannot proceed from a mere collation of proof texts. If that were an appropriate procedure, then we would find it necessary to side against the liberation of women (including giving them a significant role in the church) and against modern science with its evolutionary perspectives. More seriously, perhaps, we would violate the clear hermeneutics of Scripture itself with its continual modification and correction of the traditions which are received in any particular stage of its development.

Thus we must ask in each case whether the passage in question brings to expression a central principle of the faith or is to be understood as accidental, peripheral or timebound.

In the space available here, I must restrict myself to the Levitical texts and Romans 1:26f. (A more detailed investigation may be found in D. Sherwin Bailey's *Homosexuality and the Western Christian Tradition*.)

The two passages in the Leviticus holiness code (Lev. 18:22 and 20:13) clearly condemn (and demand the death penalty for) acts of sexual intercourse between two males (apparently anal intercourse). We must note that no reason is given for the prohibitions; they are simply listed among a whole series of such prohibitions. Since these prohibitions are found in the ritual law and are apparently equal in severity with prohibitions against drinking the blood of an animal or having intercourse with a menstruating woman, or having an ox which gores one's neighbor, their pertinence for theological ethics is generally disputed. It is sometimes asserted that the Old Testament proscribes homosexual acts because they are nonprocreative, but this connection is never made in Leviticus—or elsewhere in Scripture. Thus we must ask to what extent we consider the proscriptions against homosexual acts in Leviticus generally binding upon the Christian conscience. Unless we understand ourselves bound to all Levitical proscriptions equally, then some reason in principle must be provided for discrimination among them. We have seen that principles normally invoked to make the proscription of homosexual acts binding do not in fact justify such a procedure. We must conclude that the Levitical texts do not provide us with sufficient grounds to enforce such a proscription.

With respect to the oft-cited passage of Romans 1:26f. we must notice that Paul's mention of anal intercourse between males functions as an illustration of the consequence of God's having abandoned the gentiles to their own wickedness. Thus these acts are taken by Paul to be expressive as much of God's judgment as of human depravity. In any case, it is clear that the aim of Paul's argument in Romans is not to exclude those who perform homosexual acts from the sphere of God's grace but rather to use the example of homosexual activity as an expression of the great need which all human beings have for the grace of God which justifies the "ungodly."

So far our reflections have produced a somewhat negative result. I have argued that there is no theological principle which compels us to perpetuate the proscription of homosexual acts. Let us now turn to inquire whether there may not be in fact principles of theology which illumine the relation between the church and homosexuality in terms other than the proscription of homosexual acts.

Standing with the Outcast

One theological principle which has a clear basis in Old Testament prophecy and the teachings of Jesus is God's identification with the poor, the outcast, the oppressed. In order to apply this principle to the case of homosexuals we must ask to what extent homosexuals in our society constitute a class of oppressed and outcast persons. I do not suppose that all clear-headed and morally sensitive Christians will come to the same conclusion here. After some reflection on the legal and social plight of homosexuals in our society, I have concluded that homosexuals do, to a significant degree, fall within this category. They are persons against whom existing laws are enforced capriciously and arbitrarily, persons who are continually threatened with exposure, with loss of job and social standing.

To the degree to which the principle of identification with the oppressed applies here, the church must stand with homosexuals against those socio-political structures that deprive them of the protection of the law and the rights and privileges of full members of society. This principle has been recognized by the United Methodist Church and other churches. Moreover, it has a lasting tradition in the history of the church, whose official position has always been to shield homosexuals from the application of civil authority. Existing laws against homosexual acts are derived from the attempt of King Henry VIII to divest the church of its power and to replace it with the state in the enforcing of moral legislation.

Thus it appears clear to me that the church appropriately allies itself with many of the aims and interests of gay liberation, as it also and for similar reasons may ally itself with the aims and interests of women's liberation or black liberation. This is not to say that these expressions of liberation from oppression are equitable or stand on the same plane, or place the same demands upon us. It is rather to say that the way in which any of these movements places a claim upon us is by way of our responsibility to imitate the divine mercy which takes the place and the side of those whom society casts out and oppresses.

The Perilous Character of Sexuality

Further clarification of our problem may result if we consider the theologically ambiguous character of sexuality. I realize that many of us inside and outside the church have come to suppose that sexuality, both as condition and as act, is morally neutral at worst. In this case sexual activity, where it does not "violate the other person or oneself," may be understood not merely as morally neutral but as morally positive as well. I have myself entertained this view, but further reflection upon the biblical and ecclesiastical traditions, upon philosophical and psychological interpretations, and upon my own experience and that of others to whom I am related as pastor or friend has led me to believe that this "emancipated" view is naive at best and is even potentially damaging to any moral sensitivity at all. The more overtly sexual our relationships become, the more perilous they become as well. For in sexuality we are placed in the greatest physical and psychic proximity to one another, and thus it is here that we are most severely tempted to reduce the other to the instrument for the realization of our narcissistic desire.

Whatever proclivities toward a Manichean libel of God's creation and its goodness we may discover in the "puritanical" streams of the Judeo-Christian traditions, and however much we may deplore and seek to correct these proclivities, we must also see that here at least the seriousness of sexuality was recognized. However much we may wish to assert the goodness and even the playfulness of sexuality (I remain persuaded that we both may and must assert this against all defamations of God's gifts), we must not forget that we assert this in the face of a fallen condition in which sexuality has become perilous, fraught with the temptation to do violence to one another.

How then does this principle of the perilous character of sexuality apply to the question of homosexual "life style"? Its application means, first of all, that we cannot regard things like sexual life style or sexual "preference" as a matter of no importance or as an area in which the individual is to have free reign. These things are not morally neutral but morally ambiguous. By "morally ambiguous" I mean that they are heavy with the perils of temptation at the same time that they are or may be the good gifts of creation.

The way sexuality as a thoroughly ambiguous and perilous phenomenon in the fallen creation has been correlated to a restored and redeemed humanity is through the notion of vocation. Protestant Christian ethics have made the category of vocation central for an understanding of the Christian life. In this setting, vocation is a comprehensive designation for all that characterizes the relation of the Christian to the world of nature and society. Traditionally this notion has been applied to sexuality in terms of two vocations: marriage and celibacy. Under the protective signification of these two vocational stances, sexuality has been understood as restored to or attaining a positive status.

The Question of Sexual Vocation

Now we must ask how the category or principle of vocation applies to the situation of the homosexual (that is, one who is inclined or driven to seek persons of the same sex for sexual gratification). It is possible to argue that an unalterable tendency toward homosexuality, when it means the impossibility of traditional marriage, must also mean that one is called to celibacy (the renunciation of sexual activity for God's sake). This stance is regularly presupposed even by Protestants who do not otherwise have any use for the vocation of celibacy (e.g., Billy Graham).

The difficulty of such a position is that it equates the vocation of celibacy with the condition of homosexuality without any clear basis for doing so. In fact such a view misunderstands the character of celibacy as vocation, which is never to be confused with mere abstinence nor founded upon some "natural" inclination.

A further possible application is to agree (as Norman Pittenger does) that celibacy is not a category to be applied a priori to the situation of the homosexual. In this case Pittenger then suggests an ethic for homosexuality which approaches as closely as possible the vocation of marriage; i.e., permanent, monogamous relationships integrating sexual activity together with serious regard and love for one another.[3]

A third possibility is to inquire whether marriage and celibacy exhaust the possibilities of an obedient sexuality. Here we are on relatively new ground, I think, but it is terrain which must be explored (even if not finally colonized) if we are to be able to respond constructively not only to the questions of homosexuality but to the questions of sexual life style which confront us again and again under such headings as "open marriage" or "new morality." It is only with an understanding of vocation and the question of sexual vocation other than marriage and celibacy that a responsible Christian sexual ethic can be elaborated which is neither reactionary nor soft-headed, neither simply orthodox nor simply enlightened, but a genuine application of Christian moral insight to the contemporary setting.

It is with this principle of vocation that we enter most fully into the situation of pastoral counseling and moral guidance. The deployment of this principle here means first to insist that the homosexual is not abandoned by God or by Christ's church. The homosexual (I mean here the full range of homosexual inclination from exclusive to subliminated: this range therefore may include all of us) is confronted also as homosexual by God's grace and judgment and is summoned to a comprehensive vocation inclusive of his or her homosexual inclination.

Obedient Responses

To what use then is one of homosexual inclination to put this homosexuality? What is the vocational character of homosexual inclination? How is this inclination to be put in service to Christ? Here, I think, no a priori answer is appropriate. Here there can only properly be careful probing, conscientious questioning and obedient response.

Is homosexual inclination an obstacle to be overcome—a training ground for the will in the discipline of renunciation which prepares one for some further obedience? As a pastor I cannot rule this out, but I also cannot impose it. (Placing homosexuality in this context calls into question behavioral modification schemes for remedying an unruly homosexual inclination. Vocation entails obedient freedom, not conditioned response. I am unable to understand at all how Christian pastors can possibly recommend this "remedy" to homosexuals.)

Should a homosexual inclination be placed in an order similar to that of marriage? Here homosexuals may ask themselves whether their homosexuality is to be placed in the service of God through the establishment of a committed and enduring relationship. Such a relationship may then be understood as a witness in a world of broken and impersonal relationships to the God-given possibility of and provocation toward fidelity and trust among persons.

If we are persuaded that there may be a third category of sexual vocation, then the homosexual may further ask: How is my homosexuality to be acted out in such a way as to contribute to God's purposes for me and my fellow human beings? What are the features of a homosexual pattern of relationships which point toward or bring to expression the lordship of Christ? Responses to such a question are possible only on the part of persons who understand themselves as claimed by Christ in their homosexuality.

The kinds of responses which are made to this question on the part of Christian homosexuals will have great importance for all of us. For these responses may help to illuminate also the situation of heterosexuals for whom neither marriage nor celibacy, as traditional categories of sexual vocation, function to clarify their situation of concrete obedience to Christ.

The Forms Temptation Takes

Exploration of the question of obedient vocation in relation to homosexuality is an urgent pastoral task. It can be most fruitfully explored if we church people attempt to understand more clearly the moral ambiguity of the situation in which the homosexual is placed. We must become sensitive to the peculiar forms which temptation takes in this sphere if we are helpfully to interpret an understanding of Christian vocation in this same sphere. Let me suggest a few questions about the peculiar form of temptation to which a homosexual life style may be open. These are leading questions—not to be permitted to become a priori pronouncements about the condition of persons of homosexual inclination, history or intention.

1. Is there a peculiar form of a temptation toward relational irresponsibility here? To what extent is the choice (if it is that) of a homosexual life style a refusal of the responsibilities which others bear in connection with ongoing relationship, marriage and family? (To what extent is this temptation the obverse of a temptation, characteristic of a straight, middle-class life style, to become all-responsible as a means of self-justification?)

2. Is there a peculiar form of a temptation toward irresponsibility concerning oneself here—the temptation to blame one's genes, one's parents, one's culture for one's choices? Is there here a refusal of freedom which results in one's sinking back into sensuality?

3. Is there here a refusal of the genuine otherness of another expressed in the flight from women, from straights, etc., which results in a "community" of persons who are the mirror image of one another? Is there here a peculiar form of that temptation we all share to associate only with "our own kind"—religious, racial, etc.?

4. Is there here a temptation to reduce relationships to the most trivial possible form of encounter, severing sexuality from its integration with comprehensive relationality? (This would be the obverse of the way in which a straight marriage presents the temptation of total personal subjugation of the other person on the basis of sexual ownership.)

Now, as even this brief and arbitrary list of questions should indicate, any illumination of the peculiar temptations of a homosexual life style may also serve to illuminate the peculiar temptations of a heterosexual life style and the commonality of temptation for both. Moreover, the illumination of the peculiar forms of temptation is the necessary corollary for the illumination of the peculiar forms of vocation pertinent to a homosexual life style. By keeping the questions of temptation and vocation together, we avoid the twin dangers of simply issuing a priori denunciations of homosexuality on the one hand or a priori justifications of homosexuality on the other. Neither attitude is a way of taking the other seriously. To take another seriously is to understand the other in the light of Christ as one who in his or her concrete situation is a sinner claimed by God's grace for the vocations of obedience and freedom.

The views which I have put forward as my own in these last few paragraphs no doubt require considerable amplification and clarification. I have been able to suggest only the outline of a position—and it is also very much a position "on the way."

I would be very surprised indeed if the position I have outlined does not also need correction from various quarters. Theology functions not in a vacuum but in a dialogue with many voices. It seems to me that these corrections may come from two directions—from the Judeo-Christian heritage and from a better understanding of homosexuality (which includes above all the context of dialogues with gay men and women).

The position which I have articulated therefore is, like all other positions in matters theological, an attempt to see through a glass darkly. In these matters our capacity to see is only as great as the mutuality of aid and of correction in which the church bears witness to its hope for that dawning of apocalyptic lucidity in which we shall know even as we are known.

Homosexuality

Lisa Sowle Cahill

The increasing visibility of homosexuals in the West, especially in the United States, and the militancy of the "gay rights" movement have occasioned a torrent of writings. The methodological question of appropriate sources of insight for Christian theological ethics is not necessarily more important or more difficult here than in other areas of sexuality, but it is certainly more obvious. Particular scriptural texts have been more influential in traditional evaluations of homosexuality than of other sexual conduct. Evidence of the statistical frequency of homosexuality or psychological "health" of homosexual persons tends to confute scriptural classifications of homosexuality as a sin. A good many ethicists give great weight to sociological and psychological evaluations.

There are two distinctions which are crucial to the cogent moral evaluation of homosexuality. These are pursued with varying degrees of success in the ethical literature. The first is that between the homosexual orientation and overt genital homosexual acts. The second is that between a general moral evaluation of homosexuality (orientation and/or acts) and its justification in particular circumstances. The first distinction is fairly obvious; not all those who are sexually attracted to persons of the same sex choose to engage in genital congress with them. By the second distinction I mean to indicate that there are some acts, conditions, or relations which are valuable in themselves and are worth seeking or actualizing if to do so will sacrifice no higher value. Such acts are "normative" for conduct. There are other acts or choices which, in themselves, represent disvalues, and generally are to be avoided. However, they might be justified in circumstances where they represent the best available alternative. Although such a choice would not in general be ideal or normative, it would in a particular instance be morally commendable. To give an example, the preservation of life is morally "normative," but killing is morally justifiable in circumstances where an even greater good than human life is at stake.

In the case of homosexuality, the question of its "normative" moral evaluation depends upon whether it is in itself good or valuable for persons and therefore worth choosing. To give an answer requires a method for relating insights into value or personal goods from various sources: psychology, physiology, biblical studies, natural law, and so forth. The inquiry with regard to homosexuality consequently takes place on three levels: (1) Is homosexuality good for persons, "fulfilling," or consistent with human maturity—"humanly normative"? (2) Does this or any other consideration make either orientation or acts morally choiceworthy in themselves—"morally normative"? (3) If homosexuality is neither humanly nor morally normative, would it ever be morally justifiable to choose the orientation or acts? When?

Not infrequently, one encounters arguments which slide immediately from the first level to the third, identifying the morality of any homosexual acts with the human value of homosexuality. Others distinguish between the first two levels (the humanly valuable or fulfilling vs. the morally commendable) but assume that one moral judgment will do for both the homosexual phenomenon in general and the acts of the particular individual. Thus many ethicists argue that since the homosexual orientation cannot be considered valuable or good for persons, all homosexual acts must be immoral; or that, since loving genital acts of confirmed homosexuals cannot be considered immoral, then homosexuality must be an alternate sexual option whose value is equal to that of heterosexuality. While it is, of course, possible to argue either that the orientation is a disvalue and morally non-normative and the acts immoral, or that the orientation is good for persons and morally normative and the acts morally good, a general moral valuation and justifiability in particular cases do not stand or fall together.

Concrete factors which influence Christian views of the morality of homosexuality frequently include the following: scientific evidence of its cross-cultural frequency and of the "fulfillment" (psychological health, etc.) of homosexuals is inconclusive; the homosexual orientation is a matter of choice in a limited sense if at all; it is often not feasible for those with confirmed homosexual orientation to remain celibate; the celibate homosexual often has limited access to the goods of personal relationship while the overt homosexual may have the possibility of establishing a stable sexual friendship; in fact, few homosexuals in our society do establish permanent and fulfilling homosexual relationships. In a survey of literature on homosexuality Walter G. Muelder[1] warns the Christian ethicist not to surrender theology to descriptive social science nor to begin with a particular human condition and work out a theology to accommodate it. However, the factors cited above are not uncommonly interpreted according to two assumptions: (1) whether homosexuality is authentically and fulfillingly human or "humanly normative" can be determined empirically, if at all; (2) the humanly normative will correlate with the morally normative. Sometimes a third assumption is also made: (3) only the morally normative act ever constitutes a justifiable choice in particular circumstances.

Roman Catholics on Homosexuality

The position of the Roman Catholic church on homosexuality rests on the second and third assumptions and repudiates the first. Its logic remains act-centered. Recent official statements manifest increased understanding of homosexuality as a condition. However, neither the irreversibility of this condition nor the intentions or attitudes of the person are allowed to justify acts judged "intrinsically evil" by the norm of heterosexual, marital, procreative union.[2] Some latitude on the pastoral level is permitted if subjective responsibility and guilt are limited by the absence of truly free consent. Genital homosexual acts are said to be always "objectively" sinful but not necessarily "subjectively" so.

Roman Catholic theologians have objected to this analysis with increasing frequency. Two major complaints are registered. First, the distinction between "objective" and "subjective" sin is said not to describe adequately the situation of the moral agent. Richard McCormick[3] has pointed out that the objective moral character of any act includes not only its relation to the created order, but also the component of subjective intention, motive, or purpose. This amounts to a distinction between what I have called the moral normativeness of acts and the objective morality of acts for individuals in particular circumstances. Secondly, the analysis is said to have an inadmissible pastoral consequence: the counsel of celibacy for all homosexuals, regardless of condition and circumstances.

Some theologians, among them Charles Curran, have tried to circumvent this result without denying that homosexual acts do not measure up to the full meaning of human sexuality. It might be said that, for Curran, the homosexual orientation and overt acts are not in themselves good for persons and therefore generally right, but they are not necessarily immoral in all cases. As detailed in his "theology of compromise,"[4] such acts within a stable and loving union may offer the greatest degree of human fulfillment available to some persons. Thus there is proportionate reason to choose them as the "lesser evil" or "greater good." This view comes to terms with the exigencies of human moral agency in a world disordered by the effects of sin (the sin of humankind generally, not necessarily of the homosexual, his or her parents, etc.). Homosexual unions are for Curran a manifestation of objective disorder (non-normative) and yet also a positive moral good for individuals for whom they are the only viable alternative.

André Guindon[5] supplies a comparable analysis, using the framework of "sexuality as language" rather than that of "essential human nature." Since in the homosexual union, the conversation partner is not affirmed as truly "other," the union falls short of the ideal. The practical question is distinct from the normative one, however. The "fixated" adult homosexual may be encouraged to express sensuality, tenderness, and fecundity at the limited level possible.

The CTSA commission's *Human Sexuality* and John J. McNeill's *The Church and the Homosexual*[6] respond both to the official church position and to the "compromise" theory of Curran. A central concern of these and other responses is the total framework for judging the morality of the homosexual act. A tendency exists in much of the ethical literature (religious or not) to define sexuality in terms of erotic satisfaction and, more importantly in the theological context, of free and self-giving love. The criteria of homosexual acts then become, not physical characteristics, but (1) the erotic pleasure and fulfillment of the participants, and (2) the presence or absence of a relation of love. The act is related to the objective created order by values such as freedom, love, and the like; however, the relevance of the physical or material aspect of the act to objective values can become obscure. This is particularly the case in McNeill's book and, to a lesser extent, in the CTSA report.

Human Sexuality, for instance, recommends that heterosexuality and homosexuality be evaluated by the same seven criteria, criteria which focus on personalistic values interpreted with limited reference to the embodied nature of the person. Cautiously, the authors endorse as "reasonable" the view that homosexual acts, judged by these criteria, are "essentially imperfect." [7] However, the major determinants of the goodness of homosexual acts are the values of interpersonal affection and responsibility, rather than the objective relation of material acts to human values or Christian character.

The objective connection of acts and values is all but severed in *The Church and the Homosexual*, by John J. McNeill, a Jesuit priest and an avowed celibate homosexual. Reacting against the "physicalism" of Roman Catholic sexual ethics, he puts forth the thesis that the human person is defined by "radical freedom." [8] The book is a sustained counterargument to Curran's theology of compromise. For McNeill, the proposition that homosexual acts are permissible as the least offensive among objectively "evil" alternatives is demeaning. McNeill misinterprets

Curran and thinks the negative implications of his solution entail that the homosexual "must see his deepest and most sincere human love as cutting him and his loved one off from God." [9] The force of the distinction between "human" non-normativeness, moral non-normativeness, and actual immorality in particular cases seems to elude McNeill. He supposes that affirmation of the homosexual orientation in itself is a precondition of the affirmation of the homosexual Christian in his characteristic sexual lifestyle.

McNeill makes a distinction of his own which becomes a crucial principle of interpretation both of biblical texts and of traditional condemnations of homosexuality. He uses the term "inversion" to refer to the true homosexual orientation and acts which flow from it; the term "perversion" refers to homosexual activity indulged in by those who are really heterosexual by "natural" orientation.

McNeill interprets Scripture, in particular the Sodom and Gomorrah account in Genesis and Pauline texts, as condemning the pervert rather than the true invert. His exegesis of the Sodom story as probably condemning inhospitality is convincing. However, the explanation of the heterosexual norm, which might seem to emerge from the canon as a whole, as a product of cultural and historical circumstances, is less so. McNeill reaches the conclusion that the only general norm of sexuality yielded by the Bible is the expression of love.[10] This norm coincides with McNeill's definition of the nature of the person as free, loving, and as an end in himself.[11] Thus love is the sole human and Christian standard of sexual activity.

The major constructive effort of the work is the definition of the distinctive social purpose of the homosexual. McNeill borrows heavily from Jungian descriptions of male homosexuality to define the "special gifts" which constitute the homosexual's resemblance to the New Testament image of Christ as understanding, loving, and peace-seeking. Although McNeill denies that he replaces negative sexual stereotypes with positive ones, many psychologists would resist, and other homosexuals may resent, this unrealistic sex-role idealization.

The strengths of *The Church and the Homosexual* are the restoration of biblical exegesis to a place of prominence in Roman Catholic ethical argument, emphasis on character as the context of acts, and serious concern about the moral aspects of the actual experience of persons as elucidated in part by contemporary sciences. An outcome is the outline of social contributions of the homosexual as homosexual. Lacking, however, is a satisfactory explication of what is meant by the repeated claim that human sexuality should promote "human wholeness" and "humanization." [12] Whether the definition is approached in the language of human nature or of biblical images of personhood, it must focus on the human agent as free but also as embodied, and must be given definite content. Only on such a basis can moral norms be developed with sufficient stability and specificity to discriminate meaningfully among human acts.

Marc Oraison, priest and counselor of homosexuals, displays a similar uncertainty about the relation of the humanly normative to the morally justifiable.[13] As a Freudian psychiatrist, Oraison believes that, since homosexual genital activity is often sought compulsively and does not express sexual maturity, it is humanly, i.e., psychologically, non-normative. Yet because Oraison also is convinced that homosexual relationships are for some the best human and Christian option, he ends his perceptive experiential analysis with a lame theological conclusion: "we clearly affirm that the true moral standard is not 'nature' but love." [14]

While Oraison's book may be narrow on psychoanalytic theory and short on theological ethics, it is long on pastoral insight. It manifests two tendencies in Catholic ethics and ministry. One is a growing willingness to discard in practice and theory an act-focused analysis of "nature" in favor of a more comprehensive interpretation of the Christian moral life. The other is a serious attempt to incorporate on the theoretical as well as the "pastoral" level reflection upon the concrete experience of persons, even when that experience challenges time-honored or magisterial teachings.

Protestants on Homosexuality

The primary theological resources which Protestant ethicists bring to bear on the problem of homosexuality are biblical. Like many of their Catholic counterparts, revisionists appeal to the gospel command of love as the overriding standard of acts. An additional important source of moral reflection is the psychological and sociological exploration of homosexuality. The tendency, in general, has been to rely upon a multiplicity of sources for defining the normative in sexual morality, combined with uncertainty about or direct rejection of clear and universal specific norms. Some ecclesiastical study groups are caught between biblical texts and conflicting empirical studies. Judging that both kinds of evidence are at present inconclusive, they finally neither affirm nor condemn homosexuality. They stress the complexity of the phenomenon and of alternative evaluations and advocate the "acceptance" of gay individuals within the Christian community.

Take, for instance, the report of the Council on Theology and Culture of the Presbyterian Church in the United States, *The Church and Homosexuality: A Preliminary Study*.[15] The report is a response to a 1972 resolution of the General Assembly of the PCUS which condemned homosexual behavior as a sin, and to a proposed new resolution from a local presbytery. The latter insisted that "authorities in the field of human behavior" are "secondary guides," and that the church must base its evaluation of homosexual practice "on Scripture alone." [16] The proposed resolution cited scriptural condemnations at length, made no reference to critical perspectives on texts, and did not distinguish clearly between orientation and acts. It enjoined compassion for the individual homosexual plus pastoral counseling of homosexuals.[17] Here biblical and nonbiblical sources are definitively ranked: an empirical notion of human good is not to be identified with what is morally normative for the Christian. The morally normative, on the other hand, as for the Roman Catholic magisterium, does not allow for exceptions in particular cases.

The response of the Council on Theology and Culture is much more liberal than the earlier proposals. Carefully, the authors outline various sources for understanding homosexuality: scientific data, homosexual experience, and biblical scholarship. Scriptural references to homosexuality are discussed at length. The variety of interpretations and the evasiveness of conclusions in all areas are stressed, as is the distinction between orientation and acts.

The report turns to the Bible to formulate "a responsible Christian position" on homosexuality. It states that both the Old and New Testaments recognize "male-female relatedness" as normative in human sexuality.[18] The Hebraic-Christian tradition has "consistently" concurred in rejecting homosexuality as "unnatural and sinful." [19] The negative conclusion one might expect to follow from these assertions, given the biblical commitment of the authors, is not forthcoming, presumably because of the weight given to contradictory or inconclusive empirical evidence. The authors simply outline three alternative Christian positions on homosexuality (it is sick, healthy, or sinful), managing within each to include homosexuals in Christian fellowship and ministry. The authors call for a decision about the validity of these options, but that decision—and a clear methodology which might support it—goes beyond the content of the study.

While the PCUS study seems to await scientific corroboration for one of the diverse biblical options, James B. Nelson, in a recent article in *Christianity and Crisis*,[20] holds up a single biblical criterion which can surmount relativistic interpretations of texts relevant to homosexuality: love. Nelson's argument is similar in essential respects to that of McNeill, though his is developed in a distinctively Protestant context. Nelson appeals to the Protestant principle and states at the outset that "secular scholars" can contribute substance to this norm, since revelation continues in human experience and through nontheological disciplines.

Nelson attributes great significance to the fact that homosexuals do not choose their sexual orientation. To see this orientation as a sickness or perversion is to inhibit the self-acceptance of gays. *Therefore*, not only is responsible genital expression to be encouraged, but also "full acceptance" of the homosexual relation as expressive of love or of God's "humanizing" intentions. Following Pittenger, Nelson defines "the human" as "the loving." He declines to specify further the content of terms such as "humanizing" or "human wholeness," or to indicate whether there are any acts or relations which are less conducive than others to love and wholeness.

In a response to Nelson, John W. Espy[21] challenges the former to fill out his notion of "human wholeness" by referring the meaning of love to its biblical context of covenant. Espy gives clear priority to the biblical source of ethics and is committed to the derivation of specific norms of conduct. He emphasizes scripture's general heterosexual model and concludes that homosexual acts are incompatible with the Christian lifestyle. Espy is to be commended for making explicit his methodological choice and then attempting to develop the biblical image of personhood within its own context. However, both Nelson and Espy blur the distinction between what is morally normative and what is justifiable in particular circumstances. Nelson begins from the conviction that the lives of homosexuals, including genital expressns of love, are morally praise-worthy, and concludes that the homosexual orientation must be in itself no less valuable than the heterosexual one. Espy begins from the conviction that the Bible supports the heterosexual norm and concludes that therefore homosexual practice is sinful, regardless of the orientation of the individual.

Homosexuality is an important subject in *Male and Female*, a collection of articles on various aspects of sexuality and sex-role differentiation edited by Urban T. Holmes III and Ruth Tiffany Barnhouse as a contribution to the Episcopal church's consideration of the ordination of women.[22] The pros and cons of homosexuality are argued by four authors (Alan Bell, Charles Socarides, Norman Pittenger, William Muehl), all of whom seem to assume that the immoral will coincide with the non-normative and that the moral acceptability of homosexuality depends on whether its actual effects on the person and society are beneficial or detrimental.

Ruth Barnhouse has also written *Homosexuality: A Symbolic Confusion*.[23] She rightly deplores what she perceives as a common inclination of moralists uncritically to derive the "ought" from the "is." The task of science, she says, is to describe "what is," the task of religion to illuminate "what ought to be": scientists and theologians ought not to encroach upon one another's proper domain.

Barnhouse interprets descriptive data in the light of Freud's theory of psychosexual development and Jung's typologies of male and female. She concludes that the norm of mature sexuality is the symbolic reconciliation of opposites in the union of complementary sexes. Thus homosexuality is a "symbolic confusion" and not "a perfectly normal alternate lifestyle."[24] In an appendix, Barnhouse surmises also that the biblical ideal is "monogamous, lifelong heterosexual marriage."[25]

Barnhouse attributes moral significance to the homosexual orientation. She accepts the Freudian proposal that the individual has at some unconscious level chosen to come to terms with a conflictual situation through sexual deviance, and thus is "responsible" for his condition. The presupposition that persons are responsible for all choices, even unconscious ones, is put forth as central to both psychology and religion.[26] (The Genesis myth of creation and fall is adduced to amplify this point.) Her conclusion is that even the confirmed homosexual often (not always) can choose to change and ought to do so.

Too much in this book depends on the psychological explanation of homosexuality, including the dubious imputation of responsibility to the homosexual for his or her sexual orientation. Barnhouse seems to think that to see the homosexual lifestyle as either humanly or morally non-normative one must be able to define the basic orientation as a matter of moral choice. A further criticism concerns the internal consistency of her method. In describing the homosexual orientation as humanly non-normative and subject to a negative moral evaluation, the author herself may be deriving the ought from the is. Since the homosexual personality falls short of a standard of psychological maturity derived from empirically based psychoanalytic theory—this standard is itself a value judgment—she concludes that it is therefore immoral to choose the homosexual orientation and acts. Theologically based moral judgments actually play a very minor role in the book.

Two of Barnhouse's assumptions are also questionable. The first is that of the possibility of a value-free science which is strictly descriptive, especially when the subject of research is the human person. The second is that of the possibility of a religion which undertakes the normative task of ethics without incorporating some prior understanding of what "is" into its own perspective. In sum, can the descriptive and normative tasks be decisively separated and assigned to discrete disciplines which will pursue them independently and meet to confer once each has done its job? The is/ought problem to which Barnhouse has drawn our attention is a thorny one; her own methodological grasp of it is uncertain.

Recent writings on homosexuality are in many respects the reflection and culmination of the shift in Christian sexual ethics toward the incorporation of non-theological, especially empirical, sources, and toward greater tolerance of deviant, or at least non-normative, behavior. Accommodations to *de facto* "sexual liberation" on the formal moral level, as opposed to the pastoral level, are made with caution. As in other areas of Christian ethics, however, sexual ethicists have serious reservations about the viability of any norm, biblical or natural, which purports to be "absolute." Most can envision some extenuating circumstance or other which would make a generally unacceptable form of conduct—adultery, for example—"good" or "right."

Appendix

The following are excerpts from church statements on homosexuality.

AMERICAN BAPTIST CHURCHES

We, as Christians, recognize that radical changes are taking place in sex concepts and practices. We are committed to seeking God's guidance in our efforts to understand faithfully and deal honestly with these changes and related issues. We recognize that there are many traditional problems of family and personal life for which the church's ministries have not been adequate, but we are committed to be used by God to strengthen and broaden these ministries. In this spirit we call upon our churches to engage in worship, study, fellowship and action to provide for meaningful ministries to all persons as members of the 'Family of God' including those who are homosexuals.

THE AMERICAN LUTHERAN CHURCH, Standing Committee for the Office of Research and Analysis, 1977.

The church need not be caught up in the conflicting theories as to how widespread homosexuality is, the factors which cause or foster homosexuality, and whether it is an illness, an arrested state of sexual development, a form of deviant behavior, or a sexual expression of human nature. These are matters for the various scientific disciplines to debate and resolve. The church, however, is concerned that some human beings created in God's image are involved in homosexual behavior, that many people are hurting because of their own homosexuality or that of a loved one, and that the Scriptures speak to the entire issue.

We believe that taken as a whole the message of Scripture clearly is that:
a. Homosexual behavior is sin, a form of idolatry, a breaking of the natural order that unites members of the human community;
b. Homosexual behavior is contrary to the new life in Christ, a denial of the responsible freedom and service into which we are called through baptism;
c. God offers the homosexual person, as every other person, a vision of the wholeness He intends, the assurance of His grace, and His healing and restoration for the hurting and broken.

Nevertheless, we recognize the cries of our homosexual brothers and sisters for justice in the arena of civil affairs. We cannot endorse their call

235

for legalizing homosexual marriage. Nor can we endorse their conviction that homosexual behavior is simply another form of acceptable expression of natural erotic or libidinous drives. We can, however, endorse their position that their sexual orientation in and of itself should not be a cause for denying them their civil liberties.

CHRISTIAN CHURCH (DISCIPLES OF CHRIST), General Assembly. Study Document, 1977.

. . . The standards of membership in the Christian Church (Disciples of Christ) have always rested on confession of faith in Jesus Christ and baptism. Its standards have been "inclusive" rather than "exclusive." In support of these it has appealed to the relationships of Jesus which were inclusive, often, in fact, deliberately directed to those whom society had demeaned and cast aside. It has never acknowledged barriers to fellowship on the basis of dogma or life style. By these principles, rooted in biblical faith, it is difficult to point to any basis upon which homosexual persons might be excluded from membership.

Acknowledging . . . the wide differences of opinion, there does seem to be a minimal consensus to which the church can strive: homosexuals are persons whom God created, loves and redeems and seeks to set within the fellowship of faith communities to be ministered to and to minister. The church can affirm that God's grace does not exclude persons of differing life styles or sexual preferences, nor does the church which is enlightened by the Holy Spirit. Homosexuals may be included in the fellowship and membership of the community of faith where they are to love and be loved and where their gifts of ministry are to be welcomed.

FRIENDS, Philadelphia Yearly Meeting of Friends, 1973.

We should be aware that there is a great diversity in the relationships that people develop with one another. Although we neither approve nor disapprove of homosexuality, the same standards under the law which we apply to heterosexual activities should also be applied to homosexual activities. As persons who engage in homosexual activities suffer serious discrimination in employment, housing and the right to worship, we believe that civil rights laws should protect them. In particular we advocate the revision of all legislation imposing disabilities and penalties upon homosexual activities.

GREEK ORTHODOX CHURCH, Biennial Clergy–Laity Congress, 1976.

The Orthodox Church condemns unreservedly all expressions of personal sexual experience which prove contrary to the definite and unalterable function ascribed to sex by God's ordinance and expressed in man's experience as a law of nature.

Thus the function of the sexual organs of a man and a woman and their biochemical generating forces in glands and glandular secretions are ordained by nature to serve one particular purpose, the procreation of the human kind.

Therefore, any and all uses of the human sex organs for purposes other than those ordained by creation, runs contrary to the nature of things as decreed by God. . . .

The Orthodox Church believes that homosexuality should be treated by society as an immoral and dangerous perversion and by religion as a sinful failure. In both cases, correction is called for. Homosexuals should be accorded the confidential medical and psychiatric facilities by which they can be helped to restore themselves to a self-respecting sexual identity that belongs to them by God's ordinance.

LUTHERAN CHURCH IN AMERICA, Biennial Convention, 1970.

Human sexuality is a gift of God for the expression of love and the generation of life. As with every good gift, it is subject to abuses which cause suffering and debasement. In the expression of man's sexuality, it is the integrity of his relationships which determines the meaning of his actions. Man does not merely have sexual relations; he demonstrates his true humanity in personal relationships, the most intimate of which are sexual.

Scientific research has not been able to provide conclusive evidence regarding the causes of homosexuality. Nevertheless, homosexuality is viewed biblically as a departure from the heterosexual structure of God's creation. Persons who engage in homosexual behavior are sinners only as are all other persons—alienated from God and neighbor. However, they are often the special and undeserving victims of prejudice and discrimination in law, law enforcement, cultural mores, and congregational life. In relation to this area of concern, the sexual behavior of freely consenting adults in private is not an appropriate subject for legislation or police action. It is essential to see such persons as entitled to understanding justice in church and community.

MORAVIAN CHURCH, Synod, 1974

WHEREAS: the Christian Church has the responsibility of reexamining its own traditional sexual stance in the light of more recent interpretation and scientific evidence for the benefit of both youth and adults, and

WHEREAS: the homosexual has too often felt excluded from and persecuted by society, there be it

RESOLVED: (29) that the Moravian Church reaffirms its open welcome to all people by specifically recognizing that the homosexual is also under God's care, and be it further

RESOLVED: (30) that Moravian congregations will extend an invitation to all persons to join us in a common search for wholeness before God and persons, and be it further

RESOLVED: (31) that as Christians, recognizing our common sinfulness and the miracle of God's grace, accepting God's pardon, and together striving to help free each other from bonds of fear, despair, and meaninglessness, fitting us for lives of commitment, responsibility, witness, service, and celebration in God's Kingdom, we will share in this venture as children of God and brothers and sisters in Christ toward wholeness.

THE PRESBYTERIAN CHURCH IN THE UNITED STATES, 117th General Assembly, 1977.

That the 117th General Assembly expresses love and pastoral concern for homosexual persons in our society and the need for the Church to stand for just treatment of homosexual persons in our society in regard to their civil liberties, equal rights, and protection under the law from social and economic discrimination which is due all citizens.

Although we confess our need for more light and pray for spiritual guidance for the Church on this matter, we now believe that homosexuality falls short of God's plan for sexual relationships and urge the Church to seek the best way for witnessing to God's moral standards and for ministering to homosexual persons concerning the love of God in Jesus Christ.

PROTESTANT EPISCOPAL CHURCH IN THE U.S.A., General Convention, 1976.

Resolved, that it is the sense of this General Convention that homosexual persons are children of God, who have a full and equal claim with all other persons upon the love, acceptance, and pastoral concern and care of the Church.

Resolved, this General Council expresses its conviction that homosexual persons are entitled to equal protection of the law with all other citizens, and calls upon our society to see such protection is provided in actuality.

ROMAN CATHOLIC, Vatican Congregation for the Doctrine of the Faith, 1977.

At the present time there are those who, basing themselves on observations in the psychological order, have begun to judge indulgently, and even to excuse completely, homosexual relations between certain people. This they do in opposition to the constant teaching of the magisterium and to the moral sense of the Christian people.

A distinction is drawn, and it seems with some reason, between homosexuals whose tendency comes from a false education, from a lack of normal sexual development, from habit, from bad example or from other causes, and is transitory or at least not incurable; and homosexuals who are definitely such because of some kind of innate instinct or a pathological constitution judged to be incurable.

In regard to this second category of subjects, some people conclude that their tendency is so natural that it justifies in their case homosexual relations within a sincere communion of life and love analogous to marriage insofar as such homosexuals feel incapable of enduring a solitary life.

In the pastoral field, these homosexuals must certainly be treated with understanding and sustained in the hope of overcoming their personal difficulties and their inability to fit into society.

Their culpability will be judged with prudence. But no pastoral method can be employed which would give moral justification to these acts on the grounds that they would be consonant with the condition of such people. For according to the objective moral order homosexual relations are acts which lack an essential and indispensable finality.

THE ROMAN CATHOLIC CHURCH—Great Britain, Statement issued by the Archbishop of Westminster, 1957.

The civil law takes cognizance primarily of public acts. Private acts as such are outside its scope.

However, there are certain private acts which have public consequences in so far as they affect the common good. These acts may rightly be subject to civil law.

It may be, however, that the civil law cannot effectively control such acts without doing more harm to the common good than the acts themselves would be. In that case it may be necessary in the interests of the common good to tolerate without approving such acts.

It has, for example, invariably been found that adultery or fornication (which, however private, have clear public consequences) cannot effectively be controlled by civil law without provoking great evils.

Applying these principles to the question of homosexual acts between consenting males:

1. As regards the moral law, Catholic moral teaching is:

   a. Homosexual acts are grievously sinful.

   b. That in view of the public consequences of these acts, *e.g.*, the harm which would result to the common good if homosexual conduct became widespread or an accepted mode of conduct in the public mind, the civil law does not exceed its legitimate scope if it attempts to control them by making them crimes.

2. However, two questions of fact arise:
   a. If the law takes cognizance of private acts of homosexuality and makes them crimes, do worse evils follow for the common good?
   b. Since homosexual acts between consenting males are now crimes in law, would a change in the law harm the common good by seeming to condone homosexual conduct?

Ecclesiastical authority could rightly give a decision on this question of fact as well as on the question of moral law, if the answers to questions of fact were overwhelmingly clear. As, however, various answers are possible in the opinion of prudent men, Catholics are free to make up their own minds on these two questions of fact.

SOUTHERN BAPTIST CONVENTION, Resolution on Homosexuality, 1976.

Whereas, homosexuality has become an open lifestyle for increasing numbers of persons, and

Whereas, attention has focused on the religious and moral dimensions of homosexuality, and

Whereas, it is the task of the Christian community to bring all moral questions and issues into the light of biblical truth;

Now therefore, be it resolved that the members of the Southern Baptist Convention . . . affirm our commitment to the biblical truth regarding the practice of homosexuality and sin.

Be it further resolved, that this Convention, while acknowledging the autonomy of the local church to ordain ministers, urges churches and agencies not to afford the practice of homosexuality any degree of approval through ordination, employment, or other designations of normal lifestyle.

Be it further resolved, that we affirm our Christian concern all persons be saved from the penalty and power of sin through our Lord Jesus Christ, whatever their present individual lifestyle.

UNITARIAN UNIVERSALIST ASSOCIATION OF CHURCHES IN NORTH AMERICA, General Assembly, 1970.

Discrimination Against Homosexuals and Bisexuals: Recognizing that
1. A significant minority in this country are either homosexual or bisexual in their feelings and/or behavior;
2. Homosexuality has been the target of severe discrimination by society and in particular by the police and other arms of government;
3. A growing number of authorities on the subject now see homosexuality as an inevitable sociological phenomenon and not as a mental illness;

4. There are Unitarian Universalists, clergy and laity, who are homosexuals and bisexuals;

THEREFORE BE IT RESOLVED: That the 1970 General Assembly of the Unitarian Universalist Association: 1) Urges all people immediately to bring an end to all discrimination against homosexuals, homosexuality, bisexuals, and bisexuality, with specific immediate attention to the following issues:

Private consensual behavior between persons over the age of consent shall be the business only of those persons and not subject to legal regulations. Urges all churches and fellowships, in keeping with our changing social patterns, to initiate meaningful programs of sex education aimed at providing a more open and healthier understanding of sexuality in all parts of the United States and Canada, and with the particular aim to end all discrimination against homosexuals and bisexuals.

UNITED CHURCH OF CHRIST, The Tenth General Synod, 1975.

Therefore, without considering in this document the rightness or wrongness of same-gender relationships, but recognizing that a person's affectional or sexual preference is not legitimate grounds on which to deny her or his civil liberties, the Tenth General Synod of the United Church of Christ proclaims the Christian conviction that all persons are entitled to full civil liberties and equal protection under the law.

Further, the Tenth General Synod declares its support for the enactment of legislation that would guarantee the liberties of all persons without discrimination related to affectional or sexual preference.

THE UNITED METHODIST CHURCH, The Quadrennial Conference, 1976.

Homosexuals no less than heterosexuals are persons of sacred worth, who need the ministry and guidance of the church in their struggles for human fulfillment, as well as the spiritual and emotional care of a fellowship which enables reconciling relationships with God, with others and with self. Further we insist that all persons are entitled to have their human and civil rights ensured, though we do not condone the practice of homosexuality and consider this practice incompatible with Christian teaching.

UNITED PRESBYTERIAN CHURCH IN THE U.S.A., 188th General Assembly, 1976.

The 188th General Assembly calls to the attention of our Church that, according to our most recent statement, we "reaffirm our adherence to the moral law of God . . . that . . . the practice of homosexuality is sin . . . Also we affirm that any self-righteous attitude of others who would condemn persons who have so sinned is also sin." The 188th General Assembly declares again its commitment to this statement. Therefore, on broad Scriptural and confessional grounds, it appears that it would at the present time be injudicious, if not improper, for a Presbytery to ordain to the professional ministry of the Gospel a person who is an avowed practicing homosexual.

THE LUTHERAN CHURCH—MISSOURI SYNOD, Convention, 1973.

Whereas, God's Word clearly identifies homophile behavior as immoral, and condemned it (Lev. 18:22; 20:13 and Rom. 1:24–27); and

Whereas, The Law and the Gospel of Jesus Christ are to be proclaimed and applied to all conditions of mankind; therefore be it Resolved, That the Synod recognize homophile behavior as intrinsically sinful; and be it further

Resolved, That the Synod urge that the Law and Gospel of the Scriptures be applied to homophiles as appropriate with a view toward ministering the forgiveness of our Lord Jesus Christ to any and all sinners who are penitent.

UNION OF AMERICAN HEBREW CONGREGATIONS, General Assembly, 1977.

Whereas the UAHC has consistently supported the civil rights and civil liberties of all persons, and

Whereas the Constitution guarantees civil rights to all individuals,

Be it therefore resolved that homosexual persons are entitled to equal protection under the law. We oppose discrimination against homosexuals in areas of opportunity, including employment and housing. We call upon our society to see that such protection is provided in actuality.

Be it further resolved that we affirm our belief that private sexual acts between consenting adults are not the proper province of government and law enforcement agencies.

Statements by Professional Organizations

AMERICAN BAR ASSOCIATION, House of Deputies, 1973.

RESOLVED that the legislatures of the several states are urged to repeal all laws which classify as criminal conduct any form of non-commercial *sex conduct between consenting adults in private*, saving only those portions which protect minors or public decorum.

AMERICAN MEDICAL ASSOCIATION, Action of the Trustees, 1973.

Passed a resolution urging the endorsement of the Model Penal Code of the American Law Institute, which recommends to legislators that private sexual behavior between consenting adults should be removed from the list of crimes and thereby legalized.

AMERICAN PSYCHIATRIC ASSOCIATION, Board of Trustees, 1973.

Unanimously voted for a resolution urging "the repeal of all legislation making criminal offenses of sexual acts performed by consenting adults in private," and another resolution urged sexual practices (including homosexuality) between consenting adults in private should be removed from the list of crimes. In another resolution, the Board of Trustees voted to remove homosexuality, *per se*, from its official list of mental disorders.

The Trustees also approved the following resolution:

Whereas Homosexuality *per se* implies no impairment in judgment, stability, reliability, or general social or vocational capabilities, therefore, be it resolved that the American Psychiatric Association deplores all public and private discrimination against homosexuals in such areas as employment, housing, public accommodation, and licensing, and declares that no burden of proof of such judgment, capacity, or reliability shall be placed upon homosexuals greater than that imposed on any other persons. Further, the American Psychiatric Association supports and urges the enactment of civil rights legislation at the local, state, and federal level that would offer homosexual persons the same protections now guaranteed to others on the basis of race, creed, color, etc. Further, the American Psychiatric Association supports and urges the repeal of all discriminatory legislation singling out homosexual acts by consenting adults.

AMERICAN PSYCHOLOGICAL ASSOCIATION, Board of Directors, 1975.

The American Psychological Association supports the action taken on 15 December 1973 by the American Psychiatric Association removing homosexuality from the Association's official list of mental disorders. The American Psychological Association therefore adopts the following resolution:

Homosexuality *per se* implies no impairment in judgment, stability, reliability, or general social or vocational responsibilities;

Further, the American Psychological Association urges all mental health professionals to take the lead in removing the stigma of mental illness that has long been associated with homosexual orientations.

Bibliography

ANON. "Must Homosexuals Be Jewish Outcasts?" *Sh'ma*, Vol. 5, No. 98 (October 3, 1978), 303–05.

AQUINAS, SAINT THOMAS. *Summa Theologica*. Part 2-2ae. Q. 153, answers 2 & 3; Q. 154, answer 1.

ARISTOTLE. *Ethics*.

ATKINSON, RONALD. *Sexual Morality*. New York: Harcourt, Brace & World, 1965.

AUGUSTINE, SAINT. *De Nuptiis et Concup.*

BAILEY, DERRICK SHERWIN. "Homosexuality and Christian Morals," *They Stand Apart*, J. Tudor Rees and Harvey V. Usill, editors. London: William Heinemann, 1955. Pp. 36–63.

BAILEY, DERRICK SHERWIN. *Homosexuality and the Western Christian Tradition*. London: Longmans, Green, 1955.

BARNHOUSE, RUTH TIFFANY. *Homosexuality: A Symbolic Confusion*. New York: Seabury Press, 1977.

BARTH, KARL. *Church Dogmatics*. Part 3, Vol. 4, pp. 164–66. Edinburgh: T. & T. Clark, 1961.

BAUM, GREGORY. "Catholic Homosexuals," *Commonweal*, Vol. 99, No. 19 (February 15, 1974), 479–82.

BRILL, EARL. *The Christian Moral Vision*. New York: Seabury Press, 1979.

BUCKLEY, MICHAEL J. *Morality and the Homosexual: A Catholic Approach to a Moral Problem*. London: Newman Press, 1959.

CAHILL, LISA SOWLE. "Sexual Issues in Christian Theological Ethics: A Review of Recent Studies," *Religious Studies Review*, Vol. 4, No. 1 (January 1978), 1–14.

CAPONE, D. "Reflections on the Points Concerning Homosexuality: Declaration on Sexual Ethics," *L'Osservatore Romano* (English edition), Vol. 10, No. 414 (March 4, 1976), 9–10.

CAVANAGH, JOHN R. *Counselling the Invert*. Milwaukee: Bruce Publishing Co., 1966.

CLEMONS, JAMES T. "Toward a Christian Affirmation of Human Sexuality," *Religion in Life*, Vol. 43, No. 4 (Winter 1974), 425–35.

"A Conversation on Homosexuality," *Plumbline*, Vol. 6, No. 2 (June 1978).

CURRAN, CHARLES E. "Homosexuality," in "Sexuality and Sin: A Current Appraisal," *HPR*, Vol. 69, No. 1 (October 1968), 31.

CURRAN, CHARLES E. "Homosexuality and Moral Theology: Methodological and Substantive Considerations," *The Thomist*, Vol. 35, No. 3 (July 1971), 447–84.

DRIVER, THOMAS R. "Homosexuality: The Contemporary and Christian Contexts," *Commonweal*, Vol. 98, No. 5 (April 6, 1973), 103-06.

DUQUE, ASTERIO. "Homosexuality: A Theological Evaluation," *Priest*, Vol. 31, Nos. 3, 4 and 5 (March, April and May 1975).

EARLY, TRACY. "The Struggle in the Denominations: Should Gays Be Ordained?" *Christianity and Crisis*, Vol. 37, Nos. 9 and 10 (May 30 & June 13, 1977), 118–22.

EPISCOPAL DIOCESE OF MICHIGAN. *Report of the Task Force on Homosexuality*. Detroit, Mich., 1973.

GEARHART, SALLY AND JOHNSON, WILLIAM R. *Loving Men/Loving Women: Gay Liberation and the Church*. San Francisco: Glide Publications, 1974.

GOLDENBERG, NAOMI. *Changing of the Gods*. Boston, Mass.: Beacon Press, 1979.

GORDIS, ROBERT. *Love and Sex: A Modern Jewish Perspective*. New York: Farrar, Straus and Giroux, 1978.

HAGMEIER, GEORGE AND GLEASON, ROBERT W. *Counselling the Catholic*. New York: Sheed and Ward, 1959.

HARVEY, JOHN F. "Homosexuality," *New Catholic Encyclopedia*, VII 116–19. New York: McGraw-Hill, 1967.

HARVEY, JOHN F. "Morality and Pastoral Treatment of Homosexuality," *Continuum*, Vol. 5, No. 2 (Summer 1967), 279–97.

HERON, ALASTAIR (ed.). *Toward a Quaker View of Sex*. London: Friends Home Service Committee, 1963.

HETTLINGER, RICHARD R. *Living with Sex: The Student's Dilemma*. New York: Seabury Press, 1966.

"Homosexuality," *Christianity and Crisis*, Vol. 37, Nos. 9 & 10, (May 30 & June 13, 1977).

"Homosexuality: Resources for Reflection," *Church and Society*, Vol. 67, No. 5 (May-June 1977).

JENNINGS, THEODORE W. "Homosexuality and Christian Faith: A Theological Reflection," *Christian Century*, Vol. 94, No. 5 (February 16, 1977), 137–42.

JONES, H. KIMBALL. *Homosexuality: Sin? Sickness? Neither? Both?—A Clergyman's View*. New York: Horizons, 1975.

JONES, H. KIMBALL. *Towards a Christian Understanding of the Homosexual*. New York: Association Press, 1966.

KENNEDY, EUGENE. *The New Sexuality: Myths, Fables and Hang-Ups*. New York: Doubleday, 1972.

KOSNICK, ANTHONY, *et al. Human Sexuality: New Directions in American Catholic Thought*. New York: Paulist Press, 1977.

LOVELACE, RICHARD. *Homosexuality and the Church*. New Jersey: Revell, 1978.

MACOURT, MICHAEL (ed.). *Towards a Theology of Gay Liberation*. London: S. C. M. Press, 1976.

MCCAFFREY, J. "Homosexuality, Aquinas and the Church," *Catholic World*, Vol. 213 (July 1971), 183–86.

MCNEILL, JOHN, S.J. "The Christian Male Homosexual," *Homiletic and Pastoral Review*, Vol. 70, Nos. 9, 10 and 11 (June, July and August 1970).

McNeill, John, S.J. *The Church and the Homosexual*. Kansas City, Mo.: Sheed, Andrews and McMeel, 1976.

McNeill, John, S.J. "The Church and the Homosexual," *National Catholic Reporter*, Vol. 9, No. 38 (October 5, 1973).

Matt, Hershel, "Sin, Crime, Sickness or Alternative Life Style?: A Jewish Approach to Homosexuality," *Judaism*, Vol. 27, No. 1 (Winter 1978), 13–24.

Milhaven, John G. "Homosexuality and the Christian," *HPR*, Vol. 68, No. 8 (May 1968), 663–69.

Milhaven, John G. *Toward a New Catholic Morality*. Garden City, N.Y.: Doubleday, 1972.

Muehl, William and Johnson, William R. "Issues Raised by Homosexuality," *Y. D. S. Reflection*, Vol. 72, No. 4 (May 1975).

Muehl, William. "Some Words of Caution," *Male and Female*, Ruth Tiffany Barnhouse and Urban T. Holmes, III, editors. New York: Seabury Press, 1976. Pp. 167–74.

Nelson, James B. *Embodiment*. Minneapolis, Minn.: Augsburg Publishing House, 1978.

Oberholtzer, W. Dwight (ed.) *Is Gay Good? Ethics, Theology and Homosexuality*. Philadelphia: Westminster Press, 1971.

Oraison, Marc. *The Homosexual Question*. Jane Zenni Flynn, translator. New York: Harper and Row, 1977.

Pittenger, W. Norman. *Making Sexuality Human*. New York: Pilgrim Press, 1975.

Pittenger, W. Norman. *Time for Consent*. London: S. C. M. Press, 1979.

Rinzema, J. *The Sexual Revolution: Challenge and Response*. Lewis B. Smedes, translator. Grand Rapids, Mich.: Eerdmans, 1974.

Ruether, Rosemary Radford. "The Personalization of Sex," *From Machismo to Mutuality*, Rosemary Radford Ruether and Eugene Bianchi, editors. New York: Paulist Press, 1976. Pp. 70–86.

Sacred Congregation for the Doctrine of the Faith. *Declaration on Certain Questions Concerning Sexual Ethics*. Washington, D.C.: United States Catholic Conference, 1975.

Scanzoni, Letha and Mollenkott, Virginia. *Is the Homosexual My Neighbor?* New York: Harper and Row, 1978.

Secor, Neale. "A Brief for a New Homosexual Ethic," *The Same Sex*, Ralph W. Weltge, editor. New York: Pilgrim Press, 1969. Pp. 67–79.

Shinn, Roger. "Homosexuality: Christian Conviction & Inquiry," *The Same Sex*, Ralph W. Weltge, editor. New York: Pilgrim Press, 1969. Pp. 43–54.

Smedes, Lewis B. *Sex for Christians*. Grand Rapids, Mich.: Eerdmans, 1976.

Thielicke, Helmut. "The Problem of Homosexuality," *The Ethics of Sex*. John W. Doberstein, translator. New York: Harper and Row, 1964. Pp. 269–92.

United Church of Christ. *Human Sexuality: A Preliminary Study*. New York: United Church Press, 1977.

United Presbyterian Church in the U.S.A. *Report of the Task Force on Homosexuality*. New York: United Presbyterian Church, 1978.

United Presbyterian Church in the U.S.A. *Sexuality and the Human Community*. New York: U. P. C., 1970.

VALENTE, MICHAEL. *Sex: The Radical View of a Catholic Theologian*. Milwaukee: Bruce Publishing Co., 1970.

WADDAMS, HERBERT. *A New Introduction to Moral Theology*. New York: Seabury Press, 1965.

WELTGE, RALPH W. (ed.). *The Same Sex*. New York: Pilgrim Press, 1969.

WOOD, ROBERT W. *Christ and the Homosexual*. New York: Vantage Press, 1960.

Addendum to Selected Bibliography

ATKINSON, DAVID J. *Homosexuals in the Christian Fellowship*. Oxford: Latimer House, 1979.

CAHILL, LISA SOWLE. "Moral Methodology: A Case Study," *Chicago Studies*, Vol. 19 (Summer 1980), 171–87.

CAVANAGH, JOHN R. AND HARVEY, JOHN F. *Counselling the Homosexual*. Huntingdon, Ind.: Our Sunday Visitor Press, 1978.

Church of England. Board of Social Responsibility. *Homosexual Relationships*. London: C.I.O., 1970. "La Condition Homosexuelle: A Symposium," *Lumière et Vie*, Vol. 29 (April-May 1980), 5–99.

COLEMAN, PETER. *Christian Attitudes to Homosexuality*. London: S.P.C.K., 1980.

COOK, E. DAVID. "Homosexuality: A Review of the Debate," *Churchman*, Vol. 94, No. 4 (1980), 297–313.

CURRAN, CHARLES E. "Moral Theology, Psychiatry and Homosexuality," in *Transition and Tradition in Moral Theology*. Notre Dame, Ind.: University of Notre Dame Press, 1979. Pp. 59–80.

DOHERTY, DENNIS (ed.). *Dimensions of Human Sexuality*. New York: Doubleday, 1979.

FISHER, DAVID H. "The Homosexual Debate: A Critique," *St. Luke's Journal of Theology*, Vol. 22 (June 1979), 176–84.

GUINDON, ANDRÉ. *The Sexual Language: An Essay in Moral Theology*. Ottawa: University of Ottawa Press, 1977.

HARRISON, BEVERLY WILDUNG. "Misogyny and Homophobia: The Unexplored Connections," *Integrity Forum*, Vol. 7, No. 2 (Lent 1981), 7–13.

"Homosexuality," *explor*, Vol. 1, No. 2 (Fall 1975).

KEANE, PHILIP S. *Sexual Morality: A Catholic Perspective*. New York: Paulist Press, 1979. Pp. 71–91.

MALLOY, EDWARD. "Methodological Considerations in the Use of Sociological Considerations in Christian Ethics," *Catholic Theological Society of America Proceedings*, Vol. 34 (1979), 123–40.

National Council of Churches in the U.S.A. Faith and Order Commission. *Guidelines for Ecumenical Debate on Abortion and Homosexuality*. New York: N.C.C., 1980.

SCOTT, DAVID A. "Ordaining a Homosexual Person: A Policy Proposal," *St. Luke's Journal of Theology*, Vol. 22 (June 1979), 185–96.

VACEK, EDWARD. "A Christian Homosexuality?," *Commonweal*, Vol. 107, No. 2 (December 5, 1980), 681–84.

Footnotes

Roger Shinn

1. Reported in *The New York Times,* March 6, 1966, p. 1.

2. See Wardell Pomeroy, "Homosexuality," *The Same Sex,* Ralph Weltge, editor (New York: Pilgrim Press, 1969), pp. 3-13.

3. Daniel Day Williams, "Three Studies of Homosexuality in Relation to Christian Faith," *Social Action,* Vol. 34, No. 4 (December 1967), 37.

4. Erich Fromm, *The Art of Loving* (Colophon edition; New York: Harper and Row, 1962), p. 33.

5. Fromm refers to the Bible, among other sources, in making this analogy; but in no sense does he use the Bible as an authority. (See Fromm, p. 33.) Incidentally, he is equally emphatic that true erotic love is one-to-one love, involving a decision and a promise. (See Fromm, 55-56.) There are real differences between Fromm's conception of the "art" of loving and the Christian idea of the "grace" of love (see Rollo May, *Love and Will* [New York: W. W. Norton and Co., 1969]), but the analogies are no less impressive.

6. See Karl Barth, *Church Dogmatics,* 11 1/4, pp. 150-81, especially p. 166.

7. Helmut Thielicke, *The Ethics of Sex,* trans, John W. Doberstein (New York: Harper and Row, 1964), pp. 269-92; H. Kimball Jones goes farther in recommending that the church recognize the validity of mature homosexual relationships without "an endorsement of homosexuality." See his *Toward a Christian Understanding of the Homosexual* (New York: Association Press, 1966), p. 108.

8. Alastair Heron (ed.), *Toward a Quaker View of Sex: An Essay by a Group of Friends* (London: Friends Home Service Committee, 1963), pp. 21, 36.

9. The pastor who has given me most help in understanding this position is Neale Secor. Robert Wood, in *Christ and the Homosexual* (New York: Vantage Press, 1960) and in other miscellaneous writings, sometimes takes the position that homosexuality is an affliction and a handicap. At other times he depicts it as a divinely given way of coping with the population explosion.

Saint Thomas Aquinas

1. Cf. Aquinas, *SCG* 3, 126. *De Malo* 15, 1. *Sent.* 26, 1, 3.

2. Augustine, *Soliloqu.* 1, 10. PL 32, 878.

3. *Ethics* 2, 2 1104a. 18. Lect. 2.

4. Ibid., 7, 11. 1152b. 18. Lect. 11.

5. Origen, *In Numeros* 6, PG 12, 610. Jerome PL 22, 1051.

6. Augustine, *De Nuptiis et Concup.* 1 24. PL 44, 429.

7. Augustine, *De Bono Conjug.* 25. PL 40, 395.

8. Ibid., 16. PL 40, 395.

9. Ibid., 8. PL 40, 379.

10. Aquinas, *ST* 1a2ae. 64. Cf. *ST* 2a2ae. 152, 2 ad. 2.

11. Augustine, *De Civit. Dei* 13, 12. PL 41, 386.

12. Augustine, *De Nuptiis et Concup.* 1, 24. PL 44, 429.

13. Aquinas, *SCG* 11, 122. *De Malo* 15, 1. In I Cor. 6, Lect. 3.

14. Aristotle, *De Generatione Animalium* 18. 726 a. 26.

15. Ephesians 5:18.

16. Galatians 5:19.

17. In loc. cit. note 2.

18. I Corinthians 6:20.

19. Augustine, *Serm. ad Popul.* 9, 10. PL 38, 86.

20. Cf. Aquinas, 4 *Sent.* 41, 4, 1 & 2. Cf. *De Malo* 15, 3.

21. Gratian, *Decretum* 2, 26. I App. 2.

22. II Corinthians 12:21.

23. Galatians 5, 19.

24. Loc. cit. note 2.

25. Aquinas, *ST* 2a2ae. 153, 2 & 3.

26. Loc. cit. Arg. 1.

27. In the body of the article.

28. Aquinas, *ST* 1a2ae. 18, 7.

29. Aquinas, ST 1a2ae. 18, 2.

30. Interlinear gloss in loc. Peter Lombard 192, 89.

31. Interlinear gloss in loc. Peter Lombard 192, 159.

32. Aquinas, *De Malo* 15, 3.

33. Article I.

34. Aristotle, *Ethics* 7, 5. 1148b 29. Lect. 5.

35. II Corinthians 7:21.

36. PL 192, 89.

37. Loc cit. Articles 6 & 9.

38. E.g., Alexander of Hales.

39. Romans 1:26.

40. Aquinas, *ST* 1a2ae. 73, 7. 4 *Sent.* 41, 4. *In Rom.* 1, Lect. 8.

41. Peter Lombard, *Sent.* 4, 38, 2. *De Bono Conjug.* 8. PL 40, 379. Also, Gratian, *Decretum* 2, 32, 7, 11.

42. Augustine, *Confessions* 3, 8. PL 32, 689.

43. *Genesis* 37:2.

44. Interlinear in loc.

Robert Gordis

1. Cf. L. M. Epstein, *Sex Laws and Customs in Judaism* (New York: Bloch, 1948), pp. 135-38.

2. B. Kiddushin 82a.

3. See I Kings 14:24; 15:12; 22:47; II Kings 23:7. Sacred prostitution, both male and female, was prohibited by the Torah on religious as well as on sexual grounds (Deut. 23:18).

4. A moving account of the tribulations of the secret homosexual, followed by his public

avowal of homosexuality, may be found in Howard Brown, *Familiar Faces, Hidden Foes: The Story of Homosexual Men in America Today* (New York: Harcourt, Brace & Jovanovich, 1972).

5. See Peter Fisher, *The Gay Mystique: The Myths and Reality of the Male Homosexual* (New York: Stein and Day, 1972), p. 128.

6. For the important implications of the evolutionary process for religious faith, see Robert Gordis, *A Faith for Moderns*, Chapter 6.

7. I am indebted to my son, Dr. Enoch J. Gordis, director of the Alcoholism Center at Elmhurst General Hospital in New York and a recognized authority in the field of alcoholism research, for this information.

8. *Patur 'abhal 'asur.*

9. For a trenchant analysis of the public activities of homosexuals and a utilization by the gay liberation movement of the widespread disillusion with marriage in order to further its objectives, see "Homosexuality and the Family," *The New York Times*, August 22, 1975, by Herbert Hendin, Director of Psychosocial Studies for Policy Research and a member of the Psychiatry Department of Columbia University.

10. John J. McNeill, S.J., *The Church and the Homosexual* (Kansas City: Sheed, Andrews and McMeel, 1976). As instances of "Old Testament legalism," he maintains that the prohibitions of homosexuality in Leviticus are not binding on the Christian conscience. As for the incidents in Genesis and Judges, he declares that the sin of the Sodomites and the Benjaminites was the violation of hospitality rather than homosexuality. This may be inferred from Ezekiel 16:49-50 and Ben Sira 16:8, which describe the sin of Sodom as basically that of the arrogance of wealth and inhospitality. Father McNeill's conclusion as to the offense committed may well be correct, but it is difficult to see how the clear indication in both Genesis and Judges that homosexuality is worse than rape can be ignored.

11. Theodore W. Jennings, "Homosexuality and Christian Faith: A Theological Reflection," *Christian Century* Vol. 94 (February 16, 1977), 137-42.

12. For a balanced presentation of the problem from the standpoint of Jewish law and ethics, see Hershel J. Matt, "Sin, Crime, Sickness or Alternative Life-Style," *Judaism*, Vol. 27, No. 1 (Winter 1978), 13-24.

John G. Milhaven

1. *The New York Times*, November 29, 1967, p. 1.

2. "The Homosexual in America," *Time* (January 21, 1966), 40-41; "God and the Homosexual," *Newsweek* (February 13, 1967), 63; "The Sad 'Gay' Life," *Look* (January 10, 1967), 30-3.

3. *Situation Ethics* (Philadelphia: Westminster, 1966), pp. 103-7.

4. C. Spicq, O.P., *Théologie morale du Nouveau Testament*, 11 (Paris: Lecoffre, 1965), pp. 481ff.; C. H. Dodd, *Gospel and Law* (New York: Columbia University, 1951), pp. 42-5.

5. *SCG* 111, 122.

6. Isadore Rubin, Ph.D., "Homosexuality," *SIECUS*, Discussion Guide, No. 2 (New York, 1965), p. 3.

7. Ibid., p. 4.

8. Ibid., p. 1.

9. *Report on Homosexuality with Particular Emphasis on This Problem in Governmental Agencies*, formulated by the Committee on Cooperation with Governmental (Federal) Agencies of the Group for the Advancement of Psychiatry, Report No. 30, January 1955, p. 2.

10. Ibid., p. 3.

11. Philip H. Heersema, M.D., "Homosexuality and the Physician," *Journal of the American Medical Association* (September 6, 1965), 159 and 160.

12. Ibid., p. 1.

13. Cf. Martin Hoffman, "Homosexual," *Psychology Today* (July 1969), 43-45, 70; John McNeill, "Pastoral Counselling of the Male Homosexual," *HPR*, Vol. 70, Nos. 9, 10, & 11 (June, July, & August 1970). Studies cited by McNeill in support of the view that homosexuality is not of itself a serious emotional illness are Daniel Cappon, *Towards an Understanding of Homosexuality* (Englewood Cliffs, N. J.: Prentice-Hall, 1965); John R. Cavanagh, *Counselling the Invert* (Milwaukee: Bruce, 1966); H. Kimball Jones, *Towards a Christian Understanding of the Homosexual* (London: S. C. M. Press, 1967); Wainwright Churchill, *Homosexual Behavior Among Males* (New York: Hawthorn, 1967); Evelyn Hooker's study published in the New York Council of Churches report, *Foundations for Christian Family Policy* (1961); Michael Schofield, *Sociological Aspects of Homosexuality* (Boston: Little Brown, 1965). Hoffman refers to a report by two London psychiatrists, Desmond Curran and Denis Parr, published in the British Medical Journal in 1957, and to the responses of a number of distinguished behavioral scientists asked by the Homosexual Law Reform Society, based in Philadelphia, their opinions on the relation of homosexuality to psychopathology. Typical of the new evidence is that of psychologist Evelyn Hooker. She found thirty homosexuals, not in treatment, whom she felt to be reasonably well-adjusted. She then matched thirty heterosexual men with the homosexuals for age, education and I.Q. Hooker then gave these sixty men a battery of psychological tests and obtained considerable information on their life histories. Several of her most skilled clinical colleagues then analyzed the material. They did not know which of the tests had been given to the homosexual men and which to the heterosexuals; they analyzed the tests blind. Hooker concludes from their analyses that there is no inherent connection between homosexual orientation and clinical symptoms of mental illness. She stated: "Homosexuality as a clinical entity does not exist. Its forms are as varied as are those of heterosexuality. Homosexuality may be a deviation in sexual pattern that is in the normal range, psychologically." This conclusion is based on the fact that the clinicians were unable to distinguish between the two groups. Nor was there any evidence that the homosexual group had a higher degree of pathology than the heterosexual group. Martin Hoffman, "Homosexual," p. 43.

From a different point of view, the Catholic moral theologian Charles Curran concludes that homosexual acts might not always be wrong: "What about the cases where modern medical science cannot help the homosexual? In these cases it seems to me that for such a person homosexual acts might not even be wrong. I am not saying that such acts are ever a goal or an ideal that should be held up for others to imitate. Homosexual acts for such a person, provided there is no harm to other persons, might be the only way in which some degree of humanity and stability can be achieved. This would be a practical application of the theology of compromise. Compromise maintains that because of the existence of sin in the world a person might be forced to accept some behavior which under ordinary circumstances he would not want to choose." *Contemporary Problems in Moral Theology* (Notre Dame, Ind.: Fides, 1970), p. 177; cf. "Dialogue with Joseph Fletcher," *HPR*, Vol. 67 (1967), 828-829.

14. John McNeill, who is impressed by the evidence that homosexuality is not necessarily a disease, nevertheless notes:

"Practically all authorities agree that the first goal of counselling should be to guide the person with a homosexual problem to the heterosexual adjustment whenever this is possible.

"The person who merely fears he may be a homosexual, or is attracted to the homosexual community, should explore every avenue toward the achievement of normal heterosexual capacities and relationships. This direction should be taken independently of what one's moral judgment may be concerning homosexual practices. Even the officers of the Mattachine Society, a homophile organization, agree with this aim: '. . . on the basis of our experience—the embarrassment, shame, and humiliation so many of us have known—we would definitely advise anyone who has not become an active homosexual, but has only misgivings about himself, to go the other way, if he can.' The reason for this advice is the many problems the average homosexual encounters, which makes a positive adjustment to such a life extremely difficult." McNeill, *Pastoral Counselling*, pp. 746-49.

As a consequence, the first discernment a counsellor should attempt to establish is whether or not a given individual is a true homosexual or merely suffering from "pseudo-homosexual panic" as a result of some experience of one of the many forms of conditional homosexuality mentioned earlier in this article. This discernment is particularly important, as Hettlinger points out, in dealing with the adolescent or young adult. *Pastoral Counselling*, p. 749.

15. Ephesians 4:11-15.

Ruth Tiffany Barnhouse

1. Robert Stoller, "Overview: The Impact of New Advances in Sex Research on Psychoanalytic Theory," *American Journal of Psychiatry*, Vol. 130 (March 1973), 246.

2. Ibid., p. 247.

3. Ibid., p. 249.

4. John W. Dixon, Jr., "The Sacramentality of Sex," *Male and Female*, Ruth Tiffany Barnhouse and Urban T. Holmes, III, editors (New York: Seabury Press, 1976), pp. 236-56. This article should be read in its entirety in order to appreciate the wonderfully revealing subtlety of Dixon's argument.

5. Ibid., p. 253.

6. Sacred Congregation for the Doctrine of the Faith, United States Catholic Conference, *Declaration on Certain Questions Concerning Sexual Ethics* (Washington: December 29, 1975), pp. 8 and 9 especially. [See above appendix.]

Charles E. Curran

1. Richard R. Parlour, *et al.*, "The Homophile Movement: Its Impact and Implications," *Journal of Religion and Health*, Vol. 6 (1967), 217-34; Foster Gunnison, Jr., "The Homophile Movement in America," *The Same Sex*, Ralph Weltge, editor (New York: Pilgrim Press, 1969), pp. 113-28.

2. A. Overing, *et al.*, *Homosexualiteit* (Hilversum: Brand, 1961); French translation: *Homosexualité*, trans. Y. Huon (Paris: Mame, 1967).

3. H. Noldin, S.J., A. Schmitt, S.J. and G. Heinzel, S.J., *Summa Theologiae Moralis: De Castitate* (36th ed.; Innsbruck: Rauch, 1958), p. 39.

4. Marcellinus Zalba, S.I., *Theologiae Moralis Summa*, Vol. II: *Theologia Moralis Specialis* (Madrid: Biblioteca de Autores Cristianos, 1953), pp. 277 and 378.

5. James M. Gustafson, "Christian Ethics," *Religion*, Paul Ramsey, editor (Englewood Cliffs, N.J.: Prentice-Hall, 1965), pp. 309-25.

6. Recall the arguments proposed at the Second Vatican Council to revise the Declaration on Religious Liberty so that the document might have its primary basis in Scripture. See Richard J. Regan, S.J., *Conflict and Consensus: Religious Freedom and the Second Vatican Council* (New York: Macmillan, 1967), pp. 117-29.

7. John C. Bennett, "Issues for the Ecumenical Dialogue," *Christian Social Ethics in a Changing World*, John C. Bennett, editor (New York: Association Press, 1966), pp. 371-72.

8. Joseph Blank, "New Testament Morality and Modern Moral Theology," *Concilium*, Vol. 25 (May 1967), 9-22.

9. Derrick Sherwin Bailey, *HWCT*, pp. 1-28. An earlier denial of the traditional homosexual interpretation of the sin of Sodom was proposed by George A. Barton, "Sodom," *Encyclopedia of Religion and Ethics,* James Hastings, editor (New York: Charles Scribner's Sons, 1921), XI, 672.

10. Eugene H. Maly, "Genesis," *The Jerome Bible Commentary,* R. E. Brown, S.S., J. A. Fitzmyer, S.J., R. E. Murphy, O. Carm., editors (Englewood Cliffs, N.J.: Prentice-Hall, 1966), pp. 20-21; *La Sainte Bible* traduite en français sous la direction de L'École Biblique de Jerusalem (Paris: Éditions du Cerf, 1956), p. 25; *The Jerusalem Bible*, Alexander Jones, editor (Garden City, N.Y.: Doubleday, 1966), p. 35, merely translates the note from the original French. *Genesis: The Anchor Bible*, E. A. Speiser, editor (Garden City, N.Y.: Doubleday, 1964), p. 142.

11. Bailey, *HWCT,* pp. 57-61.

12. Thielicke, *ES,* pp. 277-84.

13. For a summary of these opinions, see John R. Cavanagh, *Counselling the Invert* (Milwaukee: Bruce Publishing Co., 1966).

14. For a critique of *Pacem in Terris* precisely on this point, see Paul Ramsey, *The Just War* (New York: Charles Scribner's Sons, 1968), pp. 70-72.

15. For an elaboration of my understanding of the theory of compromise, see Charles Curran, *A New Look at Christian Morality* (Notre Dame, Ind.: Fides, 1968), pp. 169-73 and 232-33.

16. Franklin E. Kameny in *The Same Sex*, Ralph Weltge, editor (New York: Pilgrim Press, 1969), pp. 129-45.

Helmut Thielicke

1. Cf. Gerhard von Rad, *Genesis, A Commentary,* trans. John H. Marks (Philadelphia: Westminster Press, 1961), pp. 212f.

2. W. Schoellgen, for example, when he says that "in the picture of the natural man, as painted in the Bible, homosexuality represents almost the darkest shadow, the extreme of ethical darkness." (*Konkrete Ethik* [1961], p. 410.)

3. On this interpretation, cf. my book *Theologie der Anfechtung* (1949), pp. 21ff.

4. Hans Giese (in his article "Zur Psychopathologie der Homosexualität" in *Praxis*, 1961, No. 48) proposes that we make a distinction between the terms "abnormal" and "perverse," the latter term to designate only "psychopathological forms of psychically abnormal sexual conduct." When we occasionally use the term "perverse" here in a different and more general sense, we do so only because in our special connection we wish to make use of the etymology of the Latin word *pervertere* for the analogy between what happens in the vertical dimension (the perversion of the heirarchy of Creator and creature) and what happens in the horizontal dimension (the perversion of the order of the sexes.).

5. Cf. the interpretation of this story in my book *How the World Began* (Philadelphia: Muehlemberg Press, 1961), pp. 273-87.

6. H. Lietzmann, *Kommentar zum Römerbrief* (4th ed.; 1933), pp. 33ff.

7. Cf. *ThE* 11, 2 par. 1050ff.

8. Cf. the analysis of the "borderline situation" in *ThE* II, 1, par. 688ff.

9. Abundant clinical material has been assembled in the book by Hans Giese, *Der homosexuelle Mensch in der Welt* (Stuttgart, 1958). Among the statistical materials there are also important documentations of relationships which manifest ethical fidelity; cf. especially pp. 133ff.

10. We say this despite certain rather astonishing statistics which Giese cites concerning stable "monogamous" relationships among homosexuals. Cf. ibid.

H. Kimball Jones

1. Michael J. Buckley, *Morality and the Homosexual* (Westminster, Md.: Newman Press, 1959), p. 134.

2. D. S. Bailey, "Homosexuality and Christian Morals," *They Stand Apart,* J. Tudor Rees and Harvey V. Usill, editors (London: William Heinemann, 1955), p. 49.

3. Dietrich Bonhoeffer, *Ethics,* Ebergard Bethge, editor; trans. Nevill Horton Smith (New York: Macmillan, 1965), p. 49.

4. Sylvanus M. Duvall, *Men, Women and Morals* (New York: Association Press, 1952), p. 58.

5. Helmut Thielicke, *ES,* pp. 282-83.

6. Ibid., p. 284.

7. The same could not be said of the "contingent homosexual" or the "variational homosexual," since each of these types retains a certain amount of freedom.

Unfortunately, Thielicke does not carry this view to its natural conclusion. He appears to be on the verge of saying that we should apply the same norms in judging the sexual behavior of the absolute invert that we would apply to normal heterosexuals. However, at the last moment he says that we should not. It is as though Thielicke, finding himself on a precipice and seeing where the step he is about to take might lead him, changes his mind. Thus, he concludes that, given the various problems surrounding the homosexual way of life and the strong pressures placed upon the homosexual by society, the Church should aim at helping him to sublimate his sexual desire into other creative channels (H. Thielicke, *ES,* pp. 286-87). This is a very unfortunate conclusion in that it is even less tenable than the position Thielicke tries so hard to avoid—that of recognizing and accepting the possibility of an ethically responsible homosexual relationship. Yet, it is a conclusion that has been reached from pragmatic as well as moral considerations, and it is here that Thielicke shows great insight—in seeing the need for a practicable solution (even though his particular solution is highly impractical) and for a contextual ethic which is relevant to the problem faced by the homosexual in America today.

8. Paul Tillich, *Morality and Beyond* (New York: Harper and Row, 1963), pp. 82-83.

9. John A. T. Robinson, *Christian Morals Today* (Philadelphia: Westminster Press, 1964), p. 37.

10. K. Barth, *CD,* p. 166.

11. Thielicke, *ES,* p. 272.

12. Gordon Westwood, *Society and the Homosexual* (New York: Dutton, 1952), p. 66.

13. D. J. West, *Homosexuality* (Middlesex: Penguin Books, 1960), p. 158.

14. John F. Harvey, "Homosexuality as a Pastoral Problem," *Theological Studies,* Vol. 16 (1955), 93–96.

15. Thielicke, *ES,* p. 287.

16. Havelock Ellis, *Psychology of Sex* (paperback edition; New York: Mentor Books, 1964), p. 185.

17. In Morris Ploscowe, "Homosexuality, Sodomy and Crimes Against Nature," *Pastoral Psychology,* Vol. II, No. 18 (November 1955), 44.

18. Westwood, *Society,* p. 65.

19. West, *Homosexuality,* p. 169.

20. Thielicke, *ES,* p. 287.

21. Paul Lehmann, *Ethics in a Christian Context* (New York: Harper and Row, 1963), pp. 136-37.

22. "Homosexuality," *Foundations for Christian Family Policy,* Elizabeth S. and William H. Genne, editors (New York: National Council of Churches, 1961), p. 174.

Hershel Matt

1. *Midrash Pinhas* (Warsaw: 1876), Chapter 4, Sec. 34, p. 32.

2. Some biblical passages that are commonly taken to refer to homosexuality are actually in dispute among scholars. The so-called male prostitute *(kadesh)*, for example, may possibly be not a homosexual but a pimp, or a male who engages in heterosexual prostitution. The love between David and Jonathan ("your love was for me more wonderful than the love of women," [2 Sam. 1:26]) may possibly refer to normal love between friends of either sex.

3. B. *Niddah* 16b.

4. B. *Berakhot* 33b.

5. For a further discussion of the problem of determinism, freedom, judgment, and providence, see "Man's Role in God's Design," *Judaism*, Vol. 21, No. 2 (Spring 1972).

6. B. *Nedarim* 27a.

7. They differ on the causes (some positing a hormonal or other hereditary factor; some stressing a seriously inadequate or disturbed parental relationship in the earliest years; some pointing to early traumatic sexual experience; some insisting that the causes are thus far simply unknown). They differ on the possibilities for changing to heterosexuality (some insisting that no true homosexual can change; some claiming that all who truly desire to, can be professionally enabled to; many acknowledging that, at most, perhaps a quarter or a third can change). They differ on the appropriate treatment methods for those who seek to change (psychoanalysis, analytic forms of psychotherapy, behavior modification).

8. *Avot* 2:5.

9. Even though the tradition does at times refer to sins committed "unknowingly," "under compulsion," or "inadvertently," the sinfulness of such sins consists, presumably, in sinful decisions made previously, when a greater degree of freedom obtained; or in a *culpable* degree of ignorance or negligence; or in a lack of concern for harm inflicted even though inflicted unintentionally.

10. Ecclesiastes 3:15; Leviticus *Rabbah*, Sec. 27.

11. It is sometimes urged that though certain laws concerning morality should not be enforced, they should, nevertheless, not be repealed, because a) keeping them on the books serves a moral-pedagogic function; and b) removing them would imply full moral approval of the now decriminalized behavior, thus actually encouraging the young and the "weak" to engage in such acts. Whatever the measure of validity in such an argument, it is outweighed by two considerations: a) the retention of laws that have become recognized as unjust or inappropriate increases disdain for the legal system; and b) avoidance of actual harm to known victims must take priority over possible harm to unknown victims.

12. Paradoxically, and yet perhaps understandably, such removal of blame and guilt, and the combination of self-acceptance and acceptance by others, has *in some instances*, been followed by a changeover to heterosexuality.

13. When such open and unashamed avowal of homosexuality takes the form of public protest, demonstration, and proclamation, many heterosexuals—even those who have come to grant the validity of such basic gay rights as non-discrimination in housing, employment, and public office—become resentful, impatient and angry at what they consider the "constant parading" by gays of their homosexuality. They often fail to realize that such public display is a reflection of the grim reality that denial of these basic rights is still widespread and has only very recently been reduced. When the rights of gays will have been fully accepted and their changed status inwardly assimilated by both straights and gays, both groups will obviously feel less threatened. At that point the need for public demonstration by gays will certainly diminish and perhaps even disappear.

14. Isaiah 57:3-5.

Charles E. Curran

1. *ST* 2a-2ae, q. 153, aa. 2-3; q. 154, a 1.

2. Ibid. q. 154, aa. 11-12.

3. Bailey's otherwise fine summary of the Scholastic teaching on homosexuality in *HWCT*, pp. 110-20 could be improved by a somewhat more nuanced understanding of the sin against nature.

4. John F. Harvey, O.S.F.S., "Homosexuality," *New Catholic Encyclopedia* (New York: MacGraw-Hill, 1967), VII, 117-19.

5. Ibid., pp. 117-118. Note that Thomas Aquinas proposed the same arguments.

6. Karl Barth, *CD*, pp. 194-229. This small volume brings together Barth's considerations of man and woman which appear in three different places in his *Church Dogmatics*.

7. Ibid., p. 200.

8. Ibid., p. 213.

9. Ibid., p. 214.

10. John Giles Milhaven, *Towards a New Catholic Morality* (Garden City, N.Y.: Doubleday, 1970), pp. 59-68. This essay originally appeared as "Homosexuality and the Christian," *HPR*, Vol. 68, No. 8 (1968), 663-69.

11. Ibid., pp. 61-62.

12. Ibid., p. 62.

13. Ibid., p. 63.

14. Ibid., p. 65.

15. Ibid., p. 67.

16. Ibid., p. 68.

17. *Towards a Quaker View of Sex* (London: The Society of Friends, 1963), p. 26.

18. Robert W. Wood, *Christ and the Homosexual* (New York/Washington: Vantage Press, 1960).

19. Ibid., pp. 151-74.

20. Neale Secor, "A Brief for a New Homosexual Ethic," *The Same Sex*, Ralph W. Weltge, editor (New York: Pilgrim Press, 1969). [See above, Part V, Chapter 2.]

21. Ibid., pp. 78-79. For a somewhat similar line of argumentation representing the best reasoning I found in the literature from the homophile community itself, see Franklin E. Kameny, in *The Same Sex*, pp. 129-45.

22. The various statistics proposed are naturally fragmentary and incomplete. This paragraph is based on William Simon and John Gagnon, "Homosexuality: The Formation of a Sociological Perspective," *Journal of Health and Social Behavior,* Vol. 8 (1967), 177-85. In general, the authors appear to be sympathetic to an acceptance of homosexual behavior, but they conclude from their data: "These data, then, suggest a depersonalized quality, a driven or compulsive quality, to the sexual activities of many homosexuals which cannot be reckoned as anything but extremely costly to them." (p. 181)

23. Paul Ramsey, "A Christian Approach to Sexual Relations," *The Journal of Religion,* Vol. 45 (1965), 101-13.

24. Albert R. Jonsen, S.J., *Responsibility in Modern Religious Ethics* (Washington/Cleveland: Corpus Books, 1968).

25. Karl Rahner, S.J., "Experiment: Man," *Theology Digest,* Vol. 16 (Sesquicentennial issue, 1968), 58.

26. John Macquarrie, *God and Secularity* (Philadelphia: Westminster Press, 1967), pp. 72-85.

27. Pope John XXIII, *Pacem in Terris,* n. 35-36. Original text: *AAS* LV (1963), 262-66.

28. Heinrich A. Rommen, *The State in Catholic Thought* (St. Louis: B. Herder, 1945); Jacques Maritain, *Man and the State* (Chicago: University of Chicago Press, 1951).

29. Jacques Ellul, "Rappels et reflexions sur une théologie de l'état," *Les chrétiens et l'état* (Paris: Mame, 1967), pp. 130-53.

30. Gerard Gilleman, S.J., *The Primacy of Charity in Moral Theology* (Westminster, Md.: Newman Press, 1959).

31. Charles E. Curran, "Sexuality and Sin: A Current Appraisal," *HPR*, Vol. 69, No. 1 (October 1968), 31.

32. Thielicke, *ES*, pp. 281-87.

33. H. Kimball Jones, *Toward a Christian Understanding of the Homosexual* (New York: Association Press, 1966). [See above, Part III, Chapter 3.]

34. Ibid., p. 95.

35. Ibid., p. 98.

36. Helmut Thielicke, *Theological Ethics*, Vol. II: *Politics*, William Lazareth, editor (Philadelphia: Fortress Press, 1969), p. 440.

37. H. Kimball Jones, *Christian Understanding*, p. 108.

38. A. Overing, *et al.*, *Homosexualiteit* (Hilversum: Brand, 1961); French translation: *Homosexualité*, tr. Y. Huon (Paris: Mame, 1967).

39. H. Ruygers, "Regards en arrière," *Homosexualité*, pp. 175-83.

40. "La cure spirituelle des homosexuels," *Homosexualité*, pp. 193-6.

41. John J. McNeill, S.J., "The Christian Male Homosexual," *HPR*, Vol. 70 (1970), 667-77; 747-58; 828-36.

42. Ibid., pp. 828-36.

43. Ibid., p. 831.

44. Ibid., pp. 831-33.

45. I. Aertnys-C. Damen, C.SSR., *Theologia Moralis*, J. Visser, C.SSR., editor (17th ed.: Rome/Turin: Marietti, 1956), I, pp. 250 and 366.

46. S. Alphonsus M. De Ligorio, *Theologia Moralis* (Turin: Marietti, 1872), I lib. 3, n. 565.

47. Louis Monden, S.J., *Sin, Liberty and Law* (New York: Sheed and Ward, 1965), pp. 133-44.

James B. Nelson

1. This chapter is a revised and expanded version of my article, "Homosexuality: An Issue for the Church," *Theological Markings*, Vol. 5, No. 2 (Winter 1975), and reprinted in *Christianity and Crisis*, Vol. 37, No. 5 (April 4, 1977), by permission of both editors.

2. For a description of the gay movement within the church, see Sally Gearhart and William R. Johnson, *Loving Men/Loving Women* (San Francisco: Glide Publications, 1974), esp. Chapter 3.

3. See *Social Action*, Vol. 34, No. 4 (December 1967), a special issue entitled "Civil Liberties and Homosexuality," which in spite of its date is still pertinent.

4. More expanded interpretations of the Bible on this issue may be found in numerous places. I am indebted to a number of authors, but particularly Derrick Sherwin Bailey, *HWCT;* John J. McNeill, S.J., *The Church and the Homosexual* (Kansas City: Sheed, Andrews and McMeel, 1976); Joseph C. Weber, "Does the Bible Condemn Homosexual Acts?" *Engage/Social Action*, Vol. 3, No. 5 (May 1975); Helmut Thielicke, *ES;* and H. Kimball Jones, *Toward a Christian Understanding of the Homosexual* (New York: Association Press, 1966). Especially helpful on hermeneutical issues in this context is James T. Clemons, "Toward a Christian Affirmation of Human Sexuality," *Religion in Life*, Vol. 43, No. 4 (Winter 1974).

5. McNeill, *The Church*, pp. 42.

6. Bailey first emphasized this interpretation in 1955, but since then it has been reaffirmed by others. McNeill provided a good summary of the scholarship in the intervening years, *The Church*, pp. 42ff.

7. See Gerhard von Rad, *Genesis: A Commentary* (Philadelphia: Westminster Press, 1961), pp. 205ff.; and David Bartlett, "A Biblical Perspective on Homosexuality," *Foundations,* Vol. 20, No. 2 (April-June 1977), 135.

8. McNeill, *The Church,* p. 50.

9. Martin Noth observes, "Leviticus deals almost exclusively with cultic and ritual matters." *Leviticus, A Commentary* (London: S. C. M. Press, 1965), p. 16. Norman H. Snaith also notes, "Homosexuality here is condemned on account of its association with *idolatry.*" *Leviticus and Numbers, The Century Bible* (London: Nelson, 1967), p. 126.

10. See United Church of Christ, *Human Sexuality: A Preliminary Study,* pp. 76ff.

11. McNeill, *The Church,* p. 55.

12. See Weber, *Does the Bible. . .?,* p. 34.

13. Bartlett, "Biblical Perspective," p. 141.

14. Several writers have used different labels in the attempt to understand the differing positions. Interpretations of the theological possibilities and illustrative examples, however, will vary.

15. See Louis Crompton, "Gay Genocide: From Leviticus to Hitler," (address delivered to the Gay Academic Union, New York University, November 30, 1974, mimeographed).

16. See, for example, the remarkable article by Louie Crew, "At St. Luke's Parish: The Peace of Christ is Not for Gays," *Christianity and Crisis,* Vol. 27, Nos. 9 & 10 (May 30 & June 13, 1977).

17. See Karl Barth, *CD* III/4 (Edinburgh: T. & T. Clark, 1961), esp. p. 166.

18. See William Muehl, "Some Words of Caution," *Male and Female,* Ruth Tiffany Barnhouse and Urban T. Holmes III, editors (New York: Seabury Press, 1976), pp. 167-74. Also, William Muehl and William R. Johnson, "Issues Raised by Homosexuality," *Y. D. S. Reflection,* Vol. 72, No. 4 (May 1975).

19. Jim Cotter, "The Gay Challenge to Traditional Notions of Human Sexuality,' *Christian,* Vol. 4, No. 2 (1977), 145.

20. Gregory Baum, "Catholic Homosexuals," *Commonweal,* Vol. 99 (February 15, 1974), 479-82.

21. Rosemary Ruether, in *From Machismo to Mutuality: Essays on Sexism and Woman-Man Liberation,* Eugene Bianchi and Rosemary Ruether, editors (New York: Paulist Press, 1976), pp. 180f.

22. See C. A. Tripp, *The Homosexual Matrix* (New York: The New American Library, 1976), p. 266.

23. Compare the Kinsey statistics with the more recent estimates of Morton Hunt, *Sexual Behavior in the 1970's.* A useful discussion of the comparison is in the review of Hunt's book by Wardell B. Pomeroy in *SIECUS Report,* Vol. 2, No. 6 (July 1974), 5f.

24. See John Money and Anke A. Ehrhardt, *Man and Woman, Boy and Girl* (New York: New American Library, 1972), pp. 238ff; also, McNeill, *The Church,* pp. 113ff.

25. See Tripp, *Homosexual Matrix,* pp. 236ff.

26. The therapist is Dr. Gerald C. Davison, President of the Association for the Advancement of Behavior Therapy. See Kenneth Goodall, "The End of Playboy Therapy," *Psychology Today,* Vol. 9, No. 5 (October 1975).

27. [Evelyn] Hooker's report is published in *Foundations for Christian Family Policy* (New York: N. Y. Council of Churches, 1961). See also her article, "Homosexuality," in *International Encyclopedia of the Social Sciences* (New York: Macmillan, 1968).

28. See McNeill's summary of the evidence, *The Church,* pp. 115ff.

29. Muehl, *Some Words,* p. 171.

30. See McNeill, *The Church,* p. 136.

31. Peggy Way, "Homosexual Counseling as a Learning Ministry," *Christianity and Crisis,* Vol. 37, Nos. 9 & 10 (May 30 & June 13, 1977), 128.

32. Thielicke, *ES,* p. 282.

33. Ibid., pp. 283ff.

34. Friends Home Service Committee, *Towards a Quaker View of Sex* (London: Friends House, 1963), p. 45.

35. McNeill, *The Church*, p. 148. After a publishing delay of two years, this book was finally granted an ecclesiastical *imprimi potest* (permission to publish), which does not imply official agreement with the contents but is certification that the book has met prudent standards of scholarship in regard to a controversial topic. (See McNeill's preface, esp. pp. xiif.) Some months after it had been published, however, the *imprimi potest* was withdrawn, and the Vatican ordered McNeill to public silence on the issue of homosexuality.

36. See Norman Pittenger, *Time for Consent: A Christian's Approach to Homosexuality* (revised edition; London: S. C. M. Press, 1976). See also *Making Sexuality Human: Love and Control in Sexuality* (Philadelphia: United Church Press, 1974); and "A Theological Approach to Understanding Homosexuality," *Religion in Life*, Vol. 43, No. 4 (Winter 1974).

37. See Reinhold Niebuhr, *The Nature and Destiny of Man*, Vol. 2, Chapter 8.

38. Pittenger makes this point well; see *Time for Consent*, pp. 74f.

39. See the analysis of causation theories in John H. Gagnon and William Simon, *Sexual Conduct: The Social Sources of Human Sexuality* (London: Hutchinson, 1974), p. 137.

40. Alan Bell, "Homosexuality, An Overview," *Male and Female*, Ruth Tiffany Barnhouse and Urban T. Holmes, III, editors (New York: Seabury Press, 1976), p. 142.

41. Gagnon and Simon, *Sexual Conduct*, p. 137.

42. See Cotter, *Gay Challenge*, pp. 134ff. Precisely because gay people (like heterosexuals) vary so very widely in their understanding and experience of their own sexuality, there is no unanimity among them about language. While it is clear that an increasing majority wish to be called *gay*, there are some who insist that the term ought to be reserved for those who are "out of the closet," who are open to the public about their affectional orientation. Further, some gay women strongly prefer the term *lesbian*, maintaining that their experience and life style is significantly different from that of the gay male. The language situation has some parallels to the movement from Negro to Black and (increasingly) to Afro-American. The point is that the majority group must respect and affirm the right and need of an oppressed minority to their own linguistic self-definitions. For economy of language I have generally adopted the practice which appears to be acceptable to the majority of gays—that of using *gay* to refer to both female and male persons and those who are closeted as well as those who are publicly avowed—though I am painfully aware that some readers may find this personally unsatisfactory.

43. Bell, *Homosexuality*, p. 136.

44. Psychiatrist George Weinberg calls this "homophobia," defining phobia as "an irrational, excessive and persistent fear of some particular thing or situation." While I do not believe it fair to attribute sincerely held positions against homosexuality's acceptance to irrational fears only, I also believe it important to examine the probability that fear is part of the experience of most heterosexuals on this issue. See Weinberg's *Society and the Healthy Homosexual* (Garden City, New York: Anchor/Doubleday, 1973), esp. Chapter 1.

45. See G. Rattray Taylor, *Sex in History* (New York: Harper and Row, 1970), p. 80ff.

46. Theodore Isaac Rubin, *Compassion and Self-Hate: An Alternative to Despair* (New York: Ballentine, 1975), p. 243.

47. Mary Douglas, *Purity and Danger: An Analysis of Concepts of Pollution and Taboo* (London: Routledge and Kegan Paul, 1966), p. 113; cf. p. 94.

48. See Weinberg, *Society*, Chapter 1.

49. David Bartlett argues this basic point about grace versus works of the law in his very useful treatment of Pauline theological perspectives and homosexuality. Applying the argument in Galatians regarding circumcision, he notes, "Heterosexual people insist that homosexual people should 'go straight' in order to be Christian, or ordained, or elected to office, just as circumcised Christians needed to be circumcised in order to become full

members of the Church. However, if heterosexual people and homosexual people could really hear the word that they are in a right relationship to God because of God's grace, and if they could receive that word in faith, they would not need to spend so much energy defending themselves or browbeating others." (Bartlett, "Biblical Perspective," p. 145.) My only qualification of these words is the reminder that the gay person's felt need for self-defense and self-justification is much more understandable than is the heterosexual's, given the long history and continuing presence of homophobia and homosexual persecution.

50. See Lewis I. Maddocks, "The Law and the Church vs. the Homosexual," *The Same Sex,* Ralph W. Weltge, editor (New York: Pilgrim Press, 1969). For an example of a denominational statement which strongly endorses civil liberties without making moral judgments about same-sex relationships, see "Pronouncement on Civil Liberties Without Discrimination Related to Affectional or Sexual Preference," (Minutes, Tenth General Synod, United Church of Christ, 1975) pp. 69f. [See Appendix of this volume.]

51. The first major case of a successful public referendum to rescind gay rights legislation occurred in Dade County (Miami), Florida in June, 1977.

52. In 1976 the U. S. Supreme Court affirmed without comment a lower court decision upholding the Virginia sodomy statute as constitutional. The lower court had held that such sodomy legislation was constitutional inasmuch as the state could establish "that the conduct is likely to end in a contribution to moral delinquency." This was a serious setback to the elimination of such restrictive and punitive laws. See *Doe v. Commonwealth's Attorney for the City of Richmond,* 403 F. Supp. 1199 (1975).

53. The special issues of two journals, devoted to this matter, are particularly useful: *Christianity and Crisis,* Vol. 37, Nos. 9 & 10 (May 30 & June 13, 1977); and, *Christian,* Vol. 4, No. 2 (Annunciation, 1977). *Christian* is a British theological quarterly.

54. See Way, *Homosexual Counseling,* p. 126.

55. This study was done by Martin S. Weinberg and Colin J. Williams and is cited in McNeill, *The Church,* p. 173.

56. The action was taken by the United Church of Christ Executive Council at its meeting in Omaha, October 30, 1972.

57. See David Blamires, "Homosexuality and the Church: The Case for Honesty," *Christian,* Vol. 4, No. 2 (Annunciation, 1977), 165ff.

58. Way, *Homosexual Counseling,* p. 130.

59. John Cavanagh, *Counselling the Invert* (Milwaukee: Bruce, 1960), p. 263.

60. See McNeill, *The Church,* p. 165.

61. Money is quoted by Marily Riley, "The Lesbian Mother," *San Diego Law Review,* Vol. 12 (July 1975), 864.

62. See Thomas Maurer, "Toward a Theology of Homosexuality—Tried and Found, Trite and Tragic," *Is Gay Good?,* W. Dwight Oberholzer, editor (Philadelphia: Westminster Press, 1971).

63. Chris Glazer, "A Newly-Revealed Christian Experience," *Church and Society,* Vol. 68, No. 5 (May-June, 1977), 11.

Theodore W. Jennings

1. Karl Barth, *C.D.,* Part III/4 (Edinburgh: T. and T. Clark, 1961), pp. 164-65.
2. Cf. St. Thomas Aquinas, *S.T.* 2-2ae. Q. 153, answers 2 & 3, Q. 154, answer 1.
3. W. Norman Pittenger, *Making Sexuality Human* (New York: Pilgrim Press, 1970), p. 67.

Lisa Sowle Cahill

1. Walter Muelder, "Approaches to Homosexuality and their Implications for Ministry," *Explor,* Vo. 1, No. 2 (1975), 28-50.

2. See Appendix.

3. Richard McCormick, S.J., "Sexual Ethics—An Opinion," *National Catholic Reporter,* Vol. 12 (January 30, 1976), 9.

4. Charles Curran, "Homosexuality and Moral Theology: Methodological & Substantive Considerations," *The Thomist,* Vol. 35, No. 3 (July 1971), 447-81.

5. André Guindon, *The Sexual Language: An Essay in Moral Theology* (Ottawa: University of Ottawa Press), 1976.

6. Anthony Kosnick *et al., Human Sexuality* (New York: Paulist Press, 1977), p. 204. John J. McNeill, S.J., *The Church and the Homosexual* (Kansas City, Mo.: Sheed, Andrews and McMeel, 1976), p. 130.

7. Kosnick *et al., Human Sexuality,* p. 204.

8. McNeill, *The Church,* p. 130.

9. Ibid., p. 32.

10. Ibid., p. 65.

11. Ibid., p. 196.

12. Ibid., p. 150.

13. Marc Oraison, *The Homosexual Question* (New York: Harper and Row, 1977).

14. Ibid., p. 119.

15. Council on Theology and Culture of the Presbyterian Church in the United States, *The Church and Homosexuality: A Preliminary Study* (1977).

16. Ibid., p. 119.

17. Ibid., p. 121.

18. Ibid., p. 110.

19. Ibid., p. 102.

20. James B. Nelson, "Homosexuality and the Church," *Christianity and Crisis,* Vol. 37, No. 5 (April 4, 1977); revised and reprinted in *Embodiment* (Minneapolis: Augsburg Publishing House, 1978), pp. 180-210.

21. John W. Espy, "Continuing the Discussion 'Homosexuality and the Church,' " *Christianity and Crisis,* Vol. 37, Nos. 9 & 10 (May 30 & June 13, 1977), 116-117.

22. Ruth Tiffany Barnhouse & Urban T. Holmes, III, eds., *Male & Female* (New York: Seabury Press, 1976).

23. Ruth Tiffany Barnhouse, *Homosexuality: A Symbolic Confusion* (New York: The Seabury Press, 1977).

24. Ibid., p. 151.

25. Ibid., p. 178.

26. Ibid., p. 147.